Life at
Fonthill
1807–1822

Life at Fonthill

1807–1822

From the correspondence of
William Beckford

Translated and edited by Boyd Alexander

The thought that the day is not distant
when all that I have done or am doing
will dissolve into thin air, fills me with
the bitterest melancholy.
Beckford to Franchi, 1815

NONSUCH

First published 1957
Copyright © in this edition 2006
Nonsuch Publishing Ltd

Nonsuch Publishing Limited
The Mill, Brimscombe Port, Stroud, Gloucestershire, GL5 2QG
www.nonsuch-publishing.com

Nonsuch Publishing Ltd is an imprint of Tempus Publishing Group

British Library Cataloguing in Publication Data.
A catalogue record for this book is available from the British Library.

ISBN 1-84588-069-2

Typesetting and origination by Nonsuch Publishing Limited
Printed in Great Britain by Oaklands Book Services Limited

CONTENTS

INTRODUCTION TO THE MODERN EDITION

THE period of Beckford's life covered by Boyd Alexander's selection of correspondence in *Life at Fonthill* (1957) was not a happy one. The middle-aged Beckford, leading a reclusive life at Fonthill Abbey himself confides to Gregorio Franchi, his principal correspondent, that his letters are not gay and that indeed everything is going from bad to worse. Of the many dark thoughts crowding in upon the "Abbot" was the realization that his vast income from the family sugar plantations in Jamaica was in decline just at the very time when his expenses in building the extravagant Abbey were increasing apace. That project—which he forced on at a wild pace—involved not only the replacement of his father's neo-classical mansion, but the purchase of hundreds of paintings, *objets d'art* and books to fill his new "cathedral". Building went on day and night; in 1807 at the beginning of the period recorded by this correspondence, Beckford had just moved into the still unfinished Abbey. In his desperate need for funds he was forced to sell off some of his more valuable possessions—including the much loved landscapes, the "Altieri" Claudes. At the very end of the period covered by the correspondence, he actually sold the Abbey itself for the tidy sum of £300,000 and retreated to a more modest but still stylish life in Bath.

Other matters plagued Beckford during these years, some of a personal and some of a more general nature. His sexual proclivity was now exclusively homosexual but locked up in the vastness of the Abbey, he had no outlets for his desires. His letters to Franchi, who apparently was leading a more promiscuous life in London, are replete with expressions of a deep frustration. Beckford's only recourse was to drool over the occasional good-looking member of his staff or the "angelic" Saunders, a circus performer he saw on an infrequent visit away. Travel abroad, which might have provided an outlet for these proclivities, was effectively ruled out by the Napoleonic wars.

These wars caused Beckford distress as well as inconvenience. Like many English lusophiles, he was outraged by the Convention of Cintra under the terms of which the French armies were allowed to withdraw from Portugal with all their booty. He agonised over the physical destruction of Portugal which he learnt about through his contact with successive Portuguese ambassadors and by following reports in the press. On one occasion, in 1810, the past joys of his life in Portugal come vividly to the fore when he was visited by J.P. Bezerra de Seixas, an old friend from his Cintra days. Bezerra was "full of taste and intelligence" but strolling around the grounds of Fonthill relating the woes that had befallen his homeland, he and the Abbot fell to weeping and sharing the sentiment of "tenderest *saudades*" (or nostalgia for what is irredeemably lost).

Nevertheless there were bright moments too. Beckford gained much pleasure from his landscape gardening and by his completion of the interior decoration at Fonthill, an heroic task. If he seems to be becoming an enemy of his own, earlier promise in these years, the same aesthetic sensibility that informed all the activities of the young Beckford is still in evidence. He tells Franchi that an object, which may look like "nothing on earth" when placed in one room, can assume an entirely different character in another. Setting, background, colour, space—Beckford returns to these themes over and over again in the letters showing that he has lost nothing of his extraordinary talent for display and design. Occasional excursions—to the opera to see some oriental extravaganza—broke the monotony of his routine at Fonthill which followed a rigid daily pattern of riding, inspecting the estate during the day and reading and music in the evenings. Once matters improved on the continent, he started to re-visit Paris, a city he had always adored.

Boyd Alexander's selection came from letters which Beckford wrote in Italian to Gregorio Franchi. His edition, produced at a time when he had exclusive *entrée* into the Beckford papers, was an important supplement to Louis Melville's grand collection of the correspondence (published in 1910) which had spanned Beckford's entire life. Like his other works, Boyd Alexander's *Life at Fonthill* is richly footnoted and each section is introduced by an essay setting the scene for the years of the correspondence about to be paraded. But Beckford is also left to speak for himself and the authenticity of his voice in these letters has been put to good effect by theatre producers as well as students of Beckford's life. Even with the greater access of scholars to the Beckford archive now deposited in the Bodleian Library, Boyd Alexander's English version will remain an indispensable tool of research. But more than that, its re-publication will ensure that the delights of Beckford's prose, with its idiosyncratic mix of the precise and the whimsical, will be savoured by a new generation of readers.

Malcolm Jack
London, August 2005

INTRODUCTION

WILLIAM Beckford of Fonthill was born in 1760, the only child of a late marriage. His father, Alderman William Beckford, twice Lord Mayor of London, M.P. for the City, and friend of Chatham and Wilkes, was born in Jamaica in 1710, and represented the third generation of a family which, whilst still obscure, had emigrated there in the late seventeenth century, soon to become millionaire sugar planters in the Island. The Alderman was educated at Westminster School when it was considered the best in England, and then at Balliol. Except for a brief business visit to his plantations when a young man, he never returned to the Island, and his son never set eyes on it. Instead, he busied himself with sugar operations on the London market, high finance and City and national politics. In these he pursued a somewhat noisy and tumultuous course in loud opposition to the Court and steady support of Chatham. He was cut off suddenly by a chill at the height of his career, leaving his ten-year-old son a millionaire

The boy's background was not without difficulties. His family, who had only recently bought Fonthill from an old and decayed family, were looked upon as *nouveaux riches* by their aristocratic neighbours. His father had a violent temper and a streak of vulgarity. His mother was at once tyrannical and spoiling; she was full of whims and a snob—as the granddaughter of the Earl of Abercorn she was at times irritated by her Beckford connections. Fonthill House, nicknamed Splendens, stank of money, and everywhere there was lavishness and ostentation.

The little heir must have the best of everything. So the eight-year-old Mozart gave him piano lessons when he was five. He was taught drawing and the principles of architecture by Sir William Chambers, who had done the same for George III when Prince of Wales, and was architect to the King. He was also taught drawing by the fashionable drawing-master Alexander Cozens, who had immense influence with him and fired his lively imagination. Beckford remained throughout life a thoroughly spoiled child with whims and caprices that knew no bounds. He flew into tantrums as soon as he was opposed, but collapsed in the face of difficulties; he would call loudly on his mother or tutor or agent to "devise some plan" to extricate him from them; he cursèd and blamed everyone except himself.

This arrogance and waywardness was increased by the fact that he was undoubtedly gifted and brilliant—he was considered almost a child genius. His godfather, the great Chatham, regarded him as more talented than his son, the future Prime Minister. It was unfortunate for him that his mother could not bear to part with him, for he was never sent to boarding school to mix with his equals. Instead, he was tutored at home by two worthy but prosaic and pedestrian men—no match for their scintillating pupil.

He did not leave home until he was seventeen (in 1777), when he followed Gibbon's example and completed his education at Geneva—in those days one of the intellectual centres of Europe. From this time until 1803, when the exigencies of war ended foreign travel for all but a few intrepid and hardy Englishmen, he was almost more abroad than in England, and found his sympathies wholly engaged by foreigners and foreign ways. He was voluble, excitable, and lively, and devoted to Italian opera. He became increasingly antipathetic to the average Englishman of his class and day.

He made the Grand Tour to Italy during 1780 and 1781, when he became firm friends with Lady Hamilton, the first wife of our envoy at Naples. He kept a diary, only a fragment of which exists; on his return he began to work it up (with additional material) into a travel book in letter form, which was printed in 1783 as *Dreams, Waking Thoughts and Incidents*. It was quite different from the numerous other travel books of the time, and was strongly romantic and subjective in tone. So much so, that his family, who were politically ambitious for him, persuaded him to suppress it and burn all but six copies. He again went to Italy for half of 1782, taking with him J.H. Cozens the artist, the son of his old drawing-master.

Unlike his sad and solitary later life, this period was packed with incidents and activities. His singing, playing and mimicry, as well as his wealth, intelligence and charm, made him welcome nearly everywhere; he moved in the highest society in London and Paris, playing the fool wherever he went and inclining towards rather fast women a good deal older than himself. His censorious family became worried about him, and with good cause. He was heavily entangled with his first cousin's wife, Louisa Beckford, who was six years his senior. Worse still, in 1779 he had met at Powderham Castle the son of the house, William Courtenay, an effeminate child of ten, the spoiled darling of his parents and thirteen sisters. This became the dominating and consuming attachment of his life until it ended in his irretrievable ruin.

The usual strategy was therefore adopted. He was married off in May 1783 to a girl of nearly his own age, whom he had long known, Lady Margaret Gordon, daughter of the impoverished Earl of Aboyne and sister of the future Marquess of Huntly. They spent a prolonged honeymoon in Geneva until the end of the year, returning to England in March 1784 after two and a half months in Paris. Beckford now entered parliament as Member for Wells, but immediately tired of it and applied for a Barony, the patent of which was made out through the influence of his former guardian, Lord Chancellor Thurlow.

It was at this moment, when all seemed to be going well, that disaster fell upon him like a thunderbolt, leaving him dazed and shattered. The young couple were staying at Powderham at the same time as his enemy Lord Loughborough, Chief Justice of the Common Pleas. This man was married to William Courtenay's aunt, who had at one time set her cap at Beckford, and he was also the bitter enemy and rival of Lord Thurlow. A month later, in November, Beckford was fiercely assailed in the press (at Loughborough's instigation) and accused of misconduct with the sixteen-year-old Courtenay. The punishment for this crime against the laws of England was death, and it was usual for men of the ruling class to disappear abroad in order to escape the embarrassment of a trial. But Beckford, who had a strain of toughness in him, manfully stood his ground (supported by his devoted wife, who firmly believed in his integrity), maintained his innocence, and remained at Fonthill. Either it was a trumped-up charge, or there was not enough evidence available, for his opponents did not press their case beyond these cowardly, anonymous insinuations.

This situation was, however, boring and painful in the extreme. So the following July the young couple retired to Vevey in Switzerland, where

Lady Margaret died after the birth of her second daughter, Susan, in May 1786. Beckford, who was genuinely attached to her (perhaps as a tutelary deity in the background of his life), was distracted. It was now that he was betrayed by a trusted friend, the clergyman Samuel Henley. In 1782 Beckford drafted in French his most original work, for which he is still famous, the oriental tale *Vathek*. He slowly added subsequent tales, known as *The Episodes of Vathek;* at the same time he commissioned Henley to translate *Vathek* into English, under his supervision. Henley was anxious to publish the translation, but Beckford wanted the original French version, and perhaps the *Episodes,* to appear simultaneously. His instructions on this point were quite clear. But Henley took advantage of his absence in Switzerland to publish the English text *anonymously,* with a Preface which specifically stated that the book was merely a translation of an Arabic original. Beckford's best work was stolen from him. He had no redress.

He returned to England in January 1787, hoping to settle down quietly at his beloved Fonthill. But his enemies would not let him rest in peace (they had even claimed that he was responsible for his wife's death), so in March his family shipped him off to Jamaica, the source of nearly all his wealth. But he was a bad sailor and he dreaded the climate and hurricanes of Jamaica. He therefore went ashore at the first stop (Lisbon) and refused to go any farther. He remained in Portugal until November and then travelled on to Madrid, where he stayed until the following summer. His extraordinary life in these two capitals and his persecution by the British envoys and the fussocks of the British trading community in Lisbon is inimitably portrayed in his *Journal.*[1] Portugal and its people drew him like a magnet, and he returned twice for lengthy stays, 1793–5 and 1798–9. Each of his first two stays gave him the material for a book. He selected portions of his *Journal,* cast them into letter form, added them to his suppressed and slightly altered *Dreams,* and gave the lot to the world in 1834 as *Italy; with Sketches of Spain and Portugal.* During his second stay be made a trip to the monasteries of Alcobaça and Batalha, kept a fragmentary diary, and later expanded it into *Recollections of an Excursion to the Monasteries of Alcobaça and Batalha,* published in 1835.

His last stay in Portugal was followed by two trips to Paris between 1801 and 1803, with a journey to Switzerland sandwiched in between so that he could "read himself blind" in Gibbon's library at Lausanne, which he had bought *en bloc.* As far as I can ascertain, he never went abroad again except to Paris in 1814 and 1819.

For from 1796 a great part of his energy was taken up by the planning, building and furnishing of a Gothic Abbey at Fonthill, and the accumulation of art treasures there. He employed the most celebrated and imaginative architect in the Kingdom, but also the most unbusiness-like and dilatory—James Wyatt, who was Surveyor-General to the Board of Works and a personal friend of the King. Once Wyatt had drawn the plans and seen the work started, he tended to lose interest, and it was the most difficult thing in the world to get him to inspect or supervise the later stages of a building. Matters were made worse by Beckford's mercurial enthusiasm, his impatience and his blazing temper. This combination of factors meant that for long periods the building languished. Then Wyatt was at last prevailed upon to come for a spell, or Beckford lost his temper, and the building proceeded for a while at a furious pace by day and night, with much consequent hasty and scamped work. But the circumstance most unfavourable to the durability of the Abbey was the constantly changing purpose in building it, as Beckford got new ideas. Originally it was to be a mere "ruined Convent", where he could spend pleasant hours reading and writing. But even when the final plan was hit upon, it was not built for durability, but run up in timber and cement, and intended only for occasional use. The result was that its tower fell down twice before Beckford was able to move in, and for the third and last time in 1825, after he had sold it. By 1806 the compo-cement in which the tower had been encased had crumbled in the English weather, and it had to be dismantled and re-erected or re-encased in stone. This renovation was still in progress when these letters begin and was the cause of Beckford's delay in not finally moving into the Abbey until the summer of 1807.[2]

The reason for the sale of the Abbey in 1822 is discussed in Chapter Ten. Beckford moved to Bath, where the same process of building a tower, planting, creating a garden out of a wilderness, collecting and commissioning pictures and works of art began anew, as Franchi had forecast to Beckford's son-in-law, the Duke of Hamilton, in February 1821— "new houses, new caprices, new follies, new debts; everything will disappear without one being able to prevent it." In the midst of all these activities Beckford died in May 1844, at the age of eighty four—unrepentant, unreformed and immature.

The letters begin too late to show whether the conception of Fonthill was inspired by Beckford or Wyatt. When the work was progressing well under Wyatt's superintendence, Beckford spoke enthusiastically about his genius.[3] His settled view of him is not unreasonably expressed in the letter of 23 September 1813: as far as Fonthill was concerned, his inspiration had long ago evaporated, and his sloth, carelessness and inattention were disastrous. In one or two particulars the letters are of value in their picture of Wyatt. His previous biographers, Mr Dale and Mr Tumor, have been able to find only one example of Wyatt's addiction to women, and this reference they regarded as suspect. But Beckford's incidental remarks[4] and his very nickname for Wyatt—the Whoremonger (*Bagasse*)—make it obvious that this was one of his besetting sins which interfered with his work. The other was his drunkenness. His biographers quote two remarks, both from Farington's diary, about his fondness for the bottle, but suggest that this was nothing out of the ordinary for those times. Beckford's picture of him at table shows that he had all the characteristics of the confirmed drunkard.[5] These letters also show that Wyatt charged for attendance double what had previously been recorded, that is to say, ten guineas a day, not five.[6]

The plan of the Abbey was four arms spreading in a cross from a great Octagon and Central Tower—St Michael's Gallery to the south, King Edward's to the north, the Great Western Hall and the Eastern Transept. There were three floors, the ground floor being almost entirely domestic offices and the first floor the main one.

Beckford normally lived in the south wing. His dining-room, the Brown Parlour,[3] a long low room, was on the ground floor in the south-west corner of the Abbey. One set of its pointed windows looked west through an oriel flanked by two turrets, and the other south through the Southern Cloisters on to lovely views. Its name derived from its dark oak wainscoting. It was hung with tapestries, but the dominating feature was a huge full-length portrait of Peter Beckford, the Alderman's grandfather, the founder of the family fortunes in Jamaica. The upper part of the windows had painted glass by Eginton, representing Beckford's supposed royal ancestors, and the lower parts were huge panes of plate-glass. Two tables of Sienna marble were heaped with massive gilt plate, including, perhaps, some of that for which Beckford secretly negotiated with the Regent in 1808; the plate was flanked by choice specimens of Dresden and Sèvres china. After the ancestors, the objects to which the visitor's attention was most likely drawn were a pair of silver candlesticks designed by Beckford himself. His bedroom was the Gallery Cabinet, on the second floor of the south-east tower, at the south-east extremity of the Abbey. One small window, looking south, was immediately above the fine south oriel of St Michael's Gallery. It was little more than an unheated cell, and Beckford slept in a narrow truckle bed without hangings.

The rooms on the second floor in this wing were designed as a suite for Beckford's special use, and reflect his studiousness and his liking of privacy and small living-rooms. There was the "Board of Works",[8] so named because Wyatt and others working for Beckford consulted its special collection of books on the fine arts and prints of the old masters, using the massive library table in the window recess, which looked down into the Fountain Court. Concealed in the oak wainscoting of a recess in its west wall was the door of the Cedar Boudoir, which was in an octagonal turret. Its walls were lined with books and cedar gilt mouldings and gilt Hamiltonian cinquefoils, and its window looked up the Great West Avenue. On the other (eastern) side of the building was the Vaulted Library, which ran above St Michael's Gallery. It was here that Beckford and his bookseller Clarke (Boletus) toiled up the stairs in the summer of 1818, their arms full of books of Voyages and Travels, some from the great MacCarthy Library. It ran for forty-four feet from a mirror which carried on the perspective, to the Chintz Boudoir at its north end, which looked out on to the east. The walls of this boudoir of Beckford's were covered with yellow chintz of a damask pattern and hung with a Van Eyck *Virgin and Child* and West's fearsome *Apocalypse*; a characteristic *objet d'art* was the Piping Boy, in bronze. This concluded Beckford's own private suite, and from here he was able to descend by the circular staircase in the Latimer Turret to the Vestibule of St Michael's Gallery, where he could enjoy either the sublime heights and depths of the Great Octagon or the perspective of St Michael's Gallery (on the first floor).

This gallery was the finest feature of the south wing, running for 112 feet from its magnificent south oriel to the Great Octagon, through which the perspective was continued to the Oratory at the far north end of the Abbey, an uninterrupted vista of 307 feet. Its fan vaulting ended in corbels of angels bearing emblazoned shields; its carpet was crimson with white cinquefoils. Stained-glass windows alternated on either side with marble-topped ebony tables (upon which were precious cabinets) and with bookcases curtained in scarlet and deep blue. The corresponding gallery in the north wing was called King Edward's Gallery, since it commemorated Beckford's seventy-two supposed ancestors who had at an early date received the Garter, including the founder of the Order, Edward III. His portrait occupied the place of honour in the centre of the east wall, over an alabaster chimney-piece; on either side were ranged smaller portraits of Knights of the Order, hung above bookcases. Their arms and badges were in stained glass on the pointed windows opposite, through which the western sun was filtered by double scarlet-and-blue curtains on to a plain scarlet carpet and scarlet wall paper. Looking up this gallery, the eye rested at its central point on a solitary inlaid table of *pietre commesse* from the Borghese Palace, upon which were tastefully arranged Cellini's nautilus and two other precious objects. The ceiling was quite different from that in St Michael's Gallery, being flat and of oak, reticulated in lozenges and in square panels; below it ran a frieze with seventy-two rich gartered shields of the aforesaid Knights.

In the evening these two immense galleries were lit by only two dozen candles; the visitor was insensibly drawn on by a blaze of light three hundred feet off at the far north end, which cast a wonderful glow on the surrounding gloom. One was thus enticed through King Edward's Gallery and the Vaulted Corridor, up a step into the Sanctuary, and thence into the Oratory. Here, upon an altar, stood an alabaster statue of St Anthony of Padua holding a child, and surrounded by thirty-six lighted wax candles in silver-gilt candelabra and candlesticks; above his head hung a silver-gilt lamp of antique design. The Oratory was five-sided; from each angle rose a slender gilt column from which sprang fan tracery of burnished gold, and there were five small lancet windows of bright stained glass.

The chief rooms in this north wing on the floor above were (from south to north) the Tribune Room, Lancaster Gallery and Lancaster State Bedchamber, where the honoured guests slept beneath Henry VII's purple silk quilt in an ebony state bedstead with crimson damask hangings, once graced by Colonel Peter Beckford, Lieutenant-Governor of Jamaica. Here hung *Christ in the Garden* by Bellini, now in the National Gallery. The Tribune Room, hung with crimson silk damask, had a wonderful view into the Octagon from its balcony or tribune.

The west wing was wholly occupied by one grandiose feature, the Great Western Hall. It could not be heated and so was converted in 1809–10 from a monkish refectory to a State Entrance (seldom used) into the Great Octagon. Standing at the top of a broad flight of stone steps, one looked through the great doors (thirty-five feet high but opened by the dwarf) up the Great West Avenue. Seventy feet from the floor was a massive hammer-beam roof, so studded with heraldic escutcheons that the puzzled tourists at the time of the 1822 sale wrote down "Fancy arms" in their notebooks. On the right, behind a crimson curtain in a recess, lurked the statue of the Commendatore (as Beckford called the Alderman), brooding upon the sins and ruin of his son.[9]

The Eastern Transept is particularly interesting to the reader of these letters, which describe the construction of its outside walls in 1812, its octagonal turrets and roof in 1815, its first-floor rooms in 1817–18, and the hanging of recently acquired pictures in them in 1818–19. The main purpose of this wing was to commemorate, in a grand "Baronial Hall" on the second floor, all the barons who signed Magna Carta, from every one of whom Beckford spuriously claimed descent. This hall was to be gaudy with their emblazoned shields and enriched by a library. This floor was never begun, and even the rooms on the main floor below were temporary and make-shift. The wing was huge, and dwarfed everything except the Octagon and Central Tower; its parapet was ninety-five feet high and its twin octagonal turrets at the east end 120 feet. Its southern face had three very high pointed windows which served the first and second floors; above was an arcade, intended to be a continuation of the Nunneries which ran round the Central Tower.

The wing was entered from the Octagon through the Great Portal in the Eastern Vestibule, which Beckford was constructing in June 1818, aiming at making it "worthy, absolutely worthy, of William of Wykeham". There followed a suite of rooms (the Cabinet Room[10] and Crimson and Grand Drawing Rooms) decorated and furnished to match, opening out from one another in a series of doors to form a perspective. Each room had in a curtained recess a gilt latticed south window which it shared with the floor above, a ceiling of massive beams laid close together, and silk damask hangings (crimson in the first two and Garter-blue in the third); each was a veritable picture gallery—several of the pictures are specially mentioned by Beckford, e.g. Lodovico Caracci's *Sibyl,* Dou's *Poulterer's Shop* (now in the National Gallery) and West's *Abraham and Isaac.* Here too were Reisener's secretaire (now in the Wallace Collection), and many objects mentioned by Beckford—the ebony jewel-cabinet set with rubies and emeralds, with figures designed by Bouchardon; Hume's great Ebony Cabinet, so admired by Samuel Rogers, in a recess of its own behind crimson damask curtains; van Diemen's japan coffer, which had belonged to Mme de Pompadour; the ivory cup carved by Magnus Berg; and Fiamingo's ivory vases bought in a delirium at the Margravine's sale in July 1818. And here "upon a carpet of extraordinary costliness", stood a table of Egyptian marble, "the largest slab of the kind in Europe"—alas, Beckford still had the *nouveau riche* in him and had been brought up at Splendens on such talk. Franchi's room, the Crimson Breakfast Parlour, was on the north side of this wing.

The Octagon, the central point from which these wings radiated, was the chief glory of the Abbey. In each wall was an arch eighty feet high; four of them, hung from top to bottom with deep blue curtains, gave access to the wings; the other four arches were mere recesses hung with scarlet curtains fifty feet high, above which were the pointed Batalha windows of stained glass in purple, crimson and yellow. These were modelled on the windows of the Portuguese monastery which Beckford visited in 1794, and their glass reflected a mosaic of brilliant coloured light on the floor. Between each arch ran a single slender column ending in a capital ninety feet up, from which fanned out the vaulting which supported the sixteen-sided Lantern; the great central boss in the Lantern's vaulted roof was 132 feet from the ground. Between these capitals and the points of the great arches below ran a gallery with a perforated stone balustrade and twenty-four small pointed arches; this gallery was called the Nunneries or Nun's Walk, and opened on to four small sitting-rooms for guests. It was here that Beckford stood at midnight in September 1808, watching by torchlight the huge buckets of plaster and water being hauled up through the maze of scaffolding for the stuccoing of the Lantern.

The Abbey was surrounded by lawns upon which ornamental plantations encroached in an informal and casual manner, there being no fences or straight lines. Hares, pheasants, partridges, peacocks, turkeys and all manner of fowl wandered unconcernedly and tamely upon the sward. The Great Western Avenue, a hundred feet broad, ran from the Great Western Hall due west for a mile to Stone Gate, but it was not a formal avenue like those on most estates. Due south was the American Plantation, full of rhododendron and magnolia, azalea and arbutus. Here too flourished the Angelica tree and the andromeda, the Yulan tree and the Carolina Allspice. Nearby was the artificial Bitham Lake, the haunt of water fowl, in whose serene waters the Abbey was mirrored. From the lake and its vale, the picturesquely wooded ground rose steeply to the ridge of Beacon Terrace, which led to the highest hill in the area, Stop's Beacon; beyond that lay the Norwegian Lawn with its Norwegian Hut and appropriate trees. This beautifully planted area of over five hundred acres, upon which Beckford had lavished a fortune, was surrounded by the Barrier, an unscalable wall twelve miles in circumference and a dozen feet high, surmounted by iron spikes. Half a dozen gates pierced it, but they were closely guarded and it was almost impossible to obtain admission.

There were plenty of other rides beyond the Barrier, but still within the estate—a guest could drive for twenty-two miles along these special paths without retracing his steps. There was the Great Terrace, a ridge running east along the northern boundary of the estate from Knoyle Corner for three miles to Inigo Jones's entrance Lodge. There was the drive east of the Abbey from the Barrier Gate, past the Beckford Arms inn, through the Old Park and alongside the old lake, past the ruins of Splendens, Beckford's birthplace. Across the lake from the old house were the huge grotto, the Alpine Gardens and the picturesque quarry. Beckford still used Splendens' eight-acre kitchen garden, a mile and a half from the Abbey—there was no formal garden of any sort within the vicinity of the Abbey, except for the dwarf's garden, with a sundial and fountain, and a herb garden. All these excursions were made by guests like his daughter, the Abbé and Rogers in a low Sociable a foot from the ground, painted green and drawn (on important occasions and in earlier days) by four grey ponies ridden by two small boys dressed in scarlet and gold.

An estate of this sort, with the ceaseless building, repairs and planting, was very costly to maintain. It is surprising to learn from these letters how little Beckford had available. After he sold his Somerset estate of Witham in 1811, his only remaining English lands were in Wiltshire, with a rent-roll of £4,000 a year, from which "public burdens" of £740 a year were deducted (in 1821 at any rate); he got nearly £1,000 a year from the farms he leased from the Bishops of Salisbury and Winchester, but the Duke of Hamilton's agent reckoned that Beckford did not receive more than £4,000 net a year from his English lands. His only other source of income was the quarterly allowance made by his West India merchants, which fluctuated with the erratic price of sugar. It fell as low as £750 quarterly, but as a result of the 1814 boom Beckford was expecting a quarterly of "£3,000 instead of £2,000" in January 1815; that very year sugar was beginning its long price-decline, so this would not have been paid for long. In general, his Jamaican allowance fluctuated between £4,000 and £8,000 a year during the period of these letters, and occasionally the merchants threatened to stop it altogether.

Some of the reasons for their threats, and the precariousness of Beckford's whole financial position, are given on p.295. Farington's diary abounds with gossip in the 1790s about the hugeness of Beckford's income. Even if Wyatt and West passed these figures on to the diarist without exaggeration and he noted them down accurately, perhaps we should suspect them. Beckford's *nouveau-riche* background may have made him boast about his money in order to bolster up his own importance and exact deference and service; and he was always ready to tell a tall story to anyone foolish enough to believe it. Still, whatever his income, he was incapable of living within it. Like a spoilt child his ideas had to be carried out. Like many collectors, he could not bear to let tempting objects go. So his account with his merchants became increasingly overdrawn and the unpaid interest at 5 per cent swelled the principal. Periodically Jamaican and English estates were sold to reduce this debt. And the sins of his father and grandfather were visited upon him: plantations which they had got into their clutches by dubious methods were the cause of expensive litigation. When he lost these cases he was also obliged to pay up part of the past profits which he and his family had enjoyed.

No wonder he was always complaining of a shortage of money—at a time when great treasures in the way of books and pictures were to be bought by those with long purses. Aristocrats and parvenus vied fiercely with one another at auction, but Beckford was able to spend very little at important sales.

From these letters, Farington's diary and Redding's biography, we get a good idea of how Beckford spent his day at the Abbey (the exact times altered a little with the seasons). He always rose early—at six o'clock in October—swallowed some chicken broth, and took an hour's ride. He then walked round the garden or examined the building works, returning to breakfast at ten for half an hour. From eleven he was busy with his land-steward Still (the Great Dolt) and his Clerk of the Works, George Hayter (Coxone), discussing building, timber sales and the estate; Hayter was "a pastime for two hours a day to his master".[11] From these wearying details he turned to a book (sometimes the latest memoir or travel book) and the newspapers to refresh himself for another hour or so. He then went for a very fast ride, sometimes covering twenty or thirty miles. Or he walked round the plantations with Hayter and Vincent (one of his "gardeners"), marking oak or fir for felling or inspecting new planting. On his return between half-past three and half-past four, he expected to find a letter from Franchi on the harpsichord; he immediately sat down to answer it or to complain of its absence. He dined at four in winter and five in summer. This took about an hour, for he dined in state even when he had but a single guest (the Abbé Macquin or Father Smith the artist), eating very sparingly of a number of dishes served by a great train of servants. This was followed by coffee, after which he went out again if it was still light. He drank tea at eight and supped at ten (a very light refreshment) before immediately retiring to bed. When it was dark in the evenings he mostly read books; sometimes he listened to Franchi playing the piano; sometimes he played the organ, and it reverberated down the empty, candle-lit galleries. Unless a doctor ordered otherwise or a cold prevented him, he bathed in the river every day until some time in November. He never shot, being afraid of a gun, with its kick and noise; he hated to kill any living creature, preferring game to run about tame on his lawns and plantation rides.

He hated being alone in the gloomy Abbey. So he arranged for the Abbé or Father Smith to stay for long periods when Franchi was away. His daughter Susan and son-in-law Douglas came for short periods, General Orde and Lord Roden for a night or two, and Wyatt for the building. There was no one else whom he could ask—so heavy lay the social ban upon him. When the Tory whip Billy Holmes dined at the Abbey on 23 April 1819 with four of his Parliamentary friends, Beckford had to absent himself; the honours were done by the land-steward Still!

These letters show why his neighbours and nearly everyone in society adopted this attitude. There was not merely the unproven Powderham Castle scandal of 1784; there was every reason to suspect what went on behind the closely guarded twelve-foot-high Barrier. The nicknames of the staff are significant—the Doll, Bijou, Mme Bion, the Calf. But we may well ask—what did it all amount to? Beckford's relations with the valet Richardson (Mme Bion) and the Turk seem to have been wholly sentimental. Again and again Beckford assures the jealous Franchi that the Turk is kept in his place—the occasional melting look could not overcome the barrier of his inhibitions. What he seems mostly to have needed was to be surrounded by "lively and lovely objects, cheerful, pretty faces and comely forms",[12] and he liked them "sentimental". Those who are deprived of something fundamental talk much about it and are obsessed by it. Perhaps this was so with Beckford. A good letter-writer gets carried-away, he dramatises and exaggerates his moods and feelings. Beckford was prone to this, even in conversation.[13] In London he probably felt freer to indulge himself, although the cost and the risk of blackmail or prosecution were formidable. But whatever his peccadilloes may have been, it does not follow that his relationship with low-class youths of the stable, the theatre, the circus, the Army and the slums, was similar to that with his social equals like Courtenay. The Powderham affair, which ruined his life, remains a mystery.

The letters about this side of his life are valuable for two reasons. They reveal his turbulent spirit—they show him consumed by a canker which prevented him from fulfilling the literary promise of his youth and from indulging in any serious literary pursuits until old age had quelled his frustrated passions.[14] Secondly, they show how widespread sodomy was in England and how recruits for it were found. Practically no literature on the subject is available for this period. An important scandal like the flight of Marquess Townshend in 1812 is passed over in silence even by the press. Our leaders today are greatly exercised by its prevalence; they speak as if it were a new phenomenon and a sign of national degeneracy; they frequently confess or show their ignorance about its past history. Beckford's letters will perhaps set the subject a little more in perspective.

Closely linked with this side of his personality was his attitude to religion. He was by nature a religious man. He was easily moved by the pomp and historicity, the solemnity and theatricalness of Catholic worship in Lisbon. All his æsthetic feelings, all his Rousseauesque sentimentalism found full play. But what had happened by 1807, when he had been an exile from society for over twenty years and starved of Catholic worship? He quotes frequently from the Roman service books, even if in a light vein. There are constant references to St Anthony of Padua. And Judgment was ever before his eyes. This was evidently not a belief he could laugh off, and he may have felt that his perversion could not be squared with Christianity. And so he wrote, bitterly or ironically: "How difficult is salvation! Nothing now is open or offers easy progress but the broad way which leads to the abode of the Devil."[15] Perhaps this resulted in a gradual hardening process, which on his deathbed prevented him from seeing even a Romish priest—unrepentant and yet believing—but believing without hope.

Nearly all the letters in this book were written to Beckford's best friend, the Chevalier Gregorio Fellipe Franchi, who was born in Lisbon in 1770, the son of Loreto Franchi, a Neapolitan singer in the service of Queen

Maria I of Portugal. In 1783 he entered the Patriarchal Seminary or College of Music, where all the Portuguese Royal choristers and leading musicians and singers were taught. Here Beckford met him on 28 May 1787, at the solicitation of one of the Queen's singers, Polycarpo da Silva, as the *Journal* relates:

> During sermon time I slipped away with Polycarpo and ran up a flight of wide easy steps at the top of which stood the *menino* who plays so well on the harpsichord. He took hold of Polycarpo's hand and seemed beside himself with joy at this opportunity of showing his talents. Several youths came around us. Only one was admitted into a tolerably neat room where the harpsichord was placed. The others applied their large eyes alternately to an aperture in the door, which was carefully closed and watched by a priest. The *menino* has surprising abilities and did ample justice to the glorious compositions of Haydn he played. I could have passed an hour agreeably in hearing of him and was in fact delighted; but rose up, after I had listened about a quarter of an hour, with dignity and apparent coldness … I wish much to hear the *menino* again and will return tomorrow, please the Patriarch! Polycarpo in behalf of his disciple hinted that my pianofortes would set off his talents to greater advantage. I suppose he wants me to send for him. All in good time.

Franchi became as devoted to him as a dog, and was delighted to make himself useful to Beckford, who writes:

> I have need of some young sweet-breathed animal to enliven my spirits, to run into the citron thickets and bring me flowery branches, to arrange my prints, transpose my songs, and write down the musical ideas which rush into my mind in happy moments.[16]

Franchi was a clever singer and pianist; he was good-looking and intelligent, humorous and good-natured, patient and affectionate; he soon acquired French and English; he was the same way inclined as Beckford. He became, in fact, indispensable. Accordingly, his father sent him from Lisbon in May 1788 to join Beckford in Madrid. The boy brought with him the following touching letter:

Excellency, with tears in my eyes I commit my son Gregory to Your Excellency, and recommend him to you, believing and hoping that your protection may be the true beginning of his fortune. All Lisbon envies his luck. I would gladly have accompanied him, but my obligations do not allow it. Meanwhile I hope to obtain from Your Excellency the kindness of persuading my son that he forget not to help his mother. For my own part I have the wherewithal to exist until my death. I only desire that he may show himself worthy of your incomparable protection, and I remain, with all imaginable respect, Your Excellency's most humble and obedient servant, Loreto Franchi.

He had entered Beckford's service for life.

In 1799, through Beckford's insistence and Marialva's influence, he was made a Chevalier of the Order of Christ, despite the distaste of the Portuguese Regent and the Minister in charge of such patronage. Franchi married a Portuguese woman of his own age; they had a daughter, but the women remained behind in Portugal (except for one trip to England by the daughter for her education)—Franchi disliked married life. Beckford paid him an annuity of £400; on his death his widow wrote from Lisbon to remind Beckford of his promise, given at her engagement, to continue the pension after her husband's death. After years of painful martyrdom to the gout and perhaps arthritis, Franchi died in lodgings in London in August 1828. He was buried in the St John's Wood burial ground of Marylebone Parish Church. The Duchess of Hamilton paid £10 to Hume for the purchase of a burial plot and the erection of inscribed head and foot stones (which are still there).

He kept all Beckford's letters, tying them in bundles labelled "His Excellency's letters"; his will requested their return to Beckford. The latter did get back a quantity written after 1820 and must have destroyed many of them, putting the rest in inscribed folders. An earlier group was labelled by the Duke *Lettres à Franchi—personne à voir, December 1846*, but we do not know how he acquired them. Another group of four hundred and thirty-seven letters (a small part of the series written between 1814 and 1819) was bought back for 2,000 *dollars* by Duchess Susan in 1857 from a firm in York acting as agents for a Mr Beeby. In this same group was a note dated *5 March* which must have become detached from its own pile; the writer, Mr E. Hall, offered the Duke's agent 146 letters for £50, which was paid to him. Altogether over 1,100 letters have survived. But there are none for 1820 and only three each for 1809 and 1813; so many more must have disappeared for one reason or another.

Sometimes there are letters for every day of the month, and even a "third edition" on the same day, and some cover six or eight quarto pages. Inevitably there is repetition, obscurity and tiresomeness. I have therefore had to select and prune drastically in presenting these letters to the public for the first time (none of them have ever before been published). They were written in Italian so that Beckford could express himself freely without fearing that they would be understood if they fell into the wrong hands; it was not ordinary Italian either, but freely larded with coined words, Portuguese words, French words with Italian endings, slang in several languages, etc.

Words coined from proper names are characteristic of Beckford's style, and I have as far as practicable retained them in their equivalent English form, e.g. *Coxonising, Dixonating, methoderies*. Archaic English words like *salutiferous* and *mephitic* sound ugly now to us, no longer nurtured on the classics; but I have retained them when they are interesting and characteristic. He often uses the adjective *anglicano* for "English"; he does this deliberately, in a jeering or deprecatory sense, especially when hinting at English characteristics which he dislikes; when possible, I have left this *Anglican*. He frequently uses certain coarse words in full, but I have usually printed them with dashes. In retaining or translating nicknames I have considered the effect on the reader: one can tire a little of "The Belcher", "The Whoremonger", "The Mushroom" and The Great This and The Great That; so I have retained some of the Italian nicknames instead of translating them—e.g. Rottier, Bagasse, Boletus; they have a certain charm of their own. But a few I have changed to the proper names. I have as far as possible modernised and standardised the spelling of proper names and places, but I could not bring myself to write *Sintra* for *Cintra*, and nearly retained the old double *l* in *Colares* and *Palmela*. Beckford underlined a great deal for emphasis, but I have reduced italics to the minimum. His erratic punctuation and proliferation of dashes add fascination to his manuscripts but would spoil the printed page. More often than not, Beckford started his letters directly, e.g. "Believe me, my dear Gregory"; but where he begins in our way, "My dear Gregory", I have always omitted it, without supplying dots (in all other places omissions are indicated by dots). There is a certain sameness about the endings of letters written by one man to the same person, so I have usually omitted them, leaving a few endings intact in order to give the reader an idea of their form. I have normally expanded abbreviations.

I have drawn on several letters written in French, e.g. by Beckford to the Marquis of Douglas (later Duke of Hamilton) and the Abbé Macquin, and by Franchi to Douglas. In every instance I have indicated this in the first footnote to the letter, and also when a letter was *not* written from Fonthill. In other words, except where indicated by a footnote, all the letters in this book were written by Beckford in Italian to Franchi from Fonthill Abbey.

Boyd Alexander

1.   *Journal of William Beckford in Portugal and Spain 1787–1788,* edited by Boyd, Alexander (Hart-Davis, 1954).

2.   For events at Fonthill between 1807 and 1822, see the Introductions to each chapter.

3.   18 July 1807.

4.   e.g. 5 October 1811.

5.   27 April 1813.

6.   24 June 1811.

7.   *Rutter* calls it the Oak Parlour.

8.   *Rutter* calls it the Oak Library.

9.   For a suggestive reference to this theme, see p.48, sunday <8 November> paragraph 2.

10.   So called because of the collection of precious cabinets there. *Rutter* calls this the Great Dining Room.

11.   Franchi to Douglas, 26 November 1818.

12.   p.146.

13.   "I could not help saying a thousand things which ought never to have been uttered. *Faire sans dire* is an excellent maxim, and it would have been better for me had I paid it a stricter attention. I have more profligacy of tongue than of character and often do my utmost to make myself appear worse than I am in reality." (*Journal,* p.238)

14. He did, however, draft some (if not all) of the passages of *Spain and Portugal*, (e.g. the interview with the Prince of Brazil), latterly at Fonthill.
15. 31 August 1812.
16. *Journal,* p.208

ACKNOWLEDGMENTS

ONCE again it is a pleasure to thank His Grace the Duke of Hamilton and Brandon and the other Directors of Hamilton and Kinneil Estates Ltd for such generosity in placing their papers at my disposal for a long period of time. I hasten to add that the responsibility for what appears in this book is mine, since I am almost certainly the first person to examine Beckford's Italian letters since they were recovered by the family a century ago. I am also indebted to Miss Bruce Johnston, His Grace's Curator.

Special thanks are due to Dr E.J. Dingwall and Mr Noel Blakiston, who were unfailingly ready to help with knotty problems out of their large store of erudition. I am also most grateful to Lady Campbell, Mr Martin Davies of the National Gallery, Dr Rossi, Miss Russ of Bath, Mr Babb and Miss Simison of Yale, Mr Frape of Salford Art Gallery, Mr Robin Ashton, the Librarian of the Guildhall and Mr M.W. Stone, the collector of theatricalia; Messrs Christie, Manson & Woods, and Messrs Phillips, Son & Neale; Mr George Speaight and Miss Lamb, who helped me with research, and Mr Francis Watson.

I am also grateful for help on specific points from Dr Parreaux; the Librarian of the Music Department of the Bibliothèque Nationale; the Librarian of the Royal College of Surgeons; Mr Meredith-Owens of the British Museum; Miss Carter, formerly of the History of Parliament Trust, the Secretary of the Royal Horticultural Society, and Mr. Toase of Wimbledon Public Library. I am indebted to my wife for many useful suggestions.

B.A.

GLOSSARY AND PRINCIPAL NICKNAMES

Bagasse	Wyatt
Barzaba	Beckford as boy-fancier
Bestifownes	Fownes, lawyer
Boletus	Clarke, bookseller
Cowpat	Mrs Bezerra
Coxone	George Hayter, Clerk of Works
Father Bestorum (the Father)	"Warwick" Smith, artist
Great Dolt	J.C. Still, land steward
Macaw	Lady Anne Hamilton
Mme Bion	Richardson, valet
Paradise of D. Fagundes	Portugal
Phoenix	Sir George Hayter, R.A.
Pledges	Beckford's daughters
Rhinoceros	Westmacott, sculptor
Rottier (Rottibus)	White (senior), lawyer
Sage	Dr Hicks
Saudades (Portuguese)	Homesickness
Shepherd	Marquess of Douglas (Duke of Hamilton)
Shepherdess	His wife, Beckford's daughter
Terra papale	Portugal
Yellow Poet (Yellow One)	Samuel Rogers

SIGNS AND ABBREVIATIONS

Bath (1841)   Catalogue of Beckford sale in Bath, 1841.

Bath (1845)   Catalogue of Beckford sale in Bath, 1845; unless otherwise stated, references are to 5th Day only.

Bath (1848)   Catalogue of Beckford sale in Bath, 1848; references to 3rd and 4th Days only.

Christie   Catalogue of his abortive sale at Fonthill, 1822.

Clarke   *Repertorium Bibliographicum*, Anon [Wm Clarke], 1819.

H.P.   Hamilton Papers (Beckford Section).

H.P.S.   Catalogues of Hamilton Palace sales of Beckford's books by Sotheby, and of pictures and antiques by Christie, 1882. It being clear from the text which one applies, *H.P.S.* is used for both sales. In Christie's catalogue there is only one series of Lot numbers, and Sotheby's is alphabetical, so only the Lot number is given here.

Inventory   MS Inventory in H.P. of Beckford's pictures and an tiques, 2 vols, 1844.

Phillips   Catalogue of his sale at Fonthill, 1823.

Rutter   *Delineations of Fonthill and its Abbey*, 1823.

< >   Editorial insertion. When there are no words inside, a word in the manuscript is illegible or incomprehensible.

(?)   Indicates that the reading of the preceding word is uncertain.

FOOTNOTES

These occur *at the first mention* of the name concerned, and are not usually referred to again.

1807

AT last, in the summer of 1807, Beckford moved into the unfinished Abbey. It was an irrevocable step, for he proceeded to pull down Splendens, the house by the Lake, rebuilt at such cost by his father. Unfortunately sugar (the main source of his income) now touched its lowest price since perhaps 1784, and was being sold at a loss on the English market.[1] So Beckford was henceforth constantly obliged to look for fresh sources of money; this explains his reluctant sale of two of the finest pictures in his collection, the Altieri Claudes; it also explains the launching of a disastrous Chancery suit—his attempt to revoke from the Widow Wildman the grant of an entire Jamaican plantation to her husband.

But financial troubles were not the only ones. There was the lingering and painful death of a man to whom he was much attached, his personal physician Ehrhart. There was the quarrel with Franchi, on whose sympathy and assistance he was wholly dependent. Franchi was now immersed in his own troubles and in danger of imprisonment—on behalf of another employer, the Foreign Minister of Portugal. Franchi was engaged in contraband activities aimed at circumventing the Continental blockade, and Beckford had to lend him money to get him out of scrapes.

Most wounding of all was the attack on Franchi's perverted morals by the local parson. This reminded Beckford of the countless similar attacks he had endured, and his fury knew no bounds. It was like a comic opera. He was afraid to face Parson Still himself, so turned on the latter's brother, the land-agent. Then the solicitor White was summoned from London to assist in the defence, but retired from the scene of battle as soon as possible. So Pedley, the West India agent, had to come down. Meanwhile, Franchi remained disconcertingly unwilling to take up the cudgels on his own behalf, and Beckford was left to fight alone a battle he should never have begun.

The only welcome occurrence was the appearance of a tightrope-walker at the Circus Royal, "Young" Saunders. His father, Abraham Saunders, toured the English Fairs with an equestrian show and at one time was lessee of the old Royalty Theatre. The son (whose Christian name is never given) is said to have been born in 1789, and was therefore eighteen when Beckford saw him, but would have been got up to look much younger. He is recorded as performing at the Royal Circus as early as 1800, when he was billed as follows: "Master Saunders, the celebrated Equestrian Infant-Phenomenon, will perform his astonishing feats of Horsemanship ... Master Saunders will make his First Appearance on the Tight Rope, in which he will particularly distinguish himself. He will dance a hornpipe, on the rope, with his Feet in Baskets; leap the garter nine feet high, from the stage, backward and forward; display two flags, and many wonderful Evolutions, without the Pole; and is without exception the first Infant Performer in Europe."[2] When he was *said* to be only seven, he was billed at Bartholomew Fair as "The Wonderful Child of Promise ... who is allowed to be the first Infant Performer in the World".[3]

In 1807 the Saunders family lived in "Duke Street". In July 1810, during the raid on the notorious White Swan in Vere Street,[4] one of those arrested was "Matthew Saunders of Duke Street, Aldgate". Unfortunately he was one of the two men whose occupation is not given, nor is his age. Was he Young Saunders, or one of the same family? Beckford was sufficiently interested in this case to cut out the press report and paste it in an album, and to refer to it in a letter,[5] but this is not conclusive. The Rate Books show no Saunders in Duke Street, but one in Duke's Place, Aldgate, for 1807–9 and 1811. There were eighteen Duke Streets in London in 1810, so it would have been a familiar name, and "Place" could therefore easily become "Street" in reporting and letter-writing. I think it is reasonable to assume that the Saunders of the press report, resident in "Duke Street, Aldgate", is the same as the Saunders of Duke's Place, and we note that there was a Saunders there in 1807. It is obviously possible that this is the Saunders family of "Duke Street" whom Franchi visited.

<Thursday> 5 February[6]

Our conversation last night has called up a long series of recollections which would require more time and patience than I can bestow just at this moment to memorize.

So long ago as the year of my father's death, I remember an old gentleman of the name of Bolland talking frequently and very morally upon the sad vicissitudes of human affairs exemplified in the case of Margery Maddock our unfortunate ancestress, for I think he claimed relationship through this line; and half in joke, half in earnest, used to rally me in the presence of both my parents upon my great-great-grandfather the shoe maker.[7] As no small portion of the family pride seemed to have been infused into me with the blood of the Hamiltons, I by no means relished the thoughts of this plebeian descent. I fell into a violent rage. In order to increase this little storm of infantile petulance which appeared diverting to my father and his venerable acquaintance, hints were thrown out of the low condition of another ancestor—my great-grandfather's maternal grandfather John Woodward. From all this, I rather imagine the Woodwards moved in an humble and confined sphere, and so far from inhabiting the purlieus of the Court, were strangers to any Court except that near St. Bartholomew the Less, where they were born, bred and perhaps apprenticed ...

You may gather from these circumstances that the glories of the Poles are so miserably tarnished, their cloth of gold so foully steeped in a torrent of plebeian filth, that scarce a ray of regal splendour remains. Indeed it becomes a question whether after striking a fair balance, we should not lose more than we gain by lifting up the veil which has so long covered this most singular scrap of genealogy. And yet the love of Truth, and my vivid, I may add impartial, taste for heraldic investigation powerfully impels me to pursue the research and hold up in broad day a melancholy picture of fallen degraded Royalty. Can you tell me what became of poor Campbell's collections upon this subject? You know how much it occupied him in his days of better health. He was a great offalist, and almost lecherously fond of raking among cinder heaps for the tattered remnants of former tatters, themselves too tattered even to keep a louse.

You remember the hearty laugh we enjoyed when the Woodward pedigree slipped out by chance from under one of the grand gartered achievements, with the ingenious portrait of M. Maddock scrawled upon the margin, and adorned with a tremendous long and peaked nose. I daresay you recollect my exclamation upon the discovery of this famous nose; and by it, as it peeped forth, I may be said to have pulled forth the pedigree; to be sure it was a rare handle. But joking apart, and in justice to the memory of this worthy and laborious grubster, we must allow he had taken a world of pains in writing to Chester and hunting after the miserable Maddocks from house to house through all the slop and slush of I know not how many hundred cheesy villages.

There was also wafered on to a long rigmarole of extracts from this correspondence, about half a quarter of an original mouse-eaten MS document ascribed (?) to Stow[8] concerning the erasure of an inscription on J. Woodward the Elder's tomb. Was not this the identical inscription you mentioned as having excited such a tempest of indignation in Queen Elizabeth's scraggy bosom? And yet what could she fear? The rich drops of royal blood in poor Margery's descendents were too much woefully diluted by worse than hogwash to raise the smallest alarm.

Indeed, we shall be finely puzzled, even now that we have vanquished so many difficulties and collected such a mass of proofs (?), to arrange our quarterings. How shall we manage Maddock, supposing even as you suspect the Woodwards had a right to arms? Your conjecture as to the eagle on the < > is ingenious; but you know we can admit no conjectures. After keeping so long within the severest bounds, let us not swerve from the paths of the most scrupulous veracity, and never lose sight of that excellent adage *Rien n'est beau que le vrai. Le vrai seul est aimable.*

<Saturday> 18 July[9]

... My letters were not gay, as you can imagine. Everything is going from bad to worse, everything is going to ruin. Poor Jamaica is already emaciated—it is, alas, the planters and not the sugars which have *consumption*. I do not know the dwarf with the black face[10] well enough yet to tell you about him in detail, but I am persuaded that of all dwarfs my little Pierre de Grailly,[11] whom you remember, is the most honest, adroit and useful.

We are in the midst of all the fracas and dust of demolition on the one hand and building on the other. The Tower and the great Octagon are being finished, but it will all remain unfurnished, for it is not the moment to begin. But at least we enjoy the spaciousness and the great architectural effect of an edifice which without exaggeration does honour to the great artist who has executed it; Wyatt merits and, I am sure, will receive the highest praise.[12] I assure you, my dear Douglas, that you will like it and that you will be in an ecstasy of enthusiasm, inspired by the view of this marvellous tower (like all those who have the Hamilton feeling for the fine arts).

You will forget the old palace of tertian fevers with all its false Greek and false Egyptian, its small doors and mean casements, its dauberies *à la* Casali, its ridiculous chimney-pieces and its wooden chalk-coloured columns, without grace, nobility or harmony. No, my dear Douglas, I cannot honestly regret this mass of very ordinary taste, and in my actual circumstances I believe I have performed a fine prudent act[13] ...

Undated[14]

Since Malvern is passably elevated, I think this spot will be as fitting for our reunion as the Tower itself. Preserve the most profound silence about my intentions, and before I set out try to get some information about lodgings etc. I am travelling with my own horses. If the Abbé Franchi arrives in time, he will accompany me; if not, it is the Abbé Macquin[15] who will have that honour. But lest the honour be too dazzling for the inhabitants of Malvern, it will be necessary to veil it; without this precaution they will make me pay triple or at least double. So see if you can procure me a suitable, quiet and cheap lair. I will not bring any chef—only Altina to make me raspberry cordial to drink according to the Ehrhartian rite.[16] You understand the necessity of not naming the lodger to the lodging-housekeepers for fear of a stripping. So write to me the instant that you have recovered from your voyage. I hope that dear Sousa[17] will also pay us a visit, but it may be more prudent to say nothing to him until the business of the lodgings is settled.

My retinue will consist of Altina, two or three innocents, an Abbé or two, Milne[18] to accompany my botanical excursions, Randall[19] to supervise my temporal affairs in general, and old Fowkes[20] for the ponies which will also go; I would like to add the dwarf, but that would be too much of a favour for the public—only the Abbey is worthy of him.

Tuesday 8 September[21]

… If it is at all possible, go to see an angel called Saunders who is a tight-rope walker at the Circus Royal and the certain captivator of every b—r's soul. Ah! Farewell …

Friday <11 September>

… I am afraid that the angel is no longer at the Circus. Highest heaven is where he exists. Ah what a blessed creature! How happy I would be if I could save such a beautiful soul!

Pissing Wednesday 23 September

… It is wretched weather with fog everywhere, and in this lovely sky there are no cherubim to be seen except the dwarf, the Ghoul and pale Ambrose. I can hear nothing except Mr Wyatt lamenting like a Prime Minister at the Court of the most watery and pissful Tertian Fever. He is of a deathly cadaverousness and stinks as only those beneath ground do. Ah, when will more favourable times come? Ah, when shall I be able to see the long desired ♋.[22] In the meantime, find out what you can about the site of the Earthly Paradise. Many have sought it in vain: some in Syria or Mesopotamia, some in Abyssinia, others in Ceylon, but I (according to the latest information) in Bristol.

<Sunday> 27 September

I am condemned by cruel Destiny to run a hospital and to hear of nothing but the maladies of that Bagasse Queen Charlotte[23] and the Bagasse Wyatt—how much better it would be to have some sweet invalid to dose with cordials. So if young S—d—rs wants a change of air (and perhaps of habits too) let him come to this bosky shade 'to cool his fever'.

Just Heaven! how interesting the news from Duke Street is! Ah, if you could but act as Impresario to the Court of Maria I,[24] and look out some valiant youth who could dance the tight-rope in the royal presence, as the saintly David, the king of harpists, was sought out in order to appease the furies of Saul. If only you could (and I don't see why not), it would make me so happy. "*Je sens un grand voide dans mon coeur*", as the Marchioness Lepri used to say to me;[25] and in the way that one frequently says one thing and does another, it was a little lower than the heart that the sentimental lady pointed. But such a pantomime is of small consequence to me. What matters to me is—but you know already what it is, and while you are carrying out so many commissions, execute one for me anyway. Dearest Impresario, have no fear of obstacles; the moment the beatific vision appears before your eyes, all fear (save that of God) will cease to trouble you. In view of your sympatheticness, I think you will find me not only the most charitable of human beings but also the most steadfast and reasonable.

A visit to his father, a proposition for a journey to foreign parts, and even a life-annuity—all this is possible.

> tighti tighti tighti ti
> titi tighti, tighti tighti ti

Celestial harmony, music of the spheres, you make my heart leap! Oh how I despise all the *chords* of all the lyres of all the poets! Give me only one *cord*[26] (*garni de son ange*) and …!

I descend and touch ground, and here I am at the door of the china shop. Twenty-four plates at twenty-one a piece is some price, and we haven't much money, as you know. What the devil are the plates anyway? Chinese or Japanese? God knows. Why not send one, or put them aside until I can see them? How can I judge without seeing them! What are the other trifles? And the two cups with their covers so different from any I have in my power. Ah my power, my power! It were better to be impotent, better to fall into the secure sleep of total dissolution, than to rage in vain. For pity's sake go to Duke Street and see how he is. Whisper sweetly some proposition of a flight (why not to Brazil?) with the whole Court, in splendid vessels all glittering with gold, diamonds and carbuncles. There, above the deck my little angel will be poised whilst little zephyrs play and clarinets, oboes and hunting-horns sound.

Rings of brilliants, wondrous bracelets and golden coins will rain down in abundance ...

Tuesday 29 September

I doubt if it will be in the power of the boastful D. Robert Barclay[27] to find any way at all of securing you a passage through Holland as long as the present frenzy lasts. The English, animated by the fires of Copenhagen[28] (not of Sodom), will go from prodigy to prodigy; Bonaparte will get into a mood to destroy everything, and then God knows whether even the English of Verdun, Valenciennes and other depots[29] will fall victims. Do not lose your time in vain. Return here the moment your Aranjo-isms[30] permit and do not become the dupe of D. Robert.

If your cold had not obscured your lucid intellect you would not find it so difficult to seek out the object—the loveliest under heaven. Ah what an object! What harm would there be in paying a visit to Duke Street to find out whether or not *Monsu*[31] the son of the house would be agreeable to an engagement abroad. Would this be impossible? I don't see why ... Your observations on Westminster are not unjust. The galleries especially are sublime, but the wretchedness of the choir and the iniquitous and disgusting state of the venerable chapels of Henry VII and St Edward the Confessor fill one with horror. If the building was purged by celestial Catholic fire of all the foulness of infamous Protestantism it would be capable of producing the most majestic effect imaginable. Its height is about the same as St Denis but cannot compare with Amiens: St Denis is ninety French feet high and Amiens 132! ...

<Friday> 2 October

... It would not be a bad idea to tell Mr Foxhall[32] that to your certain knowledge the Claudes[33] are adored in Paris and that the Museum is still prepared to give what it originally offered for them—5 or 600,000 *livres*. So the candidates for them would do well to conclude the matter before your departure. Once they're in France, it will be farewell for

England to the finest landscapes in the world (this said with a knowing air will have an effect). Mr Hope[34] and Kinnaird[35] are mad with the desire to purchase.

Thursday 8 October

I see clearly that poor Barzaba[36] must die of grief and sorrow just as dawn was breaking for him. The infamous cruelty of tormenting this delicate creature[37] with exertions so little suited to his tender years must distress every charitable soul. If you have the least compassion or inclination to serve an honest and pitiable old man, do see if it will not be possible, before this cruel and fatal departure for Ireland, to sow the seed of a friendship; and then, when he returns (if indeed the poor dear rascal survives), who knows whether he may not remember you and a certain kind soul full of the most human compassion who is interested in him and only seeks to discover how much would be asked should any occasion arise for his making a profitable trip. That is all—an all which should in no way be so difficult or dangerous for you to perform. One exposes oneself to no trouble or risk in making an enquiry of this kind with decency. Who is a firmer friend of decency than Barzaba? None to my knowledge. And it would make Barzaba so jubilant, so content if he could ease the destiny (hitherto not very kind) of a charming unfortunate.

My dear Gregory, I cannot live in peace until I know something more positive about this interesting creature. For heaven's sake see him, make his acquaintance, visit his wretched hovel in Duke Street, ask after his dear health, make friends with his father—and you will restore me to life. He cannot leave yet, he cannot leave so soon after a fever for fever-ridden Ireland. If you wish to please me, to oblige me, to enchant me it is in your power. One hour spent on these commissions will enable you to help me in the only thing in which I really need help. Nothing else matters. But this does matter so *very, very, very* much that unless you wish to fail in all the duties of friendship and Christian charity you will find some plausible excuse for going where my beloved has his haunts. One moment of this beatific vision will suffice to show you that I am right, and provide sustenance for a thousand conversations between us when terrible Ireland swallows up my treasure.

Happy you, to be able, in the easiest and simplest way in the world, to gild my days and breathe new life into the miserable carcass of poor, love-sick, drooling, sorrowing Barzaba.

… I would forgive everything if only you would give proof of your ability by going there—where I live, where I breathe—for elsewhere I do not exist. Ah! Ah! Ah![38]

Friday <9 October>

The poor old fellow <Barzaba> is pitiful; if you are not a Hyrcanian[39] wild beast try to please him; take serious and sustained steps to pay all possible respects, kindnesses and endearments to father, mother, brothers, cousins, sisters, etc, if they exist (without violating the laws of the chastest decency and purest morality), so that you may sow the idea (I daren't say the seeds) of a friendship or a patronage which would be the comfort of my failing years. I am certain that, if you wished to, you could help me, and greatly, without running the least risk of being persecuted by the Society for the Suppression of Vice.[40]

I know nothing of politics; I've become a miserable, doting, delirious, stuttering, doddering Barzaba.

Alleluia Saturday <10 October>

… How lovely to see that dear name! Duke Street! Duke of my soul, lead me <conducetemi> beneath your banners and I will follow you faithfully where you will, how you will, when you will. Let us march to victory, to military glory.[41] But if sweet peace be more the order of your days let us live in peace in some obscure corner. I submit to whatsoever is required—the most rigid economy, retirement from Fonthill with the consent of Mr White,[42] the most frugal lodging in Duke Street, death, Judgment, Hell, Paradise. So "I too am a painter"[43] at least in words; I have not scattered the pearls of my eloquence in vain. You are not deaf to my laments.

You ask me if I have seen the comet[44]—a fine question indeed! If this devilish thing was a coach to transport people a million leagues away from this ill-omened realm of vile and foolish prejudices, well and good, it might interest me; and if a certain traveller (whom you may already know) were willing to accompany me, and if the most fervent prayers and the severest penance could obtain for me a place in the aforesaid celestial diligence or *turgotine*,[45] I would fall on my knees, I would prostrate myself on the earth, I would pass through the rituals of death itself if this creature desired it and promised to share the same passport with me.

Barzaba is slobbering, Barzaba is good-natured, Barzaba is anything you wish; but in certain circumstances there is no energy that is too strenuous for him.

The Sunday of the Return to Life <11 October>

... In a room at Brunet's Hotels[46]—he is going to appear. Ah, how my heart beats! For God's sake, be careful, risk nothing. Shall I kiss? No, for God's sake, not yet; be discreet, moderate, collected, cold—if that's possible in the rays of the sun in full—.[47] Talk of this and that, of a contract (?), of parrots, oranges and lemons etc. Make yourself his friend, but not a lover—nothing suspicious ...[48] Decency, decency! Ah! And then, after discussing the price for Portugalising, promise to write to Portugal etc. But I'm not sure that without witnesses present the risk isn't great—discussing this face to face, alone with the angel himself in his own room in furnished apartments. Passing into the presence of God without the mediation of His saints is too rash, too—.[49] My dear Gregory, my revered and esteemed Acheron,[50] do not expose yourself to any peril—remember me, but at the same time remember the cursèd country in which, for my extreme misfortune, I live!

Thursday 29 October

I need angelic patience and celestial serenity not to be outraged at seeing a person whom I believed to be wholly dependent on myself becoming the wretched slave of God knows what set of rascals or circumstances. It is enough to make one weep and scream… You practically admit that it is not I who directs your steps. Very well! It is time, then, to devote yourself to some other kind of life. These scrapes, mysteries and speculations are too much for me. To find that the large sum I drew for you from my own pocket does not suffice; to see you exposed to a thousand vexations, a thousand uncertainties, a thousand calamities; to see you forced to flee hither and thither like a bankrupt whether your true friend and master likes it or not: all this, after the many blows that fate has rained down on me, is the unkindest, the most unexpected, the cruellest cut of all. Do you suppose that I will go on imagining that you are a person affectionately and devotedly attached to my service …?

When you were with me a few days ago, you had time to open your heart to me. Why do you torment me with suspicions and uncertainties? Am I not tortured enough as it is …? I thought I possessed in you someone capable of lightening my tedium and woes, not of accumulating them upon my head. You are lost to me, I can clearly see. And I see it with genuine sorrow. False friends and bad company have enticed you from my mode and manner of thought and action … Knowing how much I detest mysteries and reservations, how wrong you were to continue so long this fine trafficking; never to tell me what it was all about, never to ask my advice or (I might say) my orders—as to whether or not you should get involved in these things. Had you confided in me in good time (which indeed I deserved), I would have saved you a host of troubles; I would have restored you to a right frame of mind; and I would have inspired you with the desire and given you the opportunity to be a great consolation to me … Consider, before it is too late, the suffering and absolutely justifiable disgust inflicted on me by your strange position. Consider well, and renounce the fatal labyrinth which deflects you from your true and straight path—the sweet duty of showing yourself fully sensible of all that I have done for you—and could do if ever the inauspicious circumstances of our age change their mournful hue …

It is high time to give up all that is unpleasing to me—or to leave my service and enter that of someone who could content you with more than the little which is at present in my power …

Friday 30 October

Your description of the Leg household[51] is so true and so admirably executed that in spite of the sadness which oppresses me I could not help bursting into laughter. By making yourself such a good friend of the female section, you will doubtless be able to form a close friendship with the divinest creature in the Universe. By becoming the confidant of all their cares, by not putting your tongue too far into the mouths of the little girl or the little boy, by offering every now and then some little present, you will surely find yourself in an odour of sanctity with the whole family. But always remember not to advance too much money on the trip; if this comes to nothing, then good-bye to the money and beware of its being pinched by Mother Leg, aided and abetted by that rogue Father Tight-rope-walker.

... I doubt neither your heart nor your special affection for me. What I do doubt is your head, for it is too unstable, too light, too prone to follow false, stupid or interested advice. Read and re-read my letter of yesterday; it was intended to bring you back to your senses, to make you promise that, once free from the torments which have all but snatched you from me, you would never, never fall again. Anything I can do to show you that I am not illiberal, I shall do ... as long as I have something and am not down to my last farthing, you may count on my readiness to do my best for you and to treat you with generosity and magnanimity.

The poor Doctor,[52] it seems, is due for the next world; he is very weak and very ill. That's another terrible blow to me. Thus, one by one, I am losing all my best and most trusted servants: death takes some and life the others ...

Sunday 1 November

A few words will suffice, my beloved Gregory, to assure you that my heart beats in perfect union with yours. In the midst of many confused and some unjust ideas there still shines forth the simple, good and kind candour of your soul. You are right to love me and to reveal your innermost belief in my unchangeable favour. Farewell to fantasies, suspicions and threats! Let us leave the past and turn to the future; for the present is anything but kind: sugar affairs grow worse every day and much caution will be needed if I am not to become a total bankrupt … Little by little I am suspending all work on the Abbey: in two months we shall have quiet in this place. But if the cursèd Claudes aren't sold I shan't know which way to turn …

Sunday <8 November?>[53]

… What the devil is D. Domingos doing at Worthing at such a time as this? Perhaps, not knowing what to say, he is making a 'political' retirement![54] I am not in anxiety about his political skill—he is subtle enough without appearing subtle, and he knows his job. One can under stand only too well the horrible confusion in Lisbon and above all in that sad Carthage of the English at Buenos Ayres.[55] I don't wonder at your prolific Madame's fear, nor at her desire that so good a spouse as yourself should return again to start afresh the stupid business of mar riage. I detest families and offspring, but I am so sin cerely your friend that nothing will be lacking on my part (as far as is possible) to calm your torments in this respect.

I am not a doctor to be able to explain to you the Doctor's state, but it looks as if he is threatened by some horrible internal putrefaction, the result of his bad habits aggravated by his fall last year. It will be a miracle if he survives. The doctors will be in consultation at his house this morning. God knows the outcome. I am afraid … I'm none too well myself and say to you what the Doctor used to say to me … *"Ayez soin de moi, Milord, et sh'aurai soing de fous"* …

Tuesday 10 November

'Tis not possible to suffer more than I am suffering at present: the wretched Doctor almost at death's door; the weather all deluge and storm; the solitude profound; a thousand important things to discuss and no one at hand to listen, to comfort or to help me … The sugar news is so terrible that Ruin stands nigh unto my door. Already I seem to hear her knock. None too sweet is the sound of such a visitor—worse even than the Commendatore's statue in the opera *Don Juan*: pale and white and smelling of Hell.

If you have time, renew your visits to Mr White and the Boastful Baronet,[56] to see what I am to do and how I am to live; for I swear to you that I don't know myself. Remember, dear Gregory, that without all possible care on your part, without some plan for calming down the terrible state of my mind, I shall certainly fall ill. I cannot resist so many horrors massed together to torture me.

I think like you and Mr. Foxhall about West,[57] and I am acting accordingly. It is important that these famous pictures should not be thrown away for a sum inferior to their incredible and inexplicable reputation ...

<Wednesday> 11 November

... I am planning all the reforms imaginable, seeing the desperate and despairing state of Jamaica. I am stopping all building little by little: I shall leave the Octagon half-finished and without most of the mouldings; as to the other buildings, I am not giving them any more thought. Only the kitchen must be finished, and if this is completed in fifteen days, not much else need be done, so that in a month's time I shall be completely free of this cancer which is destroying me. As for other reforms, besides cutting down garden expenses, I shall perhaps be compelled to get rid of my coach- and saddle-horses and be reduced to a small number of ponies ... Ah, if Father Leg would only lodge me, what splendid economies might be effected! If you can somehow or other contrive to see the leggy Divinity I shall be very glad. I don't like the idea of your leaving London without having judged whether or not poor wretched Barzaba is justified in being so slobbering ...

The poor Doctor still hovers between life and death ...

Thursday 10 December

Since you went away, my beloved Gregory, cold, snow, loneliness and horror! And worst of all, a most fervid renewal by Mr Still[58] of all the well-known attacks on you. This time it was not the Great Dolt of a

Basha,[59] but his most protestant brother, the Rector of Fonthill. I have never heard such calumnies. In short, you can imagine the effect of such a sermon on me at a time when my spirit really is lacerated in so many ways. It is fairly evident that if I wish to live a few years longer I shall have no choice but to go away and renounce for ever a country which does not cease to persecute me and a climate in so many respects the most harmful imaginable to my constitution ... The great plan will be carried out. If I am made to suffer in this fashion, farewell London, farewell Pledges,[60] farewell everything. I advise you to lose no time in considering a return to Portugal to negotiate with the French or the Portuguese (it doesn't matter which) permission for me to come to Lisbon, settle down there, naturalise myself etc.

It is impossible to picture the extreme rage, the lofty scorn which fills my heart. I am almost suffocated. If I do not fall sick unto death it will be because God and the Saint[61] miraculously preserve me. I expect letters from you tomorrow. Meanwhile I embrace you with a fearless heart.

Friday 11 December

I should not wish, my dear Gregory, to augment your troubles by detailing mine; but it is certain that both my health and my morale are in a bad way. I suffer not a little from a hideous tedium and from the lonely aspect of this tomb of an abbey, but the worst of it is that in this tomb one does not find the rest that other graves can give. The extreme agitation into which I have been thrown by Mr Still's insolent, wholly unjust and unpardonable attack has produced a kind of nervous fever which little by little will bring about the ruin of my health. If I remain here, even for a short time, I shall die. I see from your letter of yesterday that Mr White is firmly opposed to my plan; the Boastful Baronet will probably be also. I do not and will not change: you may assure these gentlemen of this truth, so well known to yourself. I am too ill to add anything more except to assure you of my everlastingly true friendship. Farewell.

\<Tuesday\> 15 December

Yesterday I was so occupied that I did not have a moment to write a line. Yesterday your friend the Great Dolt was abused worse than Bandeira[62] by B-b-b-b barzaba. If he doesn't pass out like the latter, it will be a matter for wonder; he all but died from the effects of being shrivelled up by me. But it is not proper for the hero of the scene to boast of his own prowess, so my Chancellor, Mr White, will tell you the rest ... White is wholly devoted to you and is full of the most fervent praise of your head and your heart; this is balm to my wounded soul and will bring Mr White a Prime-minister-ship. He enjoys my full trust and favour for having taken your side ...

Wednesday 16 December

Ah, how glad the Pledges are to be rid of me and I of them! Their note of yesterday was full of consoling gaiety ... Mr White departs with instructions to bring you a thousand greetings on my behalf and an account of the terrible hurricane which lours on the horizon, ready to avenge you. I agree with that idiot Foxhall that we shall get all we are asking for the Claudes, and I am agreeable to Lord Grosvenor[63] negotiating with me for two or three small pictures which interest him. I am not at all well: I am consumed by a slight fever; I am thirsty; my bile is in motion; my whole nervous system has gone to the devil. If I don't receive some consolation soon, a change of scene or some diversion, I shall run the risk of falling ill. Think of some remedy and prepare to return here next Monday or Tuesday. Believe me with all my heart your friend.

White will make you laugh over our little scheme of entertainment for the coming carnival—a little interlude to amuse the Widow Wildman[64] and her heir, a delightful operetta, but not a comic one, I swear to you. It is called *The Apotheosis of Mr Wildman*. First violin, Mr White; Director of music, the Chancellor of the United Kingdom; the leading character, myself. This modest theatrical venture will, I hope, bring in a meagre profit of fifty thousand pounds sterling or so. Heh.

Thursday 17 December

You can't imagine the Rector's dreadful rancour and his stupid brainless malignity. Mr White will tell you what happened to him: it humiliates me to have to tell you that this same Mr Notary has not behaved with that energy which I expect from my people—which I expect and require, being an absolute and sovereign master and not so mild to handle as some have thought. Having observed my supremacy, Mr Pedley[65] has become your best friend and defender ... I must be calmed, or else the thunderbolt will fall. Look out, Mr White! I abhor *pisse-froids* and molly-coddles ...

Friday 18 December

Whilst you are in the midst of social pleasures and in the realm of diamonds I remain here in this mournful hermitage fighting to the death against the most ridiculous and infamous cabal that ever existed. It is time that you frequented Mr White to ascertain a little of what is happening and above all to encourage him to support my schemes for a just vengeance. If he doesn't support me, he won't become either Prime or Second Minister. Mr Pedley is behaving in the best possible manner as far as you are concerned. Today he is going to drub the Rector and reduce him to dust; in this Mr White failed, and was himself stunned—the poor, tremulous, rheumatic coward! The storm here was terrific, and still continues with a violence that threatens everybody and everything. I am in process of discovering my power; my resources are indeed considerable; I am still a very independent and potent lord. Mr White will tell you what I am if you ask him, and what tremendous consequences will fall on those who are wanting in respect for me. I shall prove my ancient precept

"I am not to be trifled with."

I wonder that you have had no news of me. With the exception of Monday, I have not failed to write on one single day, because there was no lack of important things to write about. I very much hope that my letters have not gone astray, because I would not like anyone to know what I am planning.

Yes, my dear Gregory, if they don't appease me, I shall depart once for all, leaving behind me solitude, hunger and ruin—that is the reward which the disturbers of my peace must expect. I order you to discuss all this thoroughly with Mr White, and to support me with all your soul, seeing what destruction I am now wreaking on your behalf and for your honour. Farewell ...

Saturday 19 December

... I do not deserve these complaints and murmurings at a time when my life is being disturbed, torn to shreds and shortened (most probably) *all in your defence.* For God's sake consult Mr White; the matter is serious. I think the law will furnish you with a remedy against your horrid slanderers. Your head must have become extremely weak to be filled with so many vapourings and chimeras. Find out from Mr White what has taken place or is likely to take place, calm yourself with him and earn his confidence; if he behaves well he will have *mine* to the full—a not unimportant thing for him.

Tormented here and tormented by your letters—it's all too much for me. Your letter of yesterday is the most ill-conceived, the most ill-reasoned and the most confused you have ever in your life written to me. You haven't understood me—a fine confusion indeed, a pleasant reward for one who is consumed with anxiety to avenge and protect you!

Sunday 20 December

I've just received from D. Domingos himself the great news. Poor Prince! The Glorious Saint be praised that he's safe. I'm replying most warmly to D.D; as Brazilian Ambassador he'll be no small personage at this Court.[66]

I've no need to write to Sir Robert Barclay to learn his opinion of your affair—I hope he'll come to Fonthill to express it: my arms are open to all your friends and closed for ever to those who have at any time abused you ... Be of good cheer, take comfort and come to your true and affectionate Protector ...

1. I have throughout taken my information on the price of sugar from Ragatz, *Fall of the Planter Class in the British Caribbean*, New York, 1928, and from his *Statistics for the Study of British Caribbean Economic History, 1763–1833*, London 1927. But his figures sometimes differ from Deerr's *History of Sugar, 1949–1950*.

2. From the Bartholomew Fair Collection in the Guildhall Library.

3. From the M.W. Stone collection of playbills, etc, now in the Victoria and Albert Museum.

4. See p.100, note 9.

5. See p.82.

6. Memorandum in English to unnamed correspondent—(Sir) G.F. Beltz, genealogist and Herald.

7. Beckford inscribed his mock design (see Insert): "Design for a cupboard stall of oak highly waxed to be erected in one of the gothic corners of Fonthill Abbey to the memory of Roger Maddock, shoemaker and Hannah Poole his wife—alas, the lineal descendant of George Plantagenet, Duke of Clarence, brother to King Edward the 4th." Hannah Poole was supposed to be descended from the Poles who married into the Plantagenets. Her daughter, Margery Maddock, married John Woodward of Clerkenwell, and their daughter married Peter Beckford, father of Governor Peter Beckford of Jamaica. It was drawn either by Macquin or Beltz.

8. John Stow, the Elizabethan antiquary.

9. French draft from Berkeley Square to Alexander Hamilton Douglas (1767–1852), Marquess of Douglas and from 1819 tenth Duke of Hamilton. His marriage to Beckford's daughter Susan (1786–1859) was mooted from at least 1804, and finally took place after prolonged financial negotiations, in April 1810. An ardent Bonapartist, he had many tastes similar to Beckford, who gives him many nicknames (e.g. Florindo and Rinaldo), but chiefly the Shepherd, his future wife being the Shepherdess; their romance was ironically pictured by Beckford as an Arcadian Pastoral, and their home and life as *Arcadia,* which Virgil portrays as a region of pastoral simplicity and happiness; Arcadians were considered the least intellectual of all Greeks, and so the name was used in a derogatory sense.

10. This is the only mention I have so far seen in *H.P.* of Beckford having a black dwarf; perhaps this was the member of his staff whom he called the Ghoul. Robert Montgomery's anonymous satire *The Age Reviewed*, 1827, p.63, mentions Beckford's black dwarf, but he may be mistakenly referring to the Swiss Pierre.

11. His full name was Pierre Colas de Grailly, but he is called the dwarf, Nanibus, or Pierrot. He was French-speaking and came from Evian.

12. For James Wyatt the architect, see Introduction, pp.15–16. Nicknamed *Bagasse* and *Bagassona,* derived from *bagascione* (a whoremonger).

13. By demolishing the old Fonthill House, known as Splendens, and using it as a quarry. Andrea Casali (*c.*1720–*c.*1783) painted its ceilings.

14. Early August; French draft to unnamed correspondent.

15. Abbé Ange Denis Macquin (1756–1823), miscellaneous writer. Professor of rhetoric and belles-lettres at Meaux, he fled to England in 1792 as a strong Royalist, and was appointed heraldic draughtsman to the College of Arms. He lived in lodgings in Bermondsey, but was an accomplished gourmet.

16. Dr Projectus Josephus Ehrhart (1786–1807), a Strasbourgian, was Beckford's private physician, and had formerly been Louis XVI's. He died at Fonthill on November 12. Beckford's letters often take off his thick Alsatian accent. For Beckford he always remained "The Doctor".

17. The Portuguese Ambassador, Domingos Antonio de Sousa Coutinho (1760–1833), a bachelor, created Count (1808) and then Marquis of Funchal (1833). Anglophile and later a Liberal; Beckford calls him *D. Domingos.*

18. Beckford's head gardener, who left in 1815.

19. Joseph Randall was one of Beckford's footmen in 1795.

20. John Fowkes was head groom.

21. This is the first letter in Italian (to Franchi) printed here.

22. An invented pæderastic symbol, referring to Saunders.

23. George III's wife.

24. Queen of Portugal, where Beckford often thought of settling.

25. The Lepri were a Roman family raised to the Marquisate *c.*1760.

26. Saunders' tight-rope. The sentence ends with a phrase too scabrous to quote.

27. Sir Robert Barclay, eighth Baronet, a Scot, who advised Beckford on Colonial affairs, and introduced his Jamaican business to the West India merchant house of Plummer, Barham & Puller. Friend of the Prince Regent, who stood godfather to his youngest son in 1807; Beckford hoped to be reinstated socially through his good offices. Nicknamed "The Boastful Baronet".

28. Copenhagen and its fleet had been bombarded for three days, and surrendered on September 7.

29. Camps for internees and prisoners-of-war.

30.   *i.e.* the contraband commissions he is undertaking for Portugal's francophil Foreign Minister, Antonio de Araujo de Azevedo, created Count of Barca, 1815.

31.   A foreign pronunciation of *Monsieur*, but perhaps also reflecting *Mon çu* (= my arse), a favourite joke of Beckford's.

32.   Edward Foxhall (died 29 October 1815), of Foxhall & Fryer, Old Cavendish Street, London, upholsterers. He is mentioned in the *Portuguese Journal* as painting and furnishing at Splendens for Beckford; he also bought important pictures for him at auction. Nicknamed the Blockhead.

33.   *The Landing of Aeneas* and *A Sacrifice to Apollo* (Beckford gives them slightly different names), painted in 1675 by Claude Lorraine. They were Nos. 69 and 71 in Royal Academy Exhibition *Landscape in French Art*, 1949–50, the Catalogue of which gives a full bibliography but the wrong date for their transfer from Italy to England, which was 1799. Nelson provided a special naval convoy for them, and the whole story of their transfer is extraordinary. Beckford bought them in 1799 for £6,825, and sold them on 12 June 1808 to a dealer Harris for 10,000 guineas; within 18 days the latter sold them to Richard Hart Davis, M.P., for 12,000 guineas! Until recently they were owned by H.R.H. the Duchess of Kent.

34.   Thomas "Anastasius" Hope of Deepdene, author and collector; or his brother Henry.

35.   Charles, eighth Baron Kinnaird.

36.   Perhaps a corruption of *bar sabä*, which in Syriac means a voluptuary. Beckford's use of the name for himself certainly includes this. Barzaba is the character he assumes when in pursuit of boys.

37.   *i.e.* Saunders, whose Circus was evidently expected to travel to Ireland.

38.   This triple exclamation is scrawled in three lines right down the quarto page, occupying over half of it.

39.   Hyrcania, a province of the Persian Empire, was full of tigers, and its inhabitants were ferocious and cruel.

40.   Founded in 1787 by Wilberforce as "The Proclamation Society"; it changed its name in 1802 and instituted proceedings against those who broke the Sunday Observance laws, were cruel to animals, ran lotteries, told fortunes, sold obscene books and prints, and kept brothels, etc.

41.   This phrase echoes the famous aria *Non più andrai* sung by Figaro to the effeminate page Cherubino in Mozart's *Marriage of Figaro*: "… now amongst warriors, smoking, drinking, with fierce moustaches, gun on your shoulder, sword in hand … you will be cheered on to victory, to military glory." This

was the aria Beckford claimed to have improvised when the eight-year-old Mozart was giving him piano-lessons in London.

42. Richard Samuel White (senior), of Lincoln's Inn, became Beckford's solicitor in 1796, after Thomas Wildman's death. His firm was White & Fownes, which, after his death in May 1817, became Fownes & White, with his son (who bore exactly the same names) as junior partner. Nicknamed Rottier (the Belcher).

43. Quoted of Correggio when he saw Raphael's *S. Cecilia* in Rome.

44. The Great Comet of 1807, first observed in Italy on September 9th.

45. A stage-coach, nicknamed after the Minister Turgot, who first established them in Paris in 1775.

46. In Leicester Square; opened about 1800 by Louis Brunet, wine and brandy merchant; taken over by Francis Jaunay, 1819; demolished about 1837. This area was frequented by foreigners, emigres and theatrical people.

47. Beckford completed this sentence with expressive dots, instead of a word.

48. The rest of the sentence is omitted as too scabrous.

49. As above, Beckford ended this sentence with dots instead of a word.

50. The name of a river connected with Hades; the Portuguese word also has the figurative meaning of grave, perdition, destruction. The idea seems to be that Franchi is leading Beckford down to Hell.

51. *i.e.* the Saunders household—the legs (in tights) of a young tight-rope walker being a conspicuous feature and attraction.

52. Ehrhart.

53. Beckford only dated this letter *Sunday,* and Franchi later wrongly added *10 Julho 1808.*

54. D. Domingos is the Portuguese Ambassador. He was in an awkward position because his country was being invaded by the French, and his Government was secretly capitulating to nearly all the French conditions, which were designed to detach Portugal from the British alliance. The Foreign Minister, Araujo, was pro-French, and he was playing a double game, making incompatible promises to both sides.

55. Ayres was a quarter in Lisbon with many English residents; Becklord substituted *sad Carthage* for *quarter.*

56. Sir Robert Barclay.

57. West, P.R.A. Like many artists of the day, he made money by acting as go-between in transactions involving Old Masters (in this case the Claudes).

58. John Still (1761–1889), Prebendary of Salisbury; Rector of Fonthill Gifford and Chicklade from 1797; born locally at East Knoyle and educated at Wadham College.

59.   James Charles Still (1758–1828), land-steward to Beckford and his hated cousin Peter Beckford. Nicknamed "The Great Dolt".

60.   *i.e.* pledges of love—his daughters; the term is also applied to Franchi's daughter.

61.   St Anthony of Padua, patron saint of Lisbon and Beckford.

62.   Bandeira's letters to Beckford and other references in *H.P.* show that this was Jacintho Fernandes Bandeira, elder brother of the First Count of Porto Covo da Bandeira.

63.   First Marquis of Westminster; his son bought the ruins of Fonthill Abbey and its pleasure-grounds.

64.   Widow of Henry Wildman, one of the three brothers who managed all Beckford's affairs (as solicitors, agents, West India merchants, and managers of his Jamaican estates) from his father's death in 1770 until they were sacked in 1801, after each of them had made large fortunes out of him. This lawsuit dragged on for years and was a great disappointment to Beckford, whose object was to set aside two deeds conveying the Quebec Plantation to Wildman in 1790–1, on the grounds that its value had been misrepresented.

65.   John Pedley (1762–1888) succeeded the Wildmans as Beckford's Agent; was his nominee in Parliament for Hindon, 1802–6, and Saltash, 1808–9.

66.   The Portuguese Regent João (later João VI) sailed from Lisbon with his Court for Brazil in British ships, only just in time to escape capture by the invading French armies. Evidently Beckford received private news of this from the Portuguese Ambassador before it was known in the British Press.

1808

BECKFORD'S main anxieties were now the procrastination of his architect Wyatt and the vicissitudes of war in the Iberian peninsula. During 1806 and 1807 he had been re-casing the exterior of the Abbey with stone, and generally strengthening its structure. Now that this task was finished, he was able to complete the Octagon and its lantern by stuccoing the interior. But this was a sublime operation needing the personal supervision of the great architect himself, and Franchi had to spend half his time pursuing him back and forth across England. Most of the summer passed in this fashion. Therefore, in order to get the work completed before the winter, Beckford made a supreme effort and issued an ultimatum to architect and builder: everything must be finished by September 30th—if not, he would sack them and stop the building. He reinforced his threats by making an unbreakable vow to his patron saint, St Anthony of Padua. This had a miraculous effect. The work continued at full blast on Sundays and far into the night. The legends that building went on at a feverish pitch by torchlight and that large numbers of men were brought from London and Windsor are not exaggerated. They were merely unfair in suggesting that the only cause was Beckford's impatience and megalomania. What other course was open when dealing with an architect like Wyatt?

In the past, when difficulties and frustrations at home became unbearable, Beckford had been accustomed to ease his sorrows in Paris or Lisbon. His eyes were still turned toward Portugal, and the fact that the French were in control made no difference to *him*—anywhere would do that was free from the hated English, who turned their backs upon him wherever they found him. His resentment reached treasonable proportions, and Franchi was to be sent, in defiance of the English naval blockade, to sound the French Occupying Power about a suitable reception for his master. Nevertheless, even Beckford could not help rejoicing at the threat to the French tyranny from the popular national risings in Spain and Portugal. Nor was his hatred of the English generals wholly self-regarding, as the letters of the 10th and 21st September show—"O poor, beloved Portugal, my own true country, how I pity you!"

Wednesday 1 June

I've always found the said Cathedral <Salisbury> poor, bare and insipid, without mystery, without ecclesiastical pomp; only the tower is any good. Bagasse's work there is infamous. Oh the disgust and stink of Protestantism (it doesn't deserve the sonorous name of Heresy). All these windows, all this light, all this glass with its small diamond-shaped panes make this shameless church look like a whore clad only in muslin—what an infamous spot. How I abhor it ...

Thursday 2 June

You are not the only one to suffer. It's true, I haven't a headache, but ceaseless nervous fever and piles. These horrible alternations between heat and cold are the death of me. Why the devil did you tell the Pledges' guardian[1] that I enjoy perfect health? Health! Devilish good health! I shudder, I groan, I feel a universal malaise etc, etc. I don't dare to bathe with the present weather. I shall treat the dew with the respect it deserves and which was so often preached by the poor Doctor. But it is cruel to leave the woods and fields and retire within the profound solitude of four walls!

... I still think that if Bonaparte triumphs in Spain, a terrible blow will be prepared against the antipathetic Island; as absolute master of the fleets of Cadiz, Carthagena, Ferrol, etc, think what he could do, especially with today's admirals, who do not possess my great Nelson's impetuous ardour ...

<*Friday*> *3 June*

... Go wherever you please, I'm sure you'll find friends. I'm certain that the Grand Duke[2] will receive you with open arms, especially when he begins to hear our song against the cursèd isle. Let us sing *bene*; let us sing *forte;* Destiny will provide the accompaniment and the *basso continuo.*[3]

Is Wythe here? If you mean *Wyatt*, the answer is no, and that it wouldn't be a bad idea to find him and explain to him in your best Della Cruscan the impolite and unworthy ridiculousness of his behaviour, so well calculated to strangle the work at the Abbey, etc. I'm sure he'll be findable all right, tomorrow being the King's birthday—a ceremony which he is never in the habit of missing. How I regret not having at my command the Capigi-Basha[4] and all his strangling mutes. If I did, the last hour of judgment would not be long in coming for Mr Hobgoblin ...

I'm sorry you haven't found any orange-flower water, and still more that with so many *bijoux*[5] on every side you haven't been able to reserve one for my poor casket ... Not knowing where to place *The Sibyl*,[6] it is possible that I shall let it go for £1,500; it is worth at least £500 more: it's companion Sibyl was sold to Russia for £8,000 even before the pictures had risen to such a monstrous price ...

Sunday 5 June

... For many people Lisbon has doubtless become unbearable, but for you it may be better than ever. If Grand Dukism has not stifled every other feeling in Junot, he will not fail to show you favour, and with his favour and that of the friendly Commissariat, one might lead a pleasant life in a thousand ways, and perhaps make some nice profit as well. In Spain one could do everything. Ah if I could go there to gather these beautiful things, they would fall into our nets cheap[7] ...

Tuesday 7 June

... Our Fate will unfold the moment you can enter *terra papale*;[8] that you will be able to enter, I have no doubt, seeing that the Captain seems to have no fear whatever of taking you with him ... The Fair Pledge writes to me that her old man[9] has gone off to enjoy to the full the society of his companion Womack (what a name!) in the forests of Lancashire. It looks as if all her favours and all her tears have been shed in vain; this breed of shepherd is not Arcadian!

Ah, my dear Gregory, not getting away from these insular mists begins to weary me a little; it is time indeed to think of our existence. In the secret recesses of Napoleon's mind the great catastrophe is being prepared; each month he increases and trains his navy; each hour his power takes firmer root. Let us profit by it before it is too late …

Wednesday 8 June

… At last they are offering me 10,000 *pounds* in earnest for the Claudes, but I want guineas. I am writing to Foxhall in this sense. Even at this price they are being thrown away, considering the British rage for this kind of art …

Sunday 12 June

… This juncture in Spain is going to be magnificent and tremendous. Terrible will be the conflict. It does not surprise me: my ideas on Castilian and Portuguese energy have always been analogous to what is passing.[10] But is this the right occasion for you? Is it not too violent, too perilous, too uncertain, too confused? Junot is not on a bed of roses …

The Claudes have at last been sacrificed for ten thousand guineas in cash—a wretched, unworthy price for *The Temple of Apollo* and *The Ship of Farinelli* …[11] Mr Clarke[12] didn't make a bad sale of my verminous cabinet of books; certain infamous Italian trash fetched seven times their original cost, but not a soul wanted Macklin's Bible with all its engravings …[13]

Mr White gives his whole-hearted approval to some sort of emigration for three years; he says it will be the salvation of everyone, as far as my affairs are concerned; but where to go is not clear, for it is impossible to travel to France via Spain, where all will be fire and slaughter; once in arms, Spain will not be placated so soon. Without a stronger magic than all his previous incantations, our great Cuckoo-Philosopher[14] won't triumph this time. He may send swarms of troops from Germany and Italy etc, but they will be sent in vain if the English stop him at sea, and the ferocious Biscayans and Catalonians on land. This is the first uncertain hour for France's star for many a year …

Friday 24 June

... The ponies came to meet me with the dwarf and his followers—the Ghoul and Bijou—not much of a jewel, I can assure you, not worth much, ill-formed and verminous *(secundum evangelium Nanum)* ...

Saturday 25 June

Since yesterday I have been in the anxious and feverish grip of a violent constipation. I am very unwell, do not dare to bathe and know not what to do. I attribute this visitation to the walk to Vauxhall.

This twisting and turning between Hanworth[15] and Windsor, and Windsor and Dixon[16] is unbearable, but the chase must not be abandoned until the quarry is caught. Once you have caught up with him, do not spare him but tell him in clear terms that, if he goes on in this way for a single day, I shall stop everything here and leave for the paradise of Don Fagundes ...[17]

It's not worth talking about Bijou—he's not of the right kind and never will be; we'll need other angels if we go to another paradise. The eclipse of dear Cooper[18] distresses me—the good, sweet, and amiable creature. With such a companion I would have experienced all the innocent delights of married life: and if an indulgent providence had blessed our union with a tender smiling offspring, what pure happiness, what a blessed existence had been ours[19] the paradise of Don Fagundes!

Sunday 26 June

Ever grieving, ever sneezing, but by dint of doses of honeyed apple-water, a little better than yesterday ... For the love of God, now that Bagasse has made himself visible profit by your favour with him to get him to look at again and re-model the infamous chairs etc of that stupid Foxhall. The Jewish Abercorn is asking 3,000 <pounds> for his Parmigiano,[20] but the Jewish Beckford won't give it.

I rely on you in everything, my dear Gregory. Visit the Shepherdess despite the great bird of ill omen: when the Seraphic Lady Anne Lamprey-

Macaw-Stiffneck (an excellent name!) is at the *opera seria*, go to the comic opera in Berkeley Square. Farewell. Ah Cooper! …

Wednesday 29 June

I am so unwell, my dear Gregory, that it is necessary to think seriously about my condition, and not to content oneself any longer with the false oracles of the learned Pitcairn.[21] I must do something. My cold is a cold and nothing more, as you know; but last night I woke up with stomach-ache, vomited a little, and then fell asleep again. This morning I feel a universal malaise, a sensation of fullness etc. All this calls for a purge or an emetic, but I don't know who should be my doctor. Somebody must be seen. Ascertain, then, who is best—Pitcairn or the Sheep's Doctor.[22] In either case, enquire about expenses and what should be given, etc … Pitcairn promised to come to Fonthill whenever I sent for him; with him or his equivalent I can no longer dispense. To continue in this fashion would be dangerous and might lead to something serious.

Tell Wyatt that unless he wants to irritate and torment me to death he must come. The confusion into which everything will be thrown, and the impossibility of finishing anything (either the Octagon or the rooms) if he doesn't come at once, is not to be borne.

Farewell, dear Gregory. Write to me, love me, and believe me, as long as I live, your friend with all my heart, Guillaume de Beckford.

P.S. Find out from the Sheep about Ehrhart's method of administering emetics.

Thursday 30 June

If one thing could draw me back from the banks of the fatal river of Death, it would be your letter this afternoon, so full of true and eloquent descriptions. Yesterday thanks to a lemon purgative I slept better, the fever having abated somewhat; but I cannot too strongly depict the discomfort of this cursèd feverish cold, and above all my distress at having no authorisation to treat myself in one way or another—by taking a purge or vomiting or bathing. So do ascertain who must be summoned. As with the hotel, I leave it to you to decide—Pitcairn and Berkeley Square, the Sheep's Doctor and the Clarendon[23] or that blackguard Brunet's; but one of them it must be. The first is the most respectable etc; the second is God knows what; about the third you know already ... Without my bathes I cannot endure existence, and in order to know when I may resume them, I do not see how I can avoid the expense and annoyance of consulting someone.

So much for my health; that of the Abbey cries out for Bagasse. Don't lose sight of him; don't let go of him until he's on his way here. If you take your eyes off him for a moment he's off. Who can ever rely on such a person! Every day now loses six. If things go on in this way it won't be possible to lodge anyone in the tower or anywhere else. The workpeople sent for from Bath, Shaftesbury and London have already arrived to complete the Octagon; the scaffolding is almost in place; everything awaits Bagasse's magic wand; the weather, everything, is favourable, if only the cursèd architect does not fail. The drawings are at Wilton, I know very well; but don't let him linger two or three days on the way on the pretext of looking for them.

To my taste the chairs are unbearable, and I don't see how they can be improved. If we don't hold a general council at Fonthill about the furniture we shall never do anything that's worth while. What with Wyatt's apathy and foolish Foxhall's immense incompetence, we shall be throwing away our money in vain, as we have so often done in the past.

... It seems to me that a withdrawal into the paradise of Don Fagundes with a copious detachment of artistes etc gathered together by the Boy of Boys will be the best course to take. Let us get the whole troupe to emigrate, along with the audience, gallery, dressing room, stalls and wings etc. What a *levée en masse*! If I were at my last gasp I would rise for this one. *Gloria in excelsis* (full organ) *et in terra papale Pax, non Pox*—I hope ...

Sunday 3 July

I quite like Dr. Regnault[24] and his medicine, which was neither purge nor emetic but the river, from which I have this moment returned refreshed. Tomorrow I'll take the usual Ehrhardic medicine, and then a bath followed by seltzer-water in whey—if the real seltzer is available; however, I think everything will be available again soon thanks to the Spaniards' energy— what magnificent, what blessed energy! The hand of God and of His saints is at last put forth from the clouds. What sublime news![25]

Tuesday 5 July

... Regnault is divinely French and not lacking in understanding and medical knowledge, but he is far inferior to the great Ehrhart ...

Wednesday 6 July

Yes, my dear Gregory, I have at last received yours of the 2nd July, but from where?—from Plymouth! Seeing your writing and that postmark, I couldn't imagine what the devil had happened to transport you to the said port. I feel deeply your Bagassian torments and the infamous sojourn far from me which this impudent carrion makes you endure.[26] Don't you think it would be better to finish with him once for all? I will, if he fails next Saturday ...

Why is so much time being lost over the bed destined for the Lancaster room? ... Hayter[27] does not know what to do with all his workpeople, gathered together and arrived from so many parts and at such great expense. His not knowing what to do, and all this vain waiting day after day is serious and ruinous for me ...

Friday 8 July

I don't like this disappearance to Windsor. Why didn't you follow him? I can't stand all this annoyance, and if you don't leave on Saturday I shall go mad ... Farewell. The only idea that I have in my head is the fear of being bagassated once again this Saturday. For God's sake see to it that he doesn't escape.

Thursday 8 September

The pig of lavish promises[28] has returned, and with him beguiling hopes of completion. A thousand rose-coloured assurances crowd about him like the hosts of little cupids that accompany their mother Venus. But what is more assured is my solemn vow to the Glorious Saint that on the 30th of this month all work will cease, whether completed or not. Meanwhile fifty more workmen are required. Yesterday, Dixonising with more than usual zeal, I cut two thousand feet of useless and superfluous moulding, so that my plan is by no means impossible, and even without an absolute miracle I believe that we shall be ready on the 30th with everything completed ... They say that Don Cloaca[29] is snugly installed at Hanworth. I am infinitely miserable as usual.

Saturday 10 September

I know only too well the delights of the paradise of D. Espriella[30] the cries by day and night, the stink of coal and bedum,[31] the insolent, insipid and stupid faces, the horrible fog, the lack of everything that makes a climate tolerable, the presence of everything that constitutes an atmospheric inferno. I don't wonder at your *saudades* etc ...

I fear the English flood as much as the Portuguese Ambassador does. I have no doubt that already thousands and thousands of deaths, massacres, butcherings, upheavals, horrors, sackings, torturings, rapings etc have come about as the inevitable consequence of the poor judgement and short-sighted policy of those who now so misgovern this drunken land. Poor Portugal! Poor provinces more than half consumed by the flames that have swept across them! If we go there, we shall find nothing save ashes moist with blood.

Sunday 11 September

... I have conquered Anglicanism at least this once. Today is no day for tomfoolery at Fonthill. Everyone is working, with the dispensation of the Saint who prefers this little error to the abomination of making me a perjurer—for I have sworn by his holy name that every one will be away by the 30th ... The last lot of people sent here are excellent. The Lantern has already been completely covered[32] and four columns are half done. The great central rose will be in place today before dinner; of the others, only two are still lacking ...

Wednesday 14 September

... I haven't time to think of Bobkin or the dwarf or any dwarfism, being busy from morning to night shouting, supervising and singing out of tune in the cursèd and interminable Octagon.

The infamous Blockhead from Old Cavendish Street[33] always sends me the most horrible mess of colours possible. I remember his hideous amaranth on the sample chair, and I certainly don't want to see a similar piece of infamy on the bed or the curtains of the Lancaster room, or on the Tribune.[34] I want a beautiful crimson. After two or three months of expense the galloons have still not arrived, and when they do they will surely be well worthy of the execrable Blockhead and the other blockheads of his crew. If damask were not so wide of price and narrow of manufacture, it might have been more suitable as material for the bed and the great Lancaster curtain; for the Tribune (one window only) I already have enough.

You are quite right not to buy anything yet for Lisbon. God knows what horrors are taking place there. On the one hand, the supreme cunning of the French, aided by their francophil Portuguese partisans; on the other, confusion among the jobbing English generals and, crowning all, our national stupidity ...

Work will stop on the Octagon on the 30th for certain, as I do not wish to break an oath sworn with heartfelt sincerity in the name of my glorious and merciful Protector. I'm off to my usual work—Hayterising, Dixonising and immersing myself in the Octagon. I embrace you with all the strength of my heart.

Thursday 15 September

I know these English *friends* only too well and am not surprised at the truly interesting tidings which I have just received. I can see, I can hear the three goddam generals drinking and fraternising with the infamous Kellermann at the expense of the poor Portuguese;[35] but I put my trust in the Glorious Saint, who with pure and Catholic hands will know how to punish these assassins and liberate his native land ...

Yesterday we worked like demons in the Octagon. The Lantern with all its roses is now complete, the twelfth column will be finished today, the sixth section of fan vaulting is in hand etc. I think everything will be ready in time ... I would much like the Ambassador to come now and talk with me freely, with no witnesses present; write to him and send me news of his plans. Farewell, dearest Gregory, the Octagon is calling me.

<Friday 16 September>

... The old pieces from the Royal silver are divine.[36] I shall accordingly start felling, being persuaded that these salvers and this plate etc will give me great pleasure ... The atrocious neglect by the great Cloaca cannot lightly be forgiven. If he comes now, it will be to see what are, perhaps, irremediable mistakes. It is true that I have some knowledge of my own, but not enough, and not to that extent which a task like the Octagon so imperiously demands. If he does not wish to bring about the final ruin of the edifice, tell him to come.

Everything is progressing as if by a miracle. A reinforcement of excellent workers has arrived, and I have no doubt that before the 30th of this month the tremendous spaces of the great Octagon will be displayed in all their sublime majesty. The last fan tracery will be begun tomorrow ...

The dwarf asks me to tell you to bring six tiny cravats and six tiny handkerchiefs for a certain large fish[37] who is so well behaved and seems so honest, charitable and kind that he deserves whatever little one can do etc, etc, etc ... Farewell. The Octagon is calling me: I hear her voice.

Sunday 18 September

... Who knows if the detestable Macaw with her well-known dark, profound and criminal arts, has not caused these words and hints to be dropped in order to bring to nothing the negotiation, drive off the Calf and abstract a little more money from my miserable purse for her starving brother?[38] The whole Berkeley Square realm fills one with pity and horror—the poor Hysteric, the stupid Egoist her sister, and the guardian dragon of so many imaginary treasures. However, I advise you, more than ever, to continue to call there until you are able to see the deplorable victim and hear from her own lips something of what is happening and what she thinks and expects will happen and whether she still believes in the faith of the Shepherd etc.

... All three of the Batalha windows[39] are already in place and produce the most splendid effect. The men are in full swing on the fan tracery, and on Monday we begin the eight big columns,[40] three men to each; so I am confident that at least the grand effects will be visible before the fatal day, the day when all the workmen with all their scaffolding and filth etc have to be sent away, to do whatever they like. After that day the only plasterer to stay will be Randall and his usual acolyte.

It's really stupendous, the spectacle here at night—the number of people at work, lit up by lads; the innumerable torches suspended everywhere, the immense and endless spaces, the gulph below; above, the gigantic spider's web of scaffolding—especially when, standing under the finished and numberless arches of the galleries,[41] I listen to the reverberating voices in the stillness of the night, and see immense buckets of plaster and water ascending, as if they were drawn up from the bowels of a mine, amid shouts from subterranean depths, oaths from Hell itself, and chanting from Pandemonium or the synagogue ...

Tuesday 20 September

If you really knew how melancholy and weary I am to the depths of my being, you would not wonder at the horror I have of your being far off. Your trips to London cause me no dismay; I like to know every morning what took place the day before; it entertains and consoles me. But such a long journey as this (long at this magic time when Paris is in China and Brazil only on the other side of Falmouth),[42] a journey whose outcome is so uncertain and which can be rendered difficult in so many ways—this is something which fills me with agony ...

Now I must tell you of a new and almost incredible piece of madness. Seeing that his repeated and obstinate lies about the progress of the work here were beginning to be of no avail, that stupid and idiotic pig Hayter has run away without a word of warning and without a scolding from me, indeed without any cause other than that already mentioned, which in any case is due to his own incorrigible bestiality. You can imagine the wonderful effect of this flight at such a critical moment. This is how I am treated by rogues, Bagasses and pigs ...

I don't understand the "impracticability" of Lisbon for me: the horrible state of affairs there may be favourable to our plans, but then again it may not! It is quite clear to me that before we can decide you must go out there to judge for yourself. I don't much like the idea of rushing to a place, first betrayed and then governed by the block-headed soldiers of this diabolic island. It wouldn't be very nice to meet General Damn-my-eyes at Monserrate,[43] Captain Blast-all at La Roche's and Colonel Kiss-my-arse at José Dias' ...

In view of the inevitable confusion caused by this flight I don't think it will be possible to make the rooms in the Nunnery habitable, and I shall not make another oath; but if they are not, what am I to do in this hideous November solitude? It were better to sail by the first Packet than to suffer in this way. If the Lady of the White Flowers[44] were not so incapable and so lacking in energy and spirit, I would suggest her coming here on her own and having the only habitable room. But really I don't know what to do and your last letter asking for orders has quite non-plussed me. It could not have arrived at a moment more calculated to lacerate my nerves and make me ill. I'm too confused and tremble too much with fever to write another word. Until tomorrow, if I'm still alive ...

Wednesday 21 September

... With these Conventionists, neither Spain nor Portugal will be liberated from the talons of the Cuckoo-Philosopher. Never has the terrible destiny that for twenty years has turned Europe upside down, been more apparent than in this last English infamy. O poor, beloved Portugal, my own true country, how I pity you! Without trust in the mercy of God, implored by the Saint, I see no ray of light ...

Sunday 25 September

... Baldock's[45] china has arrived without the accident it deserved—being broken into a thousand pieces I mean. The jar, which is certainly neither unique nor Japanese, seems destined, because of its hideous shape (a false globe) and its coarse characters, to serve as the repository of some sovereign herb in the palace of some apothecary turned King. Believe me, these fashionable ridiculosities come straight from the factory near Canton, where they cost hardly more pence than guineas here. There is no grace, harmonious colouring or any merit whatever in this horror. I had it removed from my sight at once. I beg you to tell me where I am to send it so that it may not be exposed to its just fate.

What rage for trash governs you? How is it possible for you to tolerate this monstrosity—you who have an eye capable of perceiving beauty in the opposition of colours! But this infamous and harsh garland ∽ ∽ these Anglo-American barrack-room windows ⊞ and these lavatory-like hieroglyphs ‖, ~ ~. For the love of true taste, don't let yourself ever again be indoctrinated by Baldock! It is cruel to throw away so many shillings on the transportation of monstrosities which, even when they are broken into two or three sharp pieces, are hardly worthy to help Holy Job scrape himself on his dunghill ...

We'll have time to discuss Brunet's, but on the first glance at the list of charges I don't see much difference between the two dens: eleven or twelve guineas a week for the apartments isn't very cheap ...

The effect of the Octagon develops with every hour—all the fan-vaulting finished, five of the scaffoldings down, Hayter gay and smiling, fresher than a rose, the workmen stupefied by their own progress and Sunday gone to the devil. At this very moment all is ardour, all is progress, impossible to imagine or believe even when seen. It seems that the Saint inspires them; really, the thing is more like a miracle than anything I've yet seen. Yesterday they did five of the large circular windows, today they finish the other three.[46] Eight divine little windows about which you don't yet know are in place.[47] All the stucco in the Lantern and between the great arches is finished! You see what can be done when one insists on it and the Saint lends his support ...

Tuesday <27 September>

The letters Mr White writes to me are so full of sugar disasters and of the impossibility of doing anything at present with the Plummer people[48] etc that I don't know where to turn ... Consider then whether I'm in a state to spend two or three thousand pounds on silver, however royal or beautiful it may be! I who *detest*—yes detest—letters, was not a little distressed by the long and terrifying catalogue of the Windsor treasures. For God's sake don't dream of sending so much stuff by the coach! (But on re-reading your letter, I see it has already been sent.) All this in the unhappy state in which I find myself does not fail to disturb and confuse me. I don't at all understand what is required of me: am I free to buy only a small part, or must I have the whole lot together or not at all? These things should have been explained by you verbally and not by letters which I haven't even any desire to read ... The idea of sending such heavy articles by coach wasn't very good—every farthing counts for me now, with everything going out and nothing coming in. After what Rundell[49] says, I don't expect marvels. I doubt whether the style or the shape of the silver is good. You mentioned the Lancastrian rose: it isn't likely that this fine ornament is found on silver as modern as the reign of Charles II, who only died 120 years ago ...

With hardly a guinea available, I'm obliged to draw all I had kept back to live on, in order to pay for the house, the young Shepherdesses, the pensions on Mr White's list etc, etc. The Devil take him and his administration, imbecile that he is! Since I don't want to pay eighty guineas for the misfortune of having seen the cursèd and ridiculous apothecary's piss-pot, I want to know Mr Baldock's address ...

1. Lady Anne Hamilton (1766–1846), sister of the tenth Duke of Hamilton; Lady-in-waiting to Caroline, Princess of Wales, and her devoted attendant during her Trial as Queen. Supervised Beckford's daughters ("the Pledges"); nicknamed "the Macaw" because of her beaky nose.

2. Marshal Junot, recently created Duke of Abrantes; Napoleonic Governor of Portugal.

3. The thorough-bass, meaning here "the theme".

4. A Chamberlain of the Sultan at Constantinople, one of whose duties was to execute pashas as required.

5. There is a *double-entendre* here, since *bijou* can be a term of endearment (see 24 June).

6. The *Sibylla Libyca*, also called the *Cumaean Sibyl*, by Ludovico Carracci (1555–1619). At the Lansdowne Sale of 20 March 1806 (Lot 54) it sold for £267.15s. Beckford bought it for £787.10s. in his May 1817 sale, and finally disposed of it in 1823 for 360 guineas or pounds (*Phillips*, Day 26, Lot 249); the buyer then or later was the tenth Duke of Hamilton, for at *H.P.S.* (Lot 762) it was bought by Beckett-Denison for £283.10s.; at his sale on 13 June 1885 it was bought for £105 by Cyril Flower, first Lord Battersea. It measured 9 ft. 4 in. x 4 ft., and is described by Patmore, *British Galleries of Art,* 1824, pp. 124–5, who considered it one of the finest at Fonthill.

7. Art treasures being looted by the French armies.

8. *i.e.* your Father's country (Portugal). We were blockading Portugal as an enemy-occupied State, so it was proposed to smuggle Franchi over.

9. Marquess of Douglas, who spent much time at Ashton Hall, Lancaster; he was almost engaged to Susan.

10. News of the risings against the French in Madrid on May 2nd and in Asturias on 3rd appeared in our newspapers from June 8th.

11. B. gave the picture this title because its subject reminded him of the beautiful words of a famous air *Son qual Nave* ("I am a ship") in Hasse's opera *Ataserse,* sung by Farinelli, one of the greatest of all singers, in London in 1734. Hasse and Farinelli were brought over to London with this opera in order to break Handel's monopoly. The real title of the picture was *The Landing of Aeneas* (see p.56, note 33).

12. William Clarke (*c.*1752–1830) of New Bond Street; nephew of the famous bookseller James Robson, whose partner he was, 1787–9, after which he set up on his own; published *Repertorium Bibliographicum* and several editions of Beckford, who nicknames him Boletus (the Mushroom) because he had a large head and short neck and body.

13.   Beckford sold a portion of his library anonymously at Leigh & Sotheby's on June 9th and days following; the "Italian trash" included early 16th century romances of chivalry which fetched 5 to 8 guineas each; the 7-volume Bible published by Macklin in 1800, with engravings from many artists, fetched £43.1s.

14.   Napoleon.

15.   Wyatt had a country house at Hanworth (between Teddington and Staines).

16.   There were two Dixons connected with Wyatt—John, his draughtsman, clerk and assistant, and Joseph Dixon (born c.1776), who may have been John's son, and who was one of Wyatt's pupils. Dixon is later referred to as working at Fonthill.

17.   Portugal. It is an obsolete Portuguese Christian name, which nowadays has a ridiculous association, e.g. as a nickname for an old man who stands on his dignity.

18.   Perhaps he was the horse-rider of this name who appeared in the equestrian troupe supplied by Astley to Covent Garden for certain spectacular productions, 1813–14.

19.   All this is inserted to conceal Cooper's sex; or it might refer to mock marriage-ceremonies, etc, practised in pæderastic circles.

20.   This is the *Vision of S. Jerome*, now in the National Gallery, by Francesco Mazzola (1504–40) of Parma, known as Il Parmigiano. The first Marquess of Abercorn brought it over from Rome and later sold it to George Watson Taylor. Benjamin West had written the day before to Beckford that (Sir Thomas) Lawrence had just called to say that the picture was on offer for £3,000; West advised Beckford to give 2,500 pounds or guineas (letter in *H.P.*).

21.   David Pitcairn (1749–1809), a leading physician. He was in Portugal for 18 months from 1798, so Beckford probably met him there,

22.   *i.e.* the doctor attending "the Sheep", one of Beckford's queer foreign friends; this doctor was Regnault (see below, note 24).

23.   The Clarendon Hotel was in New Bond Street. Beckford gives no punctuation or conjunctions, simply stringing the names together.

24.   J.B. Regnault (1759–1836), a doctor in the French Revolutionary armies until he was denounced as a moderate and fled, practising in London until Louis XVIII made him his consultant physician at the Restoration.

25.   The defeat of Dupont near Madrid, with the loss of 12,000 men, and patriotic risings all over Spain.

26. Wyatt executed work at Powderham Castle, near Exeter, for the notorious William Courtenay, but the date is not known.

27. George Holmes Hayter (1759–1818), son of a carpenter, elder brother of the miniature painter Charles, and uncle of Sir George Hayter, R.A.; educated at Christ's Hospital; Clerk of the Works at Fonthill for many years until his death there on 4 December 1818, described by Beckford. Nicknamed *Coxone* (from *cochonus*, a swine), because of his voracity and bulk.

28. Hayter.

29. Wyatt.

30. *i.e.* London. Beckford refers to Southey's *Letters from England by Don M. A. Espriella,* 1807.

31. I do not know the origin or meaning of this word.

32. With stucco on its inner face. All the references are to the Lantern covering the Octagon: there were eight pairs of columns in its angles; the "rose" was the central boss on its vaulted ceiling, which also had eight smaller bosses.

33. Foxhall.

34. For the Lancaster Bed, see p.18. The Tribune is probably the North Tribune Room on the second floor, opening out from the Lancaster Gallery, with a balcony looking south across the Octagon.

35. This news of the infamous Convention of Cintra did not appear in the English Press until next day, the 16th, and its text was not published until the 17th; Beckford got private advance information from the Portuguese Ambassador. Kellerman parleyed and signed for the French. Wellington was one of the generals.

36. Beckford was negotiating through Edmund Rundell (see below, note 49) to buy some of the Royal silver at Windsor, and the transaction was confidential. *Christie,* Day 10, Lot 46, and similar items may be the result.

37. The word jocularly used of the dwarf means a *pike*—a large and voracious fish.

38. This refers to the final failure of Beckford's plan to marry his younger daughter Susan ("the Hysteric") to "the Calf"—a Spanish nobleman, the Count of Egmont y Fuentes (see p.284, note 19), whom Susan had already refused in 1840. It was opposed by her guardian Lady Anne Hamilton ("the Macaw"), who wanted this heiress for her brother, the Marquess of Douglas ("the Shepherd"), who had been in the offing as a suitor since 1804 at least. "The Egoist" is the elder sister Margaret, later Mrs Orde.

39. Stained-glass windows partly filling three of the great arches of the Octagon which ran from the floor to the Nunnery Arcade; they were copied from Batalha Monastery in Portugal.

40. The columns, ninety feet high, in the angles of the Octagon, which rose from the floor to the top of the Nunnery Arcade.

41. The Nunnery Arcade.

42. Because Paris was in blockaded enemy territory closed to British ships, whereas communications must have been good with Rio de Janeiro, seat of the Portuguese Court.

43. A quinta formerly rented by Beckford near Cintra; the other two are quintas at Colares nearby.

44. Susan.

45. Edward Holmes Baldock of Hanway Street (Oxford Street), a celebrated dealer in china, glass and antiques.

46. Catherine-wheel apertures in circular architraves, one for each face of the Octagon; they were just above the Nunnery Arcade, and gave light to a passage behind.

47. Loopholes above the circular windows.

48. The West India Merchant House of Plummer, Barham & Puller (their style changed periodically), of Philpot Lane, Fenchurch Street, who managed Beckford's Jamaican business from 1807 until at least 1840. He nicknamed them P.P. Lane (from their address).

49. Edmund Waller Rundell, a junior partner in the celebrated firm of Rundell, Bridge & Rundell, royal goldsmiths, of Ludgate Hill, who employed Paul Storr.

1810–1811

BECKFORD'S daughters at last got married. Susan married in April 1810, at the age of twenty-four, a man only seven years younger than her father—the Marquess of Douglas, later tenth Duke of Hamilton. She was devoted to him—evidently as a father-figure. We cannot guess his attitude to her, for she destroyed his letters, but he was attracted by middle-aged women. Four months after his marriage he left her in London and remained away a long time in Scotland, although she was indisposed as a result of measles and her pregnancy; Beckford accused him of cold-bloodedness. He had been on the *tapis* as a suitor since at least 1804, and both sides had been seriously negotiating the settlement since 1808. The Hamiltons held out for better terms, and it is hard to resist the conclusion that for them the match was largely a question of money.

Draft Agreements in the Hamilton Papers state that the marriage will give Douglas £10,000 in cash, his wife's capital of £8,100 in 3 per cent Bank Annuities, and £2,000 annual income from Beckford's Jamaican estates (out of which Susan was to have £600 annually as pin money). One would not have expected Douglas to go through with the marriage unless the capital sums had been paid over; and negotiations had been going on so long that one must suppose that Beckford's agents had the funds available. It is therefore puzzling to find that in the summer of 1811 Beckford is ashamed of not being able to pay Douglas a large sum owing to him. It is tempting to assume that this must be the £2,000 annual income from Jamaica—especially since on June 24th Messrs Plummer, Beckford's West India merchants, refused to continue Beckford's quarterly allowance, and on November 20th he finds himself "without income from Jamaica". On July 1st Beckford wants a loan of £5,000 from the financier Cochrane Johnstone; perhaps two years of Jamaican payments were becoming due to Douglas, and perhaps this sum also included Beckford's own quarterly needs. But we cannot be certain. For in October 1811 Franchi was despatched on a special mission to Hamilton Palace; his object was to extract money from the Marquess due to Beckford! We do not know what the connection was between the money due from Beckford in July and the money owed to him in October or earlier—it seems rather a short period for an important loan. But possibly under the terms of the marriage contract of 1810 Beckford had engaged himself to loan Douglas a large sum.

The marriage of the elder daughter Margaret in May 1811 was an altogether different affair. She married against her father's will, a most serious crime in a patriarchal society, for which many fathers cut their daughters off without a penny. She even ran away to do so, leaving behind what could be construed as a rather insulting note. It was quite understandable that Beckford should not want an Orde as a son-in-law—as a family they were too clerical, had few connections, little money and no title. In particular, his daughter's suitor James was only a Lieutenant-Colonel, a younger son with no inheritance.[1] That Beckford should be angry and unforgiving for years is (for those days) understandable. But his remarks about his own daughter are indefensible and make one think that what he really hated was its being a love match.[2]

1810

Friday 22 June

I know nothing more about Gulchenrouz[3] than I knew in the great Babylon. He has not been near me (at least not here); he is very uncommunicative and singularly silent and indifferent; I doubt if he'll ever acquire much favour.

The new garden makes a great effect because of its unusual arrangement, but the drought which breeds and encourages millions of vermin and insects has almost destroyed everything. The andromeda[4] is doing fairly well and so are the American plants. That rogue Milne says that he has some magnificent magnolia shrubs, but I doubt it, like everything else he tells me.

If only that ever-accursèd (and deservedly so), wretched, stupid, infamous Bagasse were here, we could quickly have a real paradise for the porcelain where I've always thought it would look best—in the antechamber, with china-cabinets all round; I've made up my mind to arrange it there. That corner will be all a-glitter with plate glass, and very comfortable. The rooms above will not be continued because Coxone cannot proceed with out Bagasse. For God's sake see if it isn't possible to get him down here—the Abbey isn't London: beadles and bailiffs can't force the doors of the mysterious Barrier.[5]

There is a terrible lack of carpets for the gallery and the ante-sanctuary; but above all there is a lack of silver plaques for the soffit and the large expanse of oak round the portrait of King Edward III;[6] that portrait, at all events, presents a beautiful harmony of colours. Consult with Rundell how the plaques are to be made; you know about the large rose, but whether or not it is to be bright, I leave him to decide …

Today I made a start with ass's milk; I needed it, and already I think I feel better. The gardenias are marvellous …

Friday <6 July>

Here I'm getting on prodigiously with the Diplomatic Corps, and were it not for the swelling on my eye, my gums and an extreme terror of the dew,

I would enjoy myself tolerably. Bezerra[7] is full of taste and intelligence; he sees and understands everything with an incomparable fervour of spirit. The weather is favourable for walking and the walks are divinely beautiful— roses everywhere, *azareiri*[8] covered with flowers, cloud-mountains in the air gilded by the rays of the sun, the most brilliant effects of chiaroscuro, stranger than I ever before remember having seen, and due to the recent drought. I wish you were here to see these picturesque mists and, above all, to breathe the scent of Cintra and Collares, which makes poor Bezerra weep and fills him with the tenderest *saudades* ...

Wednesday 11 <July>[9]

Poor sods—what a fine ordeal, what a procession, what a pilgrimage, what a song and dance, what a rosary![10] What a pity not to have a balcony in Bow Street to see them pass, and worse still not to have a magic wand to transform into a triumph the sorry sequence of events ...

Monday 23 <July>

... Last Thursday I had a pastoral letter announcing the impossibility of making any journey, the Princess being (pregnant).[11] The sugary epistle of the self-same lady informed me "that since Douglas had explained the mystery she was condemned to the environs of London the whole summer." At the same time she asked for some fruit to adorn a banquet she was giving last Friday in Arcadia to the Prince of Wales.

... Would that everything else was as profitable as Witham,[12] where they've found lead, timber, iron, stone, staircases and chimney-pieces etc in plenty; wonderful lime half as cheap as here; stables (or at any rate a portion which has escaped demolition) which are all ready to use and quite picturesque; a walled kitchen garden capable of producing all one wants the very first year; and into the bargain 200 tons of pine ready to fell. So, if Bagasse comes I'll flourish a magic wand and in a month the Tower will rise. But without Bagasse I'll lose heart. Enclosed is a note begging him to come. Second me in this, help me, imbagassate me for God's sake.

Wednesday <25 July>

Now I am Barzaba the Gourmet. Your descriptions make my mouth water—puddings, tarts, cream, fish etc, etc. Ah my God, I must imitate Jommelli[13] who, in order to have *palpette*,[14] married his cook; I would value an artist of this sort more than Miss Long,[15] and according to my ideas the mésalliance would be no worse ...

<*Thursday 26 July*>

My mouth is still barzabising,[16] after your stories of the comestible delights of Cornwall. Let's go there. Let's occupy a hole under some crag. Let's make a cottage in the midst of a shrubbery of myrtles and laurustinus. There we will live deliciously on fish, mutton, Fonthill pheasants, etc. Sir Isaac Heard[17] would find my cooking spouse rather plebeian, but no matter—at our mature age the throat pre-eminently demands a certain care. And then—and then—if amongst so many "brothers"[18] one could find one who was a bit of a mameluke, one's bliss would be perfect ...

Today there are clouds above the Tower and the hill, and a real threat of rain—sweet, poetic, melancholy weather that recalls languid memories of Cintra and Monserrate ...

Saturday <28 July>

... Yesterday I sent the little Marchioness the most stupendous collection of flowers that have ever been gathered in that rogue Milne's kingdom: a certain very scarlet lily (*Fothergillia*)[19] of rare beauty, and various other marvels, some of which have flowered for the first time in this island; and (between ourselves) if they don't flower again it will be little loss. This craze for novelty always makes it impossible to have the good old plants (jasmin, gardenias etc) in the condition in which one ought to have them. One never finds here any more that beautiful *dolichos*[20] which used to smell so sweetly on the walls of Monserrate ...

Friday 12 October

This news of the poor Shrew is not calculated to cheer me; evidently the prolonged absence of the Shepherd is producing the worst effect—an effect which will influence the future earl or little countess in a manner only too similar to the well-known churlishness of the Hamiltons. I can't understand how any sort of business in the world can keep a true and faithful shepherd from the presence of his sweet sovereign; to me at least such a thing would not have happened, for I'm incapable of such prudent cold-bloodedness. Ah, if there was but a worthy object on the throne, how devoted, how adoring, how barzabalic I am ready to become! But here I pass my life sadly without animation of any kind, arranging books by day and in the evening listening to Father Smith[21] drumming dully on chairs and tables. I ask you whether it is not time to finish with the vegetable kingdom and transport myself where thoughts circulate with a little more speed.

... At Wardour, Longleat and Stourton trees are being felled for prices far below what they had hoped—not above £4 a fir-tree, whatever its quality. Bankruptcies and taxes (which have to be paid, bankrupt or not) have obliged many gentlemen and squirelings to fell all their plantations. In the Salisbury paper one only sees the announcements of sale after sale—sad news for me ... I am going with the deceitful Milne to visit the fellings and stop them—with the way prices are going now it is a mistake to cut too much ...

<Saturday> 10 November[22]
(the wettest and saddest day ever seen, even in this month in England!
Dies irae! Dies illa![23])

... 'Tis no longer a question of *savoir-vivre. Savoir-mourir*, before being put to the torture, mental and physical, is all that the inhabitants of the proscribed Isle have to contrive as best they can. For the future I discover only phantoms stranger and more terrifying than those in the Apocalypse. Where is the mountain that will hide us from the wrath of a God justly angered by the massacres and ravages caused by our Cabinet, so coldly hypocritical and so basely mercantile? At the recollection of Quiberon and

Copenhagen, of the siege of Saragossa and the sack of Evora, on imagining the Russian horrors in Finland, we are forced to expect a day of vengeance. I see this terrible day issuing from the sanctuary of Divine Justice. It will not dawn on Windsor or London, for the Bank, Palace, Castle and cathedrals, all will have vanished. Over deserted, smoking plains pale Napoleon will be seen galloping. It will be West's Apocalypse, his Triumph of Death, painted in the same terrible colours, a mingling of mire and blood.[24] To such scenes is our fine reign of every kind of borrowing leading us. A little more hiring of mercenaries, a few more expeditions, and our great Canterbury will have uttered his last prayer, our pious Perceval[25] his last farthing. 'Tis in vain for me to turn hither and thither: the path of salvation is nowhere discovered. Let us cover our head with the skirt of our garment and be resigned.

1811

Wednesday 6 February

Here I am in my great tabernacle of Nardoc with hardly enough light to see my pen, the most horrible cold and stinking fog, and an unbelievable sadness inspiring a hundred thousand ghosts of ideas each blacker than the other. A moment ago, to cheer me up a little, they brought me a green twig with three miserable fruits on it which looked as if they had dropped from some tattered and faded map of China …

Thursday 7 February

… The infamous Bagasse will lose us time as usual, I don't doubt: as he detests Rottier he won't appear at the Abbey until many days, perhaps weeks, after Rottier's departure. One Rottier is worth a thousand Bagasses. Would to God that he had never been born and that the Turks, Moors and Arabs had been not merely circumcised but castrated before inventing their pointed saracenic-gothic architecture—the cause of my ruin. The devil take them.

Farewell until tomorrow, dearest Gregory. I'm going to get on my horse and take advantage of a miserable bit of sunshine.

Sunday 16 June

Here everything is gradually lapsing into antiquity—grass up to the very doors, etc. The lake[26] looks as if God had made it, it is so natural, without the least trace of art; I don't say it is marvellous, for its banks are too flat, but it spreads itself grandiosely and the swans look as if they are in Paradise. Am I not a poor Adam without an Eve? Who will be my Eve? Miss Long, and Miss Butterfly[27] into the bargain?

… The new round tower is bulky and much too big; I don't like its proportions.[28] Suspecting as much, Coxone hasn't put on the battlements.

One can't trust the infamous Bagasse in the slightest thing. Every day brings new proofs of his negligent apathy. Just imagine, the pinnacles have had to be fixed in the following divine manner with wooden spars!

So the Macaw will be delighted to find a most comfortable hold for her poisonous talons. When I saw this horror I thought I would faint!

Farewell, dear Gregory. Milne, more rascally and corpse-like than ever, awaits me. I'm going to plough my way through this sea of greenery, this Universe of leaves, this immense grave-yard which is more of a limbo than an elysium. Farewell. I would not have taken up my pen for anyone else in the world, which is a proof that I am all that you could wish me to be for you. I embrace you with sincerity in my heart.

Saturday 22 June

… I'm very impatient to know the result of the great sale at Christie's, especially whether Lord Yarmouth[29] (who swallows up everything) has swallowed up the fine Leonardo da Vinci.[30] From what you have written I don't doubt that this picture has very real merit—what a pity not to have seen it before my departure; that's what one gains by burying oneself away from London.

I shan't know anything tomorrow before my return from Witham. I'll go out early to Coxonise among the pines that still remain to be sold; I'll sell as many as I can. I shan't have any more pity for Witham, you may be sure; advantage shall be taken of everything one possibly can … I regret infinitely the fatal necessity of seeing here once again that cursèd, infamous Bagasse; but come he must, and if he won't come soon, I'll send for Jeffry Wyatt.[31]

I really believe that the half-stupid, half-cadaverous, half-impudent Rottibus is destined to make me blow my brains out. How is it possible to expose me in this way to the just complaints of the poor Shepherd? What

I suffer in this respect can only be expressed in the language of Hell: cries, screams, execrations and curses! If I knew how or where to turn, I should soon finish with Mr Rottibus, I can assure you …

You can't imagine what pretty frost was to be seen on the windows of my tower at six o'clock this morning! I have never experienced such a devilish change of climate, like those alternations of heat and cold of which one reads in *St. Patrick's Purgatory*[32] and which form the special diversion of damned souls. In a short time winds or zephyrs will be blowing. But nothing will matter to me; I'll be indifferent to everything and dead to everything.

Monday 24 June

The moment which I have been so long expecting seems now to have arrived. Messrs Plummer have refused further payments, and here I am without a penny! It seems to me that it is now absolutely necessary to pursue Mr Rottibus daily until some remedy is found, and especially to consult with Mr Cochrane Johnstone[33] about what can be done. A change of system and of merchants must take place without delay. As to my sufferings. I do not pretend to be able to describe them. It is enough if I assure you that since Mr White's last letter I have fever and diarrhoea.

The pinnacles will remain protected as they are now; you need have no anxiety about plans for spending money here. I am not in a position to give £10 a day to the negligent and ruinous Bagasse. The fault is entirely his and not poor Coxone's. If Coxone had not made the pinnacles secure in his own completely crude way, all the poor, childish, ignorant mechanics of stupid, lazy Mr Wyatt would have been no good. He is a man who carries with him perdition, ruin and disgrace, as is proved by the Abbey, Wilton, Kew[34] and the House of Parliament etc, etc.[35] I don't wish to dirty the paper by writing about him …

I am still full of regret at not seeing the Leonardo da Vinci; it must be quite divine, gentle and touching, like all the *genuine* works of this great master, when they are well preserved and not daubed in the style of Father *Tetonasso's* Holy Family …[36]

Friday 28 June

This tiresome business of the Marquess is killing me! I am rendered the unhappiest of mortals at the thought of this vile slave[37] of the Macaw, with the face of a damned soul, complaining about me and cursing me ... For God's sake leave neither Rottier nor Cochrane Johnstone in peace until they've found the cash for the Marquess. Tell my daughter that unless I see her and the child here, I shall be really unhappy—these are not just words ...

Farewell, my dear Gregory. Pity me and beg the Saint to extricate me from this bitter pass.

Saturday 29 June

In the bottom of my heart and in the intimate recesses of such little judgment as I have in those matters which in English are called Business, I approve, and have always approved, of Mr White. I doubt if there exists a truer friend and, even in his profession, a person of more acute or sound intellect. He is a hundred thousand times preferable to C. Johnstone. I don't need a pulpit to proclaim my perseverance in projects of economy. I am ready to do whatever is resolved upon by my old, zealous and trusted friends. Make your proposals and then see whether or not I have the strength to carry them out ... Poor boastful C. Johnstone—what a nose Rottibus had! Yes, let's trust him after all and retrench.

For the last twenty-four hours it hasn't stopped raining—a sad occurrence for the hay. Tomorrow if it doesn't deluge I shall return to Witham to mark pines. They are buying everything that we are willing to fell ...

Monday 1 July

... I do not pretend to be so ill that I lie in bed unconscious or delirious with a raging fever; but I suffer a good deal when I see the way in which God knows what form of negligence exposes me to the just lamentations of the pallid Shepherd. I have no doubt that the Macaw will take advantage of these bunglings by Rottier; the seeds of a great estrangement between the Shepherd and myself have already been scattered ... The Shepherd is nothing but a sad mixture of weak intellect and strong self-interest. I am sorry for my daughter if she is not the ruler: to follow someone incapable of leading is worse than death ... I don't pretend to expect marvels from C. Johnstone, but he must be a poor speculist if between all his friends and speculating brethren there cannot be found a loan for £5,000.

... The little picture[38] is divine—as good a bargain as the Luke of Holland.[39] It represents the Duke of Alençon and has on the back the cypher of Charles I of England; I have no doubt that it comes from the Royal Household. A truly beautiful thing! I was not wrong to insist on having it, and thanks to your prudence it did not cost much—indeed quite the contrary. The date turns out to be 1569, years after the death of Holbein. I don't know who the painter is, but I recognize his hand; we shall find out his name in due course. Here are the fruits of a bit of good judgment on my part and crass ignorance on Christie's.[40] How many things one might do in London in the course of a year with presence of mind and presence of money!

Saturday 5 October
(Saturday of a hundred thousand devils)

This fine abode has once more become Demosthenes' Lantern or the Temple of the Winds. Never in my life have I heard a more horrid whispering, a more cursèd din. Yesterday evening was a masterpiece of this sort. Almost the whole night long I seemed to hear all the carts in creation carrying all Bonaparte's artillery in perpetual motion! Truly I can't live in this way—it isn't living at all. Here's the result of the wise advice not to complete the Pavilion.[41] Had we proceeded with the work when I first had the idea, I should not now be exposed to these insufferable torments. Curse the infamous Bagasse a thousand and again a thousand times! Once the sale[42] is concluded it will be in my power to pay him; but he will not get a penny, he will only get curses from me as the reward for his stupid negligence.

"Where, infamous Beast, where are you? What putrid inn, what stinking tavern or pox-ridden brothel hides your hoary and gluttonous limbs?" Find him if you can and tell him that his presence is a *necessary evil*.

Tuesday 8 October

I'm not surprised at any stinginess in that Scottish quarter. All illnesses are contracted through excessive intimacy, and it must be admitted that the Marchioness was by no means ill-disposed to catch the narrowness, frigidity and baseness of her illustrious consort—so much so that I expect to see this sublime couple become a by-word for avarice and intolerable pride. Already they are in very bad odour with me, I swear to you. Over and over again I repeat that nothing moves them but self-interest—masked or not makes no difference, for it is self-interest and nothing more. Neither filial affection nor a sense of honour will ever spur them on; the only thing that will animate these automata to action is the idea of securing what, without this Parismatic[43] operation, will never fall to them (not a penny of it).

Wednesday 16 October

Horrid weather, putrid weather, Comet[44] weather, weather worthy of Father Bestorum, who is here once again, in high spirits after placing one of his miserable daughters in the bosom of the Eternal Father! In this at least he shows good sense and good taste. I was not born to be so fortunate. Ah, if the measles had carried off the infamous Ordure before the scandalous marriage, what a blessing it would have been![45]

... I can well believe you about the horrid food in the York Tavern[46] and the coarse faces of all these provincial beasts. But I would not fly from a nice York patapouf[47] if Providence sent him to me. Everything that the most excellent Lady Providence sends should be received with the utmost respect. In my extreme poverty I would not be hard to please. What most confounds and disgusts me is a certain kind of frigidity and insipidity like Mme Bion's[48] (the devil take you, you blond beast).

By dint of howling (more worthy of wolves and bears than of a mere swine like him) Coxone has managed to get more than half the money paid to him. Yesterday I went myself to Witham to encourage him. I might have been in Norway—such were the sights and smells: pine-wood huts; pines, on the ground in a strange and splendid disorder, some already stripped, others being stripped, with and without bark; a hundred and more work-people—youths and old men, cooking, working, shouting;

carts and donkeys; columns of smoke rising from out the abyss of green; and here and there the bright light of new-lit fires. In short, a spectacle worthy of being painted. Never again will Witham appear so beautiful. A rainy and unequal sky added to the general effect.

Tomorrow Coxone returns. Today he has been selling 500 more trees which I marked in order to make the scene still more dramatic; and, thank God, it all sells very fast and at the best price. They are buying from Bristol in order to send it—guess where—to Jamaica! ...

Thursday 17 October

I receive and I reply, my dear Gregory. You are right to admire so ardently the rich and magnificent cathedral of York. I doubt whether there exists another Gothic pile so immense and at the same time so ornate. One's eyes are consoled by this profusion of painted glass, escaped from so many political upheavals or restored by well-born people like the present Archbishop (a real gentleman).[49] What a contrast to the ruin on the Continent! Ah if only they had the good sense to restore the true Faith in all its venerable splendour—what a paradise this earth would become!

... We are still having very fine drizzle and eternal mists, with a heat worthy of the divine comet which causes it. Farewell, dear Gregory, until your news from the ducal Palace.

Saturday 19 October

I perfectly recollect Durham and its imposing position above the river, etc—its group of palace and castle buildings makes a superb effect. Its Cathedral must have been sufficiently solemn and rich when all its altars were resplendent with reliquaries and lights and when St Cuthbert was the object of the most extravagant pilgrimages; nevertheless, our gothicisms are always too mean—quite otherwise sublime are Amiens' arches and Rheims' stupendous entrance. I no longer speak of Beauvais and S. Nicaise: they no longer exist. The Beelzebubic Revolution and the weather enlisted in its aid made them disappear. S. Nicaise was sold for its stone to Santerre,[50] and Beauvais, having been despoiled of its lead, collapsed of its own accord after a great tempest in December 1802.[51]

For three days now we have had a species of spring here, but the falsest, the most deceiving and the most ridiculous imaginable. All the orange trees are again covered with flowers; the most agreeable little mushrooms are sprouting up everywhere; the birds are singing and the butterflies fluttering round—but not *the* Butterfly I long to see; so of what use to me is this new-fangled spring? None at all, I swear, save to inspire some hopes of seeing this infamous realm of cruel, bitter, coarse and hypocritical brutes ended by a stroke of the tail of the comet. Ah, dear comet, suppress the suppressors,[52] the false novelists,[53] the false prophets, the false Kings and the false Shepherds ...

Tuesday 22 October

... The Royal Circus at York and the boy! I don't like travelling, but if you could find out where this divine object has his abode, I would take to the road. Will this young horseman be part of the troupe? In pity's name, they are not all Hyrcanian tigers. Find out whither he has flown. I don't wish to languish in this way for the whole of my life without any beatific vision. I am tired to death of contemplating such painful ugliness, I who am more sentimental etc than ever. Rather than suffer thus it would be better to die.

But now to proceed. Good God, how vivid you are in your description of the 18th of the Kingdom of the Cinquefoils![54] The most Serene Lady does very well not to write; I'm not interested in news of all that riff-raff which she has the misfortune to entertain. What expenses! All this lavishness doesn't look as if payments are going to be made <to me> ...

Here I am being imbestified with poor Father Bestorum, very melancholy, very downcast and very low (?), without a ray of light save that which sparkles in your letters, without hope and without appetite for anything in the world except the divine apparition of York.

Rides, carriages, Archibalds,[55] the Most Serene Lady's loved ones etc don't interest me at all. They are not the people for me nor I for them. O that the Comet would fall on them in a shower of a hundred thousand million vipers, and that, torn asunder by deadly bites, they might be dragged by their inwards into the bottom of the eternal pit! Ah my dear Gregory, I am neither able nor wish to tell you how much I suffer in every way and how tired I am of being alive.

Thursday 24 October

Thank you my dear Gregory, for such clear and detailed information about Hamilton Palace. I knew from prints how miserable the design of the grand gallery was; but the lions as you describe them to me—all shining, majestic and noble, and the general effect of all this crimson,[56] the golden eagles, the great vases and onyx-coloured oak panelling must be very impressive, but barbarous. I did not think that the proportions were so great; they didn't appear so on the plan which Bagasse had.

The very thought of all these expeditions to taverns to dance and wolf picnic suppers etc is enough to make me sick; it must be a disgusting spectacle for the Marchioness and is a fresh proof of the degeneration of everything in this world! Blessed abbey, save and defend me from such riff-raff and riff-raffery as this! Grow, you forests, raise yourselves, you walls, and make an everlasting barrier between me and them. I shudder even at this distance—horrid, infamous, low, vile confusion! If the mad expenditure involved in all this does not serve as a cause, or at least as a pretext, for their not paying up, you can count yourself lucky. Would to God that you were already paid, dispatched and on your way to this pure and sacred residence, which, whether I'm alive or dead, shall never be profaned—*at least by them*, if they don't take more care to put me in a good humour and save the honour of the House.

Not a whisper so far about the Infamous One, curse him. Father Bestorum is making pretty views of the Abbey and its surroundings; they will make a nice little volume like last year's but much superior. I am not dissatisfied with him. Work is already in progress on the tower and the pavilion but if Bagasse doesn't come everything will go to the devil, and I shall become more rabid than a dog and will stop everything.

The weather continues to be tolerable, rather damp but with quite consoling rays of sunshine from time to time. The dwarf (making a frightful grimace at the pornography you sent me) has just brought in some wild strawberries which fill the whole room with the sweetest smell. An incredible thing, this Comet and its effects! ...

Friday 25 October

... God deliver me from all this and return you here as soon as possible, and inspire my poor daughter to take refuge in this sacred place, where one does not mix with vermin, titled or otherwise, in mere eating-houses; where one is not exposed to the vilest of all heresies—the Scottish heresy; and where Missis All-dugs, the great sow, provides better fare than all your banquets. And then the patent lamps, stinking and flickering, the diabolic music,[57] the sad sound of crashing crockery etc, etc! I see, I hear, I smell everything. I'm almost beside myself with rage and horror on reading your letters of the 20th and 21st which arrived by the same post. Fine words those of the Shepherd about me! He is right to envy me, and would do well to imitate me.

O ho, now, a post-script, and what an interesting post script! A boy jack-ass, and a jack-ass after my own heart (?). Would it not be possible to inspire his divine mother to bring this fair treasure here? In that case I should become all sugar and the most paternal of all fathers. If I have to spend my whole life with objects as insipid, monotonous and frigid etc as Mme Bion etc I shall become of so dark and extravagant a humour, so harsh and evil-tempered, that in tormenting everything which I see and which touches me I shall end up by tormenting myself to death. Countess Pox,[58] more than half dead, fills me with disgust and pity ...

The quarry in the ruins of the pavilion[59] (the one facing the water, I mean) has been opened up, and produces the finest stone imaginable, all ready to put in position. Nanibus jumped with joy on hearing that the Marchioness is coming. *"Eh bien, elle fait bien; cela lui coutera moin que tout ce train. Elle aura les plus belles fleurs du monde et je la fera monter sur ma Jenni."* Who can resist such a prospect? Not the Marchioness, I hope. Farewell, dear Gregory.

Sunday 27 October

… This catalogue of people who are at last to leave the Palace is none too brilliant—second-rate the whole lot: Lady Cunningham, Lord Primrose,[60] Sir Hew Hamilton[61] of bastard race etc, etc. Small fry indeed! It was not worth breaking one's head, purse and porcelain for company such as this.

… If I am not to be exposed to the last degree of despair, it is necessary, absolutely necessary that I should see (at least see) the object concerning whom you let fall a few words in your penultimate letter to grieving Barzaba.

<*Tuesday*> *29 October*

I do not know what you mean about Hamilton Palace park being neither magnificent nor grandiose. In descriptions at least, I know nothing more powerful than your sketch of those alpine crags, immense oaks and profound deeps, those leafy abysses, impenetrable to the wind, out of which rise the ruins of the ancient castle. It must be imposing, it must speak to the soul! Would to God that something or other might speak to my soul—I am always so melancholy, receiving as my only consolation the most wretched letters from Rottier. It seems that he hasn't a farthing, not even enough to pay the quarterly for the Harley Street house! …[62]

The Marchioness has her ways and I have mine; unfortunately they are entirely opposed. Her silence about the Ordure is sufficient proof of this. I am highly displeased by her lack of consideration for me in sealing with red wax[63] as if she did not share my just indignation, my legitimate horror …

Friday 1 November

The news of your withdrawal from the Palace of Meanness is fine and pleasing … I don't wonder that the hares there are so good; the great poverty and natural sterility of these Scottish acres must suit them better than the rich amenities of the Abbey kingdom of Fonthill …

Everything you write in your letters of the 27th and 28th (which arrived here today without being "missent to Manchester") is very interesting, but not in the way that Barzaba would like. They pass like flashes of lightning, these rare, fugitive eulogies of yours of a jack-ass, a patapouf etc. It is cruel not to be more discursive, and more generous in giving me hope of some consolation for my poor eyes, which have no object to feast upon except a Mr Prudent Well-Sealed-up and a Mme Bion, now definitely become Mr Richardson … Some remedy must be found; otherwise my desperation will lead me to some horrid end. Hasten, yes hasten your steps …

Tuesday 5 November

You must have become State painter of the Magotesque[64] Idols of New Zealand. What an infamous miniature has just fallen out of your letter of the 30th October which I am holding! The dwarf, who was standing beside me, has turned his back, shrugging his shoulders and shouting, "*C'est un peu fort repeter toujour les meme choses. Est-ce qu'il nous prend pour des imbeciles?*" Such a picture is well suited to accompany the Gospel according to the Pretty Boy which you send me; the description as well as the poetry is enough to make one vomit.

I hope that by now you are already on your way. If I were not, by some special and mysterious grace of Providence, unboreable, I should long ago have been beneath ground. To be alone is nothing to me; but to see every day the old-maidish melancholy, so typically English, of that wretched Father Bestorum with his oily, stupid sighs is almost too much; this dryness penetrates one's spirit like dampness one's body … I'm very sorry to have lost the opportunity of seeing Mrs Siddons in Macbeth and as Catherine of Aragon etc.

Saturday < 16 November >

I hope to God, my dear Gregory, that the Ordure intrigues will fall into their own mire. Heaven save me from being mixed up with people so far removed from my own sphere. With me it is all or nothing, and doubtless it will be the latter, seeing that the affair is going very slowly,[65] and not at a gallop as the unworthy Rottier had written to me. This whole race of Ordes stinks for me, and I doubt whether it would be in their power, even with the most splendid titled gilding, to disguise their native smell in such a way as not to disgust my nose. Yes, yes, Orde, write to Ireland, consult Rottier, return to your hovels, dawdle as much as you like. You will be, I hope, for ever and ever exiled from me and from all that I possess. Go to Cousin Bigg, disprove your genealogy if you can. Off! Off!

I have no great opinion of youths recommended with such ardour by their mothers, sisters and friends. This one will be some ragamuffin—and we have enough ragamuffins here. Take no steps until we have talked it over together.

Wednesday <20 November>

You may joke as much as you like, but I swear to you that this Witham infamy,[66] added to the truly ruinous conduct of my unworthy Rogue Merchants and their satellites in Jamaica, makes me see everything in saffron and turn that colour myself. Tell Mr Rottier that seven per cent per annum won't free me from anxiety; what I want is the sum owed to me. Without it, I will not be answerable for the violence I shall commit, nor for my health, nor for my life ... Ah my God, how unhappy I am! I no longer care about Bagasse or the Tribune or anything. For me everything is buried in this tomb of Witham ... I'm almost losing hope, my brain is in a ferment. Around me I see nothing but ruin in a thousand shapes. I was on the point of calling an abrupt halt to the work, but felt too sorry for poor Coxone. Explain to Mr Rottier that I shall be afflicted by more than madness, fury and torments if I continue to be thus deprived of my just expectations by a band of thieves.

I regret immensely having incurred new expenses in Harley Street. I feel everything like St Bartholomew when he was flayed alive, and I feel it so terribly that soon the froth will be trickling from my mouth like a mad dog—and Mr Rottier may be sure that it will bite him. Who the devil ever neglected the affairs of a master and friend as he has done? Shame! Infamy! This is like killing me. To lose my property without any benefit, to find myself without income from Jamaica, and with a thousand debts to pay—what a position!

My dear Gregory, you know me well enough, but nothing I have ever experienced equals what I feel in these circumstances. My illusions have vanished into thin air. Even before this fatal failure, Mr Rottier had drawn, from the sum set aside for me, from the sum kept back from the proceeds of timber at Witham, £2,000 for the purchase of land at Fonthill. Curse that purchase! Curse the Abbey and all that surrounds it! Curse the beasts in my affairs who have tolerated merchants and Zinckes[67] etc who reduce me to a state of beggardom.

I can't go on. I fall to the ground. I have quite a lot of fever—like a touch of the sun. I don't know where to turn; it's either death for me or another mode of life. I am agitated to the very limit.

1. James Orde (c.1772–1850) later became a General. His grandfather, a clergyman who married a clergyman's daughter, was a younger son; and so was his father, who married the heiress of Weetwood Hall, Northumberland; James never inherited this, being a third son. One of his elder brothers was a clergyman, and one of his sisters married a clergyman named Moises.

2. For example, he writes about her: "I don't care who is 'in the family way'…; if by this *somebody* you mean Mme Ordure, I spit anew and I curse anew with all my heart—the vilest, lowest animal." (6 April 1817.)

3. The original Gulchenrouz was, in *Vathek*, an effeminate and beautiful youth. The great Babylon is London.

4. Bog or Wild Rosemary, an evergreen heath-like shrub with pink flowers in sprays at the end of its branches, flowering in May and June; it hates drought.

5. The wall surrounding the inner property of Fonthill. The bailiffs were probably occupying his London house.

6. Copied by Mathew Cotes Wyatt (1777–1862), James' second son, from a picture at Windsor. The whole paragraph is about King Edward's Gallery, named after Edward III.

7. J.P. Bezerra de Seixas (1756–1817) figured prominently in the *Journal* and had already been Envoy to the United States, Holland and Russia. He finished up just before his death as acting Prime Minister at Rio, holding practically every portfolio, and this killed him.

8.   The Portugal Laurel (*Prunus lusitanica*).

9.   Beckford wrote *Tuesday 11,* but the 11th was a Wednesday. He refers to what he read in the *Morning Chronicle* of Tuesday the 10th, which he would probably have received the next day. This was one of the most notorious cases of the period, when a large number of men and youths, members of a group called the Vere Street Coterie, were arrested at the White Swan in Vere Street, Clare Market, on the Sunday night. The newspaper describes their procession to and from Bow Street next morning. Those who were discharged as not guilty were roughly handled by the mob, amongst whom low women were prominent, and barely escaped with their lives; one of these was a Saunders (see p.36).

10. *i.e.* "what a collection of people".

11. Beckford did not put this word in a bracket, but obviously inserted it to make the sense clear (Susan having left a dash or blank in her letter!).

12. Witham Friary, between Bruton and Frome. The Wyndhams built an 18th century house here, which they sold to Alderman Beckford, whose son pulled it down; he sold the whole property of 2,300 acres in October 1811 to a land surveyor, who quickly sold it at a good profit to the Duke of Somerset.

13. Niccolo Jommelli (1714–74), Neapolitan composer.

14. The fleshy filaments hanging from a fish's mouth (its barbels).

15. Catherine Tylney Long, millionaire heiress of the deceased Sir James Tylney Long, Bart., of Draycot House, Chippenham. She came of age that October, marrying William Pole-Wellesley (see p.125, note 42) in 1812.

16. Drooling. Franchi is travelling in Cornwall with his daughter, just landed from Lisbon at Falmouth.

17. Garter King-at-Arms.

18. A hit at the Methodists, whom Beckford detested. A *mameluke* is a catamite (the Egyptian mamelukes had a bad reputation in this respect).

19. Not a lily, which it resembled, and with which it was in those days confused, but *Nerine Curvifolia*, at that time called *Amaryllis Fothergillii*. It was introduced into England in 1788, and was a greenhouse plant.

20. A genus of sub-shrubs and twining herbs, one species of which is called Hyacinth Bean.

21. John Smith (1749–1831), nicknamed "Warwick" and "Italian" Smith, an artist who was President of the Watercolour Society. Nicknamed Father Bestorum because his age made him "father" of all the "beasts" at Fonthill.

22. To Macquin in French.

23. *Dies irae, dies illa* is the first line of a Latin hymn about the Day of Judgment, sung as the "sequence" in the Mass of Interment (one of the Masses for the Dead), and now translated in *Hymns Ancient and Modern* 398, and *English Hymnal* 351.

24. Although it is possible that B. refers to West's *Opening of the Sixth Seal*, which hung at Fonthill, it seems even more likely that he is thinking of *Death on the Pale Horse*, the sketch of which was exhibited in Paris, 1802.

25. Spencer Perceval, the Prime Minister.

26. The new lake just south of the Abbey called Bitham Lake (not the old lake in front of Splendens).

27. A "butterfly" is a pathic boy; such persons were given names like "Countess Papillon".

28. Rutter's plan shows only two *round* towers at Fonthill—the Latimer Turret (which was very small) and the Great Staircase Tower, in the angle between the western and northern arms, which gave access to the Nunnery rooms. Unless the tower B. describes was later demolished, he is probably writing of the Great Staircase Tower, especially since in 1812 he was still trying to complete those rooms for guests.

29. Third Marquess of Hertford. His son left his pictures to Sir Richard Wallace, and they formed the basis of the Wallace Collection.

30. This supposed Leonardo was Lot 33 in the Duke of San Pietro's sale at Christie's on the day Beckford writes; it fetched 3,000 guineas. It was the portrait of a brunette in a white bodice and low embroidered turban, with an emerald-green curtain behind.

31. Nephew of James Wyatt; he changed his name to Wyatville in 1824, when he began the reconstruction of Windsor Castle.

32. A mediæval legend about St Patrick's descent to Purgatory.

33. Hon. Andrew James Cochrane-Johnstone, M.P. (born 1767), youngest son of the eighth Earl of Dundonald, and uncle of the famous Admiral. One of the worst adventurers of his day. In February 1814 he spread false news of Napoleon's death, enabling him to speculate successfully in the Funds; for this he was tried and found guilty, but fled the country, disappearing for ever.

34. Wyatt was employed on additions at Wilton House until his procrastinations forced Lord Pembroke to dismiss him and stop. At Kew he spent half a million on an unfinished Gothic Palace, demolished 1827–8 and probably constructed in cast-iron.

35. B. may be referring to the cutting away of the walls of St Stephen's Chapel, in order to enlarge accommodation for the Commons; but more probably to Wyatt's building in 1800 of a new House of Lords within the old Court of Requests (the White Hall), and to his conversion of adjoining buildings into offices for the Lords. It was all executed in a slipshod manner, and constructed of timber covered with plaster (as at Fonthill, where timber was covered with cement). This helped the rapid spread of the 1834 fire, which destroyed the lot and proved B. a remarkable prophet.

36. *i.e.* a *Holy Family* owned by "Father Tetonasso" (*teton* = teat), an unidentified picture-dealer or collector.

37. Marquess of Douglas, supposed to be under the influence of his sister, Lady Anne Hamilton (the Macaw).

38. Lot 18 (where it is called a Holbein) in the anonymous sale at Christie's, June 21st, which included pictures formerly owned by Walsh Porter and W.E. Agar; Hume, acting as Beckford's agent, bought it for 19 guineas. It appears as a Federigo Zuccaro in *Christie*, Day 7, Lot 73, and then in *Inventory*, I, p.16; since then it has disappeared.

39. Lucas van Leyden (1494–1533). Beckford mentions this picture twice more, describing it as "the beautiful Lady" (24 July 1818); it is therefore *Christie*, 7th Day, Lot 68, "Lady reading a Missal in the interior of an apartment, a vase on a table before her", and is in *Inventory*, 1, p.16.

40. James Christie the Younger, son of the firm's founder.

41. A wing of Splendens had not been destroyed. That summer it had been planned to reconstruct it as a winter residence for B., sheltered from the winds.

42. Of Witham.

43. I do not know what this word means, or its derivation, unless it is coined from *Parismus, Prince of Bohemia*, a popular Elizabethan romance of chivalry by Emanuel Ford, many times reprinted up to 1790.

44. The Great Comet of 1811, one of the most spectacular of all, with an unprecedented visibility of seventeen months; it shone through the night for many weeks. Napoleon thought it augured success for his Russian campaign.

45. For his daughter Margaret's (1785–September 1818) marriage to Colonel Orde, see p.80.

46. Franchi was staying in York, on his way to Hamilton Palace.

47. Patapouf is slang for a catamite.

48. Although this nickname must be connected with the fact that its bearer, the valet Richardson, was fair (*biondo*), it may also be a recollection of the poetry of the Greek Bion, author of *The Dirge of Adonis*.

49. Edward Harcourt, Archbishop 1807–47.

50. The Abbey-Church of S. Nicaise in Rheirns was sold for its stone in 1798 to a friend and confederate of the revolutionary leader Santerre, who made enormous profits from the sale of State properties.

51. This is untrue (the Cathedral still exists), but Beckford's manuscript Reading Notes in *H.P.* show that he got this statement from p.182 of G.D. Whittington's *Historical Survey of the Ecclesiastical Antiquities of France … to illustrate the Rise and Fall of Gothic Architecture in Europe*, 1809. Whittington did not repeat his mistake (actually he meant only the *choir* of the Cathedral) in the 1811 (2nd) edition.

52. Perhaps this refers to the Society for the Suppression of Vice (see p.56, note 40).

53. Probably a hit at his half-sister Mrs Hervey, the novelist.

54. Hamilton Palace and its inmates; cinquefoils appear in the ducal coat-of-arms.

55. Lord Archibald Hamilton, M.P., an ardent political reformer and an active member of the Opposition; brother of the tenth Duke of Hamilton. Nicknamed "Brother Crotchet".

56. The family's colour; Beckford repeated this prominently at Fonthill as part of his claim to be descended from the same family.

57. Douglas was fond of playing to guests on his collection of old violins; or this may refer to bagpipes.

58. A typical nickname at that period for a catamite; he was on Beckford's staff.

59. This refers to a wing of Splendens which had been demolished; evidently its stone was to be used to reconstruct the remaining wing as a winter residence. *Nanibus* is the dwarf.

60. Fourth Earl of Rosebery.

61. Perhaps Sir Hew Dalrymple-Hamilton, fourth Baronet.

62. From the beginning of 1811 until Michaelmas 1817 Beckford rented No. 6 Upper Harley Street (to which he addresses hundreds of his letters to Franchi), now No. 100 Harley Street. It now bears the plates of *eleven* doctors, headed by a Knight. It was here that he sold his pictures and furniture in May 1817. I do not know whether it is the rent or the house-keeping allowance that the solicitor is unable to pay.

63. Beckford was sealing with black wax as a sign of mourning for the disobedience of his elder daughter in marrying Orde. Franchi broached Beckford's complaint to the Marchioness and jotted down in pencil on the back of this letter her proud reply (in French): "She bore the mourning in her heart; it was not a subject about which she wished to write."

64. From French *magot*, a grotesque china figure, usually grinning and pot-bellied.

65. Refers to promises by Orde to use his influence with friends in the Prince Regent's circle to get Beckford a peerage; if he was successful, Beckford would recognise the marriage.

66. Purchasers of his property at Witham were delaying payment.

67. Frederick Burt Zincke, who had been managing Beckford's Jamaican estates since 1808.

1812–1813

LATE in the day, Beckford embarked upon his most ambitious project at Fonthill. But Wyatt had only a year more to live, and the new Eastern Transept,[1] the fourth arm of the Abbey, remained unfinished for ever. Its construction was in full swing in August, on the grand scale. With characteristic childishness Beckford hoped to keep it secret from his lawyer White (Rottier) and to build at such speed that by the time White discovered this treason against his necessary plans of economy, his remonstrances would be in vain and nothing could be curtailed. Wyatt's delay in arriving to supervise the work was therefore doubly irritating. Once more Beckford delivered an ultimatum, and once again he was victorious (which Wyatt's clients very seldom were), for Wyatt arrived on Monday, August 24th. Beckford's one fear was that there would soon be a "hint" of his departure, but fortunately he was in one of his manic moods. Meanwhile, the land-agent Still had privily informed White of what was afoot, and the lawyer was due down on the 1st September. The building operations mentioned in June are a separate series, apparently taking place at the Octagon end of the northern arm of the Abbey—there was always something going on at Fonthill in the way of reconstruction and re-decoration.

Beckford often vouchsafes a flash of insight about himself, and none is more telling than his remark on August 17th: "Some people drink to forget their unhappiness. I do not drink, I build." He lived under unbearable strain, and he hints that he might have found easier release from this tension had life in England favoured the indulgence of his perversion.[2]

1812

Sunday 26 <January>

... I hoped to find in some little corner of your last letter a Solomonian word or two, but—nothing; you were Marchioness-ing, I know, but logic and Barzaba are two points as opposite as the poles: poor grieving Barzaba does not reason when he thinks of the beatific vision. For pity's sake, make some effort to discover the only talisman which could draw me out of a state (more than half sick) of melancholy nothingness. I shall not p— freely until I see that ivory door, David's Tower etc, etc. Let us chant litanies, rogations and ardent supplications; let us see whether all are deaf to our prayers, and if they are let us die in the odour of old goat, if not of sanctity ...

Tuesday 28 January

... It costs me much, I swear to you, to stay here and listen to the roaring of the winds. All last night, I fancied I heard the ghosts in *Volugenso* (?)[3]—sobs and groans and dying lamentations. I shall certainly leave on Saturday.

I'm afraid it will be difficult to discover the sweet enchantress of York. I don't expect that you'll find him in the nest where you think. Doubts, fears, uncertainties, frenzies, etc agitate the heart of Barzaba. Meanwhile he sings more or less like the Babylonian Brute,[4] letting out roars and half-musical, half-wild cries, putting the winds to shame. Yesterday evening in the midst of a tremendous din the dwarf came in saying "*Qu'est que c'est donc, je croyais entendre le Diable?*"

... It's only by dint of perseverance that one can do anything with Cochrane Johnstone; it's a difficult alchemy to condense his vapours—the confounded, mawkish, pompous braggart! ...

Thursday 30 January

… Today saw the departure of the horses, the Monkey, Marion, the whores and the fruit of the womb of Madame Figley;[5] they arrive in London, God willing, on Saturday … The darkness here is so general that one should not increase it by purchasing a dismal damask! Farewell, my dear Gregory.

Tuesday 16 June

Everything here is lovely and green; but it is not for mountains or valleys, however green and lovely, that I am looking. It is other objects, objects which I certainly do not find here and which I want to find more than ever, that are interesting and dear to me. What are forests without fauns, or thickets from which there does not emerge some gay frolicsome clown of a satyr, making his sport? …

The rising Tower produces the most sublime effect—a truly palatial kind of castellation; the oriel is perfect—just as I had imagined it. The interior advances rapidly and is absolutely dry so that one will be able to fit it out and furnish it in twenty days at the latest. You must hurry up the chairs.

I sincerely hope that no new indisposition will prevent you from conferring with Mr. Fownes[6] on the urgency of the payment of £2,000 on the 1st of July next. Without that I shan't know what to do. I have very little coming in (I shall scarcely get £170 for timber) and without some help the debts will pile up, and I get desperate at letting everything go to utter ruin. That beast Rottier seems to favour the Plummers and pays no attention to me.

The poor animals Caroline and Spotty, recognising the carriage from a distance, shot towards me like arrows and, jumping on my lap, showed their genuine delight by innumerable barks and licks. They're lovelier and more attractive than ever, and I adore them—a hundred times more than the other limited, chilly, touchy members of my family. Goodbye, goodbye, I'm going out for a walk with them …

Ash Wednesday (at least from the colour of the sky), but the so-called 17 June

... The clouds are making water and the peacocks screeching in such a mournful manner that really, if it were not for the transports and frenzies of affection shown in every look and every lick of my adored family, I would go off my head ... The monotony of these eternal dense dark woods wearies me to the extinction of every spiritual faculty. Everything is strangled and suffocated by vegetation. Cutting is useless—the more one cuts, the more it grows. One would have to cut down two thousand firs to have room to breathe. The value of the forests is increasing to such an extent that it is calculated that in less than twenty-five years they would yield more than £200,000 if felled ...

I don't care a fig for the Matron[7] and her intrigues—the best intrigue for me would be to take in my arms some object worthy of a little tenderness; it's cruel to hear talk of fair boys and dark Jade vases and not to buy them ...

Coxone is getting on with the room which is replacing the foppish Douglas tent;[8] it will have excellent proportions. Unfortunately the oriel does not come down to the bottom: it was impossible owing to certain beams (not joists) which could not be touched. But the oriel itself is divine; there'll be a table beneath it—that's all. The carpet is not bad, of a very rich yellow and a kind of embroidery, as I had imagined it. I have not seen it yet in the Sanctuary ...

Thursday 18 June

Yesterday sun and rain strove with each other, and there were intervals of gold and blue. Today the worst possible weather has conquered and everything is of the colour of the interior of Noah's ark! ... I don't mind from what wood the fauns come, provided they come! To live without them is worse than death. The poor castrated pheasant which was so familiar has died, and Benjamin has died, eaten by a fox. I'd almost like to follow suit. Without the consolation of Figley and Nephew, I would close my eyes for ever. Too much cannot be said for these animals. They show a gentleness, an affectionate tenderness that goes to my heart, and they havenever been so lovely, plump, sleek and clean.

... It is necessary for you to think about the preparation of pills and some oil and pomade to feed my hair and keep my head fresh and moist. It is important to confer with Regnault about this. There is talk of rum oil and of this and that, but I don't want to risk infecting my head and perhaps bring on headaches. The last water for my eyes which Regnault gave me is useless. What the Doctor gave smells of camphor, and without camphor I don't think that any water is any good for me.

Repeat to Mr Beneficed Fownes, a hundred times if necessary, that there is no way of escaping the payment of £2,000 on the 1st July next, if they desire to sugar for me. If they decide not to, I'll write to the great Sucribus; he promised in his last conversation to find merchants in the space of six days after my communication who would be quite ready to undertake all that is asked on the 25th March next, and meanwhile to make quarterly advances in full for July, Michaelmas and Christmas ...

Saturday 20 June

... After reading White's letter you won't be surprised that I deny myself everything, that I have changed the whole arrangement of the new room. Instead of painting and gilding etc, I am leaving the roof with joists without mouldings; I am putting paper and not moreen, ordinary glass instead of plate-glass etc. It's a frightful state of affairs. Nor will you be surprised either that I don't think about Bottles⁹ in spite of their perfection and the great pleasure they would have given me, and that the chests (notwithstanding their great suitability in the room for which they were destined) make me leap and turn somersaults with pain, rage and fear! Law-suits, as you see, hang over me like rocks, three quarters hollowed out, over the heads of passers-by. What good are fine letters from Jamaica? They speak of the future—the attractive future which is always vanishing into thin air. The horrible present condemns me to every kind of privation—purse trouble and the trouble which is a hundred times worse than all others—boy trouble.

Wednesday (for me) of Ashes and Passion, 24 June

Anxiety and melancholy devour me to the marrow. Neither my health nor my brain can resist much longer: one or the other will have to crack. Either death or insanity—that's what I'm expecting …

Thursday 25 June

… I wish to goodness there would be a sale of the menagerie of the present Marquess Townshend[10] with Parliamentary license and patent to lick and barzabise what one bought as much as one liked. Without something of this sort neither Plummerisms,[11] nor salvers, nor jade, nor trifles, however lovely, could induce me to sacrifice here the brief existence which remains to me …

Tuesday 30 June

I'll be as fond of Arcadia as you like provided they don't write to me—dispensing with a pen is worth a hundred times the insipid half-hypocritical jargon about the Saint and Figley etc, etc which they suppose to be sauce for my pork …

The rooms are almost finished, all in wood as in the old Swiss monasteries (*Notre Dame des Hermites*[12] or the Capuchins at Fribourg), and very clean and exceedingly dry …

Wednesday 1 July

I would like to leave at once, yes at once, on pilgrimage to this Holy Land[13] of which you speak to me so clearly, to kiss the relics and do the *via sacra* with all the devotion of ancient times. Who knows whether among the blessed proselytes one may not find some sweet soul weeping and lamenting the horrible and barbarous exile of the great Apostle of the said divine law. Such piteous tears will not be shed in vain. Faith assures me that in a few years (if England herself survives) the unlucky Orpheus will return more splendid than ever to touch his tearful lyre and once more nake the brute beasts dance ...

What the devil is C. Johnstone up to? There's another person who will not come to a good end. But the Hero! The Hero is predestined to glory according to my scriptures; discreet, modest, silent—short in speech, long in thought—there is stuff in that man to become one day a cloak of ermine and gold.[14]

What did you think of the bibliomaniac prodigies of the Devonshire Dunce and the Blandford Braggart? Worthy friends and disciples of the judicious Florindo! What a crowd, what a repast, what beaks ...[15]

Thursday 2 July

... Not a syllable from Morlands[16] about yesterday's payment. I suppose it did not take place. For the love of God go to Lincoln's Inn and kicking down the door (with, of course, an artificial foot) shout "Who's there?" in my manner; and calling Mr Fownes a double-dealing traitor etc, proclaim a seismic cataclysm upon Messrs Plummer's, something worse than the new volcano on the island of St Vincent.[17] These Plummer people are not up to much, even according to Rottier; his letter of today does not say anything nice about them. Sugar is not rising; the amount sent, instead of surprising Rottier, only seems to him *tolerable*; and he complains of their fine system of loading almost everything on one boat, not of course in my interest but in theirs in more than one way. It is horrible to see how I am always sacrificed on account of shameless thieves. The Wildmans never acted worse than this. The shame of it! But I shall know what to do, and I will do it!

... Poor Fulibus![18] I think very highly of him. Memories of Portugal will always be the memories nearest to my heart. I embrace you affectionately, my dear Gregory, and offer on your behalf my solemn and sincere vows to the Saint.

Sunday 5 July

... The picture has come. I will not say that it is worthless, but twenty-five guineas would be an ample price for it. It is not by Mabuse[19] but by a certain German who resembles him—from a great distance. Sixty-five guineas! Well, well—not from me certainly. Infamous draperies, infamous colour, infamous ornaments; the faces are delicate enough and it is all very pure and tolerably well preserved, but the price is too high. It will be sent back tomorrow. When one thinks of my fine Luke of Holland for fifty guineas and this badly designed scrap at sixty-five—my God! How squeezed the Madonna is in her corner[20] and what hands!

Monday 6 July

The black chairs are *ad interim* in the Octagon, where they look just like seats in a chapter-house. Everything depends on the way objects are placed, and where. Horrors in one place discount beauties in another ...

Thursday 9 July

... Before your departure from London tell Bagasse not to renew again his treacheries and negligences. Oh my shame, oh my blushes! Am I to suffer this traitor again! Am I to wish once more for a definite date to be fixed—only for the renewal of his costly deceptions! Shame, shame (not *sham-sham*!)[21] ... Since I want to make a few trips to Bath and Winchester etc after Arcadia's departure, it would be a help to know exactly when he intends coming ...

Sunday 16 August

The medicine-coloured sky and depressing wind have ended with a tremendous purge of rain. We'll get nothing dry at the Abbey this year ...

From the infamous Swine *nothing*! And yet for his sake I have to expose myself to the terrible shouts, screams and lamentations of the desperate Rottier! As I do not doubt that the said Rottier will scent something suspicious in my discouragement of his journey to Fonthill, it will be as well to make him scent the kitchen, telling him that the poor people, no longer able to bear the deathly vapours of that subterranean oven, have begged me on their knees for better quarters. This will explain (*tant bien que mal*) a certain *brouhaha*, a little concourse of people, that cannot fail to jump to his eyes—and his ears too. Yes, I must tell him, that moved with compassion, I have given my consent to a tiny piece of work, a trivial operation which is going to begin tomorrow and will be finished in two or three months— building gently, and oh! so slowly, and with all the economy of a Father Guardian of the poorest of monasteries.[22]

According to Rottier's letter, he proposes to arrive on the 1st of September, so that if the Infamous One does not turn out to be the worst Swine in the world, and quite beyond the Pale, we have all the time we need. I hope to receive on Tuesday some ray of light; enough to illumine the darkness of the most shameful cesspool known to the annals of architecture ...

Monday 17 August

Today, at five in the morning, a great confusion and Coxone's voice shouting "You, Sir, take care how you drive on the green!" *Nine* carts discharging stone with a noise like thunder—which gives some hope of the completion of the business. Tomorrow two further carts are promised and at least forty cartloads a day. I am suffocated with rage against the miserable and cursèd Swine.

The weather, after the purge of the day before yesterday, has cleared up. The sun shines in great splendour—for others, but not for me. For me it illumines days of the utmost sadness. Some people drink to forget their unhappiness. I do not drink, I build. And it ruins me. It would be cheaper to find another distraction, and if the wretched Rottier would only pimp for me a little, I would save a good deal. Would I were in London—there at least one can see Butterflies. I will not answer for the folly in which my present condition may land me, but I have spoken and written so much on this theme that I am sick and tired of it ...

It is midday and already the whole courtyard is beginning to be covered. Twenty cartloads (and large loads at that) have already accumulated: eight are at the stables unloading and six loading, and as many more opening the ground for the foundations. Rottier will find himself in the Tower of Babel and may curse like a priest of the false gods in the Old Testament. Let anyone curse who will—to the honour of God and in the name of the Glorious Saint

Edificabo ecciesiam meam.

A fine slaughter at Salamanca! What will be done with so many prisoners?

Tuesday 18 <August>

The heat and these eternal ridiculous tormentings by Bagasse will make me go mad and throw up all the works. I swear that if he does not leave with you I will have everything stopped and go on a journey God knows where. This utter indifference to all that concerns me and his own honour, these repeated and renewed proofs are too much for me. If tomorrow I do not receive clear and positive news, I'll make an end, I'll stop everything. Perhaps I shall make some temporary kitchen, but I promise in all sincerity that Mr Wyatt shall never eat anything that it produces. I am not made to be treated in any way but my own, and those who think the contrary make a mistake, and must suffer for it. I beg you, then, I command you to explain to him the necessity of making a decision. If he goes to Bilgewater[23] first, I'll not receive him here. The time he stops doesn't matter to me; it'll be sufficient if he stays three or four days and not more—that's time enough for all I want. Let him escape to Bilgewater when he likes after making his appearance *here*. But *here* he must come in your company or renounce the building and me for ever ...

Wednesday 19 August

Were I not bound by an unbreakable oath, you may be quite sure that Mr White would not complain in vain of this new ruination. I bitterly repent the vow, but it is made and no human power can recall it.[24] I don't doubt that the Great Dolt gave Mr White the information, which has probably made him almost beside himself. I understand the deplorable Bagassonades and approve your prudence in not making offers in my name. I desire only three or four days now, and his return at the end of November, by which time, if the least faith can be placed in Coxone, the building will be ninety feet high. Today there is a fresh throng (?) of people and carts; everything grows like Carthage under the auspices of Dido.

... I have no wish to buy manuscripts without seeing them; such a procedure may suit the Shepherd, but certainly not me; if Mr Chardin[25] doesn't take the trouble to cross the sea we shall not be doing much business together. A thousand guineas for variorum and Elzevirs, indeed! I'd rather give that for some "volumes" (you know quite well the sort I mean) which I so much need that there is almost no price I would not pay to get them. ... How are we to be free from the Great Cesspool before the first of September, the day on which the afflicted Richard Samuel Rottier will arrive like the prophet before King Saul, proclaiming misery and total ruin! Poor Rottier! I feel to the very marrow the anguish which this new piece of abbatial folly is too well calculated to inspire. Who the devil has kept him so well informed? It must be the Basha.[26]

I hope to hear from you what you are doing, miserable forgettor— whether or not the pill has been forgotten, whether sugar is rising or falling, and whether you have been unable to find eatable cassava. Farewell, my dear Gregory. A hot rain is falling; it is almost stifling; yesterday, thunder and lightning and killing heat. I don't much care when I die—my life isn't exactly Paradise ...

Thursday 20 August

Seeing all these people, hearing all this noise of carts etc without seeing the Swine gives me a fever and almost convulses me with rage ... Coxone possesses the most sublime means of fulfilling the great and sacred vow. It seems that the Glorious One is taking part. The best stone-workers are coming from near and far, all zealous, all capable, and all willing to submit themselves to the rule of Coxone. For the love of this stupendous work, don't let the unworthy Bagasse go, inspire him. If this is at all possible, it will only be with the aid of the Saint; with him what miracle may we not expect? ...

Friday 21 August

The person who has to make the supreme decision on the height of ninety feet etc is my dear (if he comes) Bagasse. As I have already said, the means are in his power—stone and stone-masons. I have not had a letter from the said Swine but one from Foxhall announcing the Hegira, *i.e.* his departure from London next Sunday. The Lord confirm it! ... So I hope Monday will be the day of Bagasse's arrival and of your return ...

Wednesday <26 August>[27]

Up to now there is no sign of the disappearance of Bagasse. He works with a brio, a zeal, an energy, a faith that would move the largest mountain in the Alps. 'Sweetness'[28] performs wonders and Coxone miracles; it seems that he and all his people are under the direct inspiration of the glorious Saint.

For pity's sake don't forget the proposed cottage; this *low* (but at the same time high) relief[29]—so lucky (?), so whimsical, has given me such favourable ideas about the site of Hounslow that I couldn't ask for any other Paradise. Whoever pimps with this end in view won't pimp in vain to give life and health to poor afflicted, wrinkled Barzaba! Farewell until Friday.

Sunday 30 August (sad, gloomy and cold)

I didn't expect to take up this exercise again so soon: what a sad departure yesterday and what a mournful wind—it seemed to carry you away like a dry leaf.

The hellish sufferings of the miserable Rottier are ever before my pitying eyes, murdering all peace ... My angelic Bagasse has not yet breathed the slightest word or *hint* of departure. He is all ardour and zeal as never before. We are lengthening the building just the least little bit—it will have seventeen Nunnery arches instead of fifteen. O Rottier, Rottier! What will that poor wretch say, when to the tune of twenty carts, to the hum of sixty workmen, to the dull creaking of twenty-four wheelbarrows, he alights at the door of the Abbey? What, oh what will he say? I have as many daggers in my heart as the image of Our Lady of Sorrows! Where is the balm for these wounds? Where is the drug for such torments? Where is the cure for so serious (well-nigh mortal) a sickness? I know—I know—I'm going to say it—it's at—Hounslow.

Monday <31 August>

A fine thirty-first of August! At seven this morning it was still night, a cold raw dampness pervades everything and plays the devil with one's system. I think no place will do me so much good as the hot sands of Hounslow (so healthy! so pure!).[30] There, in a rude cottage surrounded by a few pines and a wall, I'd finish my days in the lap of Platonism and devotion, educating the little rogue (?)!

My dear, angelic, most p-p-p-p-perfect Bagasse is killing himself with work: every hour, every moment, he adds some new beauty. The towers are eighteen feet in diameter and will provide rooms of fifteen feet in every sense—except common sense, as the afflicted and terrified Rottier will infallibly say. Poor fellow, how sorry for him I am! Every moment the confusion and babel increases—shouting, pissing, cursing ... But tomorrow, tomorrow (if the unhappy man arrives) what terror! What heart attacks! And with every reason: a great structure like this is enough to give the idea of national ruin. Oh my God, how easily I could be satisfied with less outlay—the cottage at Hounslow, ... a little pimping by Rottier, and all will be saved! How difficult is salvation! Nothing now is open or offers easy progress but the broad way which leads to the abode of the Devil.

Tuesday 1 September

I do not believe that my Angelica[31] has any more idea of going than I of abandoning the hope of rousing the Beloved Sleeper[32] of Hounslow. So, according to your letter, Rottier is on his way. I don't doubt that he is coming in the hope of putting an end to these ruinous operations. Would God that they could be stopped. Nobody is more unhappy or more cordially repents of the vow than I. But there is no way out. I have made another vow—I really have—which will remedy everything: if the building is not finished by next Christmas, I will bid my last farewell to the Abbey and to Fonthill. Then I will become grossly, enormously, formidably rich and will escape to some agreeable site, with the retinue that I desire in preference to all goods or titles and to all glory present or future ... Adieu, my Bagasse is calling me.

<Tuesday> 1 December[33]

... Yesterday I heard the Royal bird singing. He warbles wonderfully and with infinite grace. There was an enormous crowd in the Chamber, which pushed and jostled and elbowed in the most gross, brutal and indecent fashion, just as if Sir Isaac Heard with a basket of patents for baronies and baronetcies was at the end of the course to reward the most agile. In the Park and squares a mournful silence; no acclamations, but some muffled catcalls at sight of the bizarre, half-Cossack costume of the mounted Guards[34] ...

1813

Friday 23 April, freezing[35]

… Caroline has just augmented my family by ten little ones as delicate and pretty as those Saxon porcelain poodles, white with black ears, that one used to see on the mantelpieces of our Dowagers. Tell my dear Anguise[36] this happy news, accompanying it with a series of endless embraces. My dear Douglas, I am also your endlessly affectionate W.B.

Tuesday <*27 April(?)*>

Almost the entire human race gets bored in one way or another. But not I: even my own complaining does not bore or destroy me (by special grace of the Saint), and I shall go on complaining, shouting and Rottificating until the money is paid.

My Bagasse shows a moderation at table worthy of a Carthusian monk, and a shameful flush that is the colour of port-wine with a bush.[37] Certainly, if I could be bored, it would be in his company. Ah my God, how slow, silent and null he is! Ah, my dear Marchioness, you at least aren't like that! I can picture the charming family dinner in Grosvenor Place. I'll leave tomorrow … There is a certain something inside me which tells me that I am destined for a tedious succession of sufferings and calamities, poor wretched old beast that I am! Farewell.

Saturday 18 September

Rottier is here, more jubilant than I've ever seen him—all sugar, all rum. He speaks only of thousands and tens of thousands,[38] leaping on poor Bagasse's tomb; if he was Nephew he would lift his leg and piss on it. He is not yet rid of his Orde-mania, nor is he willing to admit that all this is chimerical and that the Colonel (*alias* Captain Storm or Wind-splitter) is the greatest swaggerer in the island with the sole exception of Cochrane Johnstone. He has shown me various boastful letters which only go to confirm him in his ridiculous hopes.[39]

I see from the buying mania which dominates you that we are well on the way to ruin. Oh my God, so many things! I trust to the Saint that they are not junk and unworthy of this sanctuary and refuge of Good Taste. I don't doubt the fineness of the little Greek pictures,[40] but (between ourselves) this kind of thing doesn't amount to much. "Chinese ivory vases" I can't understand, but trusting in what you say I hope they won't look dreadful beside the Magnus Berg.[41] It is hard not to be able to see these things, and many others that are going to fall into the great yawning gullet of Wellesley Poole![42] It costs nothing to see things, and seeing them, few are the objects that one regrets. Everything unknown seems a treasure, as the Latins say in one of their truest proverbs; distance softens the sharpest rocks and lends enchantment to what, nearer, loses all value.

… I'm so tired of seeing the building languish and so bored by everything around me, and particularly by the icy manner of Mabuse's Madonna,[43] that I'd like to run away, Heaven knows where, with some great Jock—one of those that abound in that earthly paradise of yours (certainly not in mine!)

<Thursday> 23 September[44]

I have perused with sensibility, I might even say with tears, the lines you composed in honour of poor Wyatt in the consoling letter which I have just received from you. My dear friend, it will ever be a great loss for this building, should I take it into my head to finish it. But alas, my poor Bagasse had already sunk from the plane of genius to the mire; for some years now he has only dabbled about in the mud, and I carried on my back the same burden that I carry now. Poor, wretched Bagasse, he shewed no interest in what was passing here; he gave me the slip in the most unworthy way in order to hasten to Mr Codrington's, and from there you know whence he hastened! Frightful and foolish catastrophe which one cannot too greatly deplore.

… We complain, as you well know, with our 50,000 maladies, but despite all we are passably well and will go far unless they overturn us too …

1.   See Introduction, p.19

2.   See August 17th and the end of the letters of August 30th and 31st.

3.   I take this to be a mis-spelling of *Vologeso*, an opera by Sacchini, to which Beckford similarly refers later.

4.   Nebuchadnezzar. Elsewhere Beckford gives this nickname to poor mad George III, so this may refer to him.

5.   The Monkey was a youth on his staff, and so perhaps was Marion; the whores were the chamber-maids; Mme Figley was Caroline, one of Beckford's dogs.

6.   James Somerville Fownes, partner of the solicitor White. The payment is the quarterly allowance from Plummer's, Beckford's West India merchants.

7.   Mrs Orde.

8.   Storer's *Fonthill*, p.22, describes "a bedchamber lined with hangings of blue, strewed with white mullets, the original arms of the House of Douglas, and drawn together in the form of a tent". He places it in a tower at the north-east corner of the Octagon; perhaps it is this. The *Gentleman's Magazine*, 1822, Part I, pp.326–7 mentions this room; but these articles reproduce whole slabs of Storer's 1812 book, so that its mention in them does not prove that it still existed in 1822.

9.   Chinese porcelain vases.

10.   George Ferrars Townshend (1778–1855), third Marquess; better known by his courtesy titles of Lord Chartley and Earl of Leicester. A notorious character, disinherited by his father; his wife left him within a year of their marriage, filing a bill against him for non-consummation, May 1808. Beckford's letter of July 1st indicates that he had just left the country (probably to avoid prosecution). As a result, his house and furniture at Richmond were about to be sold. He died in obscurity near Genoa.

11.   Quarterly payments by Plummer.

12.   The famous monastry of Einsiedeln in Switzerland.

13.   A region in St Giles' Parish, London (the Seven Dials neighbourhood), the haunt of vice, crime and poverty. The "Apostle" is Lord Townshend.

14.   Admiral Sir Thomas Cochrane, tenth Earl of Dundonald, one of the great men of the nineteenth century, liberator of Chile, Peru and Brazil; nephew of the swindler Cochrane Johnstone.

15.   Beckford refers to the sale of the library of the third Duke of Roxburghe, the first time that a four-figure sum was given for a single printed book at auction. The hitherto unparalled prices were due to the fierce competition between Lord Spencer, the sixth Duke of Devonshire and

the Marquess of Blandford; the latter was forced to sell his purchases here at enormous loss in June 1819, and Becklord was one of the buyers at the lower prices. Florindo is the Marquess of Douglas; *Florindo and Daphne* was the title of one of Handel's earliest operas, but whether B. took it from this I do not know.

16. Morland, Ransom & Co., of Pall Mall, Beckford's bankers.

17. Mt Soufrière erupted on May 1st with the loss of over fifteen hundred lives, and rendered three thousand homeless.

18. Pedro de Sousa Holstein (1781–1850), created Count, Marquis and then Duke of Palmela, the most distinguished Portuguese of his day, several times Ambassador in London, Foreign Secretary, and President of the Council of Ministers; represented Portugal at the Congress of Vienna, 1815.

19. Jan Gossart, called Mabuse (c.1472–1536), a Fleming influenced by his travels in Italy. It was Beckford's frequent habit to decry what he really wanted to buy, and he invariably complained of its price. But at the last moment he often could not bear to part with what he had been sent on approval, or he even changed his mind after he had returned it. So it is possible that this is the picture entitled *The Wise Men's Offering* in *Inventory,* I, 10, and *H.P.S.* 76 (sold for £525).

20. Beckford uses the French *niche,* which might also mean *recess* or *alcove.*

21. Presumably Becklord refers to Franchi's mis-spelling.

22. In this and the following letters Beckford refers to the commencement of the Eastern Transept of the Abbey (see p.19).

23. John Egerton, eighth Earl of Bridgewater, for whom Wyatt was building Ashridge.

24. A vow made to St Anthony to complete or stop the new work by a certain date—similar to the vow made in 1808.

25. Auguste Chardin, of 19 Rue St Anne, a leading French book seller and collector, dealing for Beckford since 1791. His own large library specialised in illuminated MSS, books printed on vellum. variorum and Elzevirs; he sold it off in portions at different dates, including 1812 (it was this portion which was being offered to Beckford). He died at a great age in December 1826, and was nicknamed the Dotard.

26. Mr Still (the Great Dolt).

27. Mis-dated by Franchi *19 Agosto.*

28. Nickname for Philip Wyatt (c. 1780–4836), youngest son of James Wyatt, and a scapegrace always in debt. He worked in his father's office until the latter's death, and then often assisted his brother Benjamin Dean Wyatt, e.g. in

altering Apsley House for Wellington and in building Londonderry House, Park Lane. His nickname probably refers to his charm or plausibility.

29.   Literally, *bas-relief.* To hide his meaning, Beckford talks in architectural terms, but he is really referring to *low* relief with a youth at Hounslow, which at this date was still an unenclosed heath inhabited by gipsies "and other loose persons", and with a barracks.

30.   An ironical reference to the fact that large quantities of manure and vegetable waste were dumped here in order to improve the soil of the heath for cultivation.

31.   Wyatt. Angelica is the capricious heroine of Ariosto's *Orlando Furioso.* Becklord later gives this nickname to Susan.

32.   A reference to the legend of Endymion, a beautiful youth whom the Moon Goddess visited nightly whilst he was asleep in a cave. Beckford's remark also has a less creditable meaning.

33.   To Douglas in French from London, describing the opening of Parliament by the Prince Regent for the first time for eight years.

34.   Beckford here mentions a revolutionary change in our Army uniform. The Life Guards and other cavalry units had been put into a new uniform that autumn, prior to their departure for active service in the Peninsular. Instead of the old half-moon cocked hat, they wore a crested brass helmet with plume in front and black horse-hair tail behind; their old long coats were replaced by coatees with less gold lace. This was rather similar to the uniforms of the Russian Imperial Guard, though not in any way Cossack.

35.   To Douglas in French.

36.   Pet name for his grandson, the future eleventh Duke of Hamilton, now just over two. Beckford's dogs were small spaniels—perhaps King Charles II or other toy spaniels.

37.   *i.e.* inferior port-wine—a reference to the old saying "good wine needs no bush" (a bunch of ivy formerly being the vintner's sign). The whole paragraph makes it clear that Wyatt was a confirmed drunkard.

38.   The price of sugar was rising fast, in anticipation of the defeat of France and the opening of the European market.

39.   Of a peerage for Beckford through influence at Court.

40.   Franchi's accounts for 1813 mention the purchase of "3 Greek paintings". They may be *Christie,* Day 2, Lot 62, three illuminated miniature paintings of Saints of the Greek Church in a black and gold frame in three compartments. Beckford thought sufficiently highly of them to exclude them from the sale to Farquhar in 1822.

41. A magnificent carved ivory cup by the Norwegian sculptor Magnus Berg (1666–1739), described in *Phillips*, Day 15, Lot 573.

42. William Pole Tylney-Long Wellesley, fourth Earl of Mornington and nephew of the Duke of Wellington. He had recently married a millionairess, and was running through all the money he could.

43. The blonde valet Richardson (Mme Bion), who, probably because of his chaste "Richardsonian iciness", reminded B. of a Madonna painted by the Fleming Mabuse—perhaps in the picture mentioned on p.113

44. To Douglas in French, about Wyatt's death in a carriage accident near Marlborough, when travelling with his client Christopher Codrington from Dodington Park, Gloucestershire.

1814

UNTIL the Napoleonic wars, Englishmen had taken Continental travel for granted. But cooped up in their damp and foggy Island for eleven years, the re-opening of the Continent after Napoleon's abdication in April 1814 must have been one of the great moments of their lives. The pleasure was increased a hundredfold because Paris, the art-market of Europe, was brimful of books, pictures and works of art to an extent that has never been equalled before or since. For about twenty years the French armies, with their attendant commissioners, had been ransacking the treasures of palaces, churches and monasteries all over Europe for the collections of Napoleon and his generals. In France itself the Revolutionaries had broken up the Royal collections of works of art. Now these treasures were being disgorged, and it was Englishmen who had the money to buy them.

Beckford was in a better position to profit from this than he had been for some years. From the low point of 1807 sugar had more than doubled in price, to stand in 1814 at its highest for half a century or perhaps ever; its price had increased by two-thirds since 1812. In June he therefore despatched Franchi to Paris to buy and set side things on approval for him, before everything was swallowed up by the swarms of Englishmen who descended on Paris. He himself arrived in October, and the French capital did not fail to stimulate him in every way—witness his vivacity and enthusiasm in the Royal Library (now the Bibliothèque Nationale) on October 31.

But in such a situation it was impossible to be rich enough, and Beckford was no longer really wealthy by contemporary English standards. This, combined with his typical collector's acquisitiveness and his recollection of the days of his youth when he could bid at auction against an Emperor, produced a terrible conflict within him, admirably summed up on December 7, after he had bought a Gerard Dou: "sighing and groaning to buy one moment and at having bought the next—it's the most delirious and feverish existence imaginable."

No wonder that the situation in the ballet-pantomime *l'Enfant Prodigue* (November 7) affected him so strongly—"the young and ingenuous son of a too indulgent father" who had ruined his life, wasted his opportunities and dissipated his fortune, and who was an exile in the desert, a prey to melancholy and remorse.

<Sunday> 2 January[1]

I vow, my very dear Douglas, that all these compliments of the season after the English fashion do not suffice for my happiness. I would much prefer a little turn round Rheims where, whilst contemplating the finest Gothic portal in the universe, one is filled with hopes of dining on *pâtés de foie gras*, truffled saveloys, turkeys *au suprême* and pigs' trotters *à la St Menou*. All that is better than our mince pies and legs of pork with pease-pudding.

But do not think that we are advancing so swiftly towards the consummation of our miseries and the beginning of a better era. Not at all. I no more expect peace than the success of Lord Castlereagh's arch-fine negotiations. The divisions are already sown in the Allies' incomparable platband; a trifle will make them spring up, and we will begin all over again worse than ever.

It is said that nothing equals the warlike ardour of our sublime Regent, neither his devotion to the Bourbons, nor his certitude of reconquering America, nor his veneration for M. Bernadotte and consequent respect for the budding talents of Prince Oscar.[2] 'Tis a pity that they do not make the latter espouse Mlle of Wales who (they say) does not at all like the poisonous future destined for her[3] ...

Tuesday 25 January

... Nature and the human society round me are like the grave: there is pale Ambrose, infamous *Poupée,* horrid Ghoul, insipid Mme Bion, cadaverous Nicobuse, the portentous dwarf, frigid "Silence",[4] and Salisbury Plain ...

Really I don't know how you'll be able to travel. At present there is heavy snow. To give a terrific idea of his journey to Hindon, the dwarf said to me *"la neige est aussi haut que moi"*.

Coxone has returned to life! Here he is with the plans; on seeing them, I'm convinced that Dixon's presence will be very useful here. I'll pay his journey and I'll make him a present of £50 very willingly *provided* I can have Dixon incognito without anything being said to His Bitterness Benjamin[5] or His Sweetness Philip. I have an idea—an 'improvement' that will at once increase the building's beauty and decrease expenses. Ten days will be enough for all that is required of Dixon—exactly the time that I shall probably remain here ...

Thursday 27 January

... They have opened the pictures—the Brueghel[6] all yellow and blue like certain arras, and of a brilliance that does not invite the venerable Bellini[7] to be its companion; the two cannot go together. The Brueghel has not suffered from the hand of Pizzetta; it is transparent and pure, but the figures seem to me a little scraped and the velvet (the glazing) of Rottenhammer has been gone many years. Nothing more rich and palatial than the frame of the Bellini; it is a masterpiece of ebony and carving—colour, gilding, all is as it should be. I have already returned them to the darkness—not yet knowing where to put them and not wishing to profane objects of such beauty. Both in their kind are distinguished and rare, but they have been paid the last farthing they will ever fetch. That rogue Forster would not have found elsewhere such a respectable price for this fine tangle of fish and flowers, monkeys, and maritime and pastoral produce ...

In this cruel weather what will become of that old demoniac Jennings?[9] Doubtless before departing he will sell all the best he has—but not to me. On the contrary, he will try to prevent anything ever falling into my hands—like the cursèd Pest of Strawberry Hill,[10] and like the greater part of your adored islanders. They die with envy every time the image of this New Jerusalem of an abbey enters their minds. Let them die and let us meanwhile profit therefrom when God wills. I embrace you in sincerity of heart.

<Friday> 28 January[11]

... How right you are, my dear Friend, to appreciate a good cook. I prefer an article of this sort to all the architects in the universe. Give me good dishes, and I will abandon spires, battlements and pinnacles to anyone who wants to pile them up on top of each other. My trees occupy me much more than my buildings. I have planted vastly this autumn (several hundred acres), and I shall recommence the moment it pleases Heaven to have pity on the earth and rid us of the snow and ice. I swear to you, however, that we are not freezing at the Abbey—on the contrary, the temperature of my apartments is worthy of Russian palaces; 'tis your fault if you have not already tried them. What a curse it is to be so far from you, with so many things to say.

Doubtless you have seen in Viscount Cathcart's last despatch that their Divinities the Emperors of Russia and Austria have crossed the Rhine ("after Divine worship") and have thrust themselves up to the neck into France. Capital, provided they don't break their necks in with drawing! At least they won't shiver, with so much exercise and a nice little conflagration here and there.

Your Chevalier Drummond is very amiable. I thank him heartily, and although I already possess all that has been written on both sides about his learned and singular work, I shall look forward with pleasure to receiving (especially at your hands) the copy which he has the goodness to reserve for me ...[12]

Sunday <30 January>

Curse it—no letters from me, and I've written every day without fail— fine testimony to the public zeal for facilitating correspondence. Shame, shame! Boletus' books arrived today, and the wine[13] from God knows what Jew; I hope it'll be superior—the price certainly is. But patience, patience—why so much hurry? It may be good, but the quantity isn't small and it must cost a lot; don't you think twelve shillings a dozen is much too much? But what (more than anything else) I find too much is the precipitation, or rather over-eagerness with which they want a reply ... I have no hope whatever of a genuine and unspoiled Hellish Brueghel[14]—I can believe a thousand times more in Purgatory than in this ... Here's the dwarf for the letters, irritating me more than the church bell ...

Monday 31 January

… Yesterday there was sunshine, and Milne's paradise was all gilded and full of sweet smells of pine-apple, violet and cyclamen; the vine and the fruit trees are beginning to bud; every day this place becomes more immense and beautiful …

Monday 7 February. Dies Irae

A horrible and baleful night! Black, stormy and cold, with intervals of sickly, fevered moonlight—a kind of evil omen spread through all the air. I thought I heard dreadful cries and wailing—who knows whether at that moment there passed the damned soul of base Wildman, accompanied by a thousand devils leading him in pomp to the dolorous city, to the realm of eternal woe.

What I know for certain is that the lack of all which was promised me has not given me a smiling prospect. To return to London and find so much to pay, and nothing coming in, is hard … With me there is no end to paying. The wine will be expensive, and this morning I gave Willis[15] £46 for the waggon bill for three months to December inclusive, and there is still £20 to pay for January. I owe the London tailor nearly £200 for suits, liveries etc; £188 is owed for harness …

Saturday 12 February

A "gem" by Teniers[16] (a pastiche or imitation of Michael Angelo) won't be a gem in my opinion, I think. Few, very few, are the Paolo Veronese[17] which are worth 900 guineas or even half that. I don't like these painters, and even if I did I'm not in a position to give large sums …

To give, give, give—extravagant prices in terror of Mr Wellesley-Pole, is to take the true path of shocking and ruinous folly. I'm only Barzaba as far as *living* pictures are concerned—neither wood nor canvas can seduce me. Sixty guineas was the ridiculous sum asked for the Rottenhammer; you ought to know that for this fine gent one doesn't pay that—he's third-rate.

Thursday 10 March

My dear Child, since you want it so tenderly and yet so despotically, the incarnation of the most serene Gumputty[19] must descend at your door. No ear, however great and insensitive, could remain deaf to such dear, to such amiable prayers. Despite my inveterate laziness I will take the road on the month and the day which you indicate to the High Priest Franchi, who is charged with all details concerning this walking Temple.

The dwarf cannot contain himself for joy in anticipation of the journey and above all of the reception which he flatters himself *le cher petit* will give him. "So you think", I said, "that the little one loves you like sugar?" "Yes", replied he, "like the best bon-bon in the universe"...

Hayter came here to consult Dixon ... about certain battlements for M. Bouffetaut's paradise. Naturally nothing to me was more urgent than to ask him for news of my 'family'.[20] "Thank God, Sir, they are well, but made a terrible noise when they found you was gone; and as for My Lady-I-forget-what's-her-name, it was cruel to hear how she cried." Having heard me so often and so gravely speak of my adored Caroline and her mishaps and of her father Viscount Fartleberry etc, in the simplicity of his heart the poor Pig thought it was necessary to speak of her with respect! But since not everyone knows how to behave, Scammel the groom, who came with the horses, said to me "the poor bitch, Sir, was troubled a good deal." What would you—some call her 'My Lady' and others 'Bitch'—alas, these two qualities are sometimes united together.

I cannot imagine by what special grace you so vigorously resist the inclemency of this horrible winter. The snow is falling in great flakes, and the sharp and piercing humidity of a kind of frozen rain accompanying the said snow sends to the Devil all who have not already sold themselves to him. They say that dear Bonaparte's pact with him is about to expire and that soon, like Dr Faust, nothing of his grandeur will remain save the most infernal and sublime smell of sulphur—for you know that Burke said that there was something sublime about really great stinks. However, may we end up and live in peace in a better atmosphere!

The Margravine[21] always maintains that it is to *canals* that we owe our terrible fogs and the frosts that afflict us. I found her the other day on her knees before a villainous heap of greenwood, blowing like one possessed; there were no flames—except in her eyes which, without exaggeration, looked like street-lamps. "Mr Beckford" said she, "I told you the atmosphere, owing intirely to the canals with which they are stripe-ing this wretched Country, is so thick that no smoke can ascend." And then—puff, puff, puff. You can have no idea of the scene! She is as bent as Sir Isaac Heard and as wrinkled as Carabosse,[22] and her black soutane, just like the Wood Daemon's[3] domino, gave her a sorceress' air enough to make one tremble, However, I escaped without being changed into an animal or bird.

The next day she returned my call, laying an immense visiting-card as big as Milord Mayor's invitation cards. I am carefully preserving it; Franchi proposes to fill and illuminate it with God knows what arabesques. What a pity that you do not want to frequent her—her absurdity would delight us both. I know no one on our planet (I do not speak of the moon) who can be compared to her. Since our last meeting she has fortified herself in extravagances, Thondertentronckism[24] and all the German virtues to an unbelievable extent. She is Schiller and Kotzebue[25] personified—all sentiment, paradox, chiaroscuro and rhapsody impossible to describe. Add to this the disposition of a hater of the first order—"a thorough good hater": she abominates Mme de Stael, she execrates the Prince Regent, she detests the knock-kneed, lily-livered Liverpool and all his colleagues. Ah, if only she condemned the King of Prussia too! ...

Monday 11 April (hotter than August)

A forest of flags on the great Tower, almost 800 feet from the ground, announces that Napo*coglione*[26] is on his Island ... Up to now I don't altogether like what's happening in Paris—still too many Serene Highnesses, Princes and Dukes *in partibus*; if he doesn't take care, Greenhorn[27] will become, without knowing it maybe, President of a Jacobin's club; ... And poor England the Paymistress—nobody speaks of her—it's all Russia, and Prussia just a tiny bit too. It's a moment truly unique in the earth's annals. Talleyrand is more in evidence than ever, and Sieyès with his nose outside his mole hill, sniffing what's going on and saying what ought to be done.

... Ah, what must the Marquis be feeling,[28] muttering between his teeth at the noise of the cannon and at the raising of the laurels of Victory to crown the white flag of the House of Bourbon, already reborn to Light and to Glory. In the midst of so much rejoicing, to tell the truth I myself am solitary and sad. Yesterday's sun did me no good; tomorrow I'm taking medicine—we'll see if this will help me. Farewell, my dear Gregory, my Easter[29] hasn't yet come—God knows when my Resurrection will take place—at the moment I'm buried alive.

Wednesday 13 April

... A fine exit indeed for Mr Bonaparte—£240,000 a year isn't bad. That's how one placates the unhappy shade of the Duke of Enghien.

Franchi to Douglas. Saturday 18 June

... You ask me for details about the Abbey. I would like to give you satisfactory ones, but that is impossible if I tell you the truth. Almost all that the villainous Bagasse built has been dismantled (to forestall finding ourselves buried in its rotten ruins); all the walls in the Fountain Court have been very solidly rebuilt in stone; the chimney-flues have been changed, together with a thousand other errors which sooner or later would have damaged the edifice—this is the work upon which we have been engaged for the last two years. The kitchen has been finished, and with its adjoining offices it is the finest bit in the Abbey ...

You have no need, my Lord, to contrive anything—anything at all—to please your dear father-in-law. He likes you as you are, because you are just what he likes in those who interest him. So present yourself unchanged at the Abbey and you will see how you will be embraced and fêted; you will have good dinners, excellent *pâtés* and delicious truffles; in short, we will do all we can to keep you as long as possible and to shew you the sincerity of our love.

We are very afflicted to learn that my dear Sovereign suffers so much. Nothing grieves her Father more than her suffering state; notwithstanding that the doctors assure you that her afflicting state will shortly take a happy turn, he does not cease to be very grieved and very unquiet with regard to her, for he loves her and is as sincerely attached to her as you, my Lord ...

Tuesday 28 June [31]

The Shepherd is consigning himself to the Devil at not being able to betake himself immediately to Paris. *You* are the object of his trembling envy! He thinks you are going to buy everything and bring it all to St Anthony's feet ...

The other day Colnaghi[32] praised to the skies two cases of books arrived for Signor Spencer[33]—apparently that rogue Edwards[34] has been in Paris reaping his harvest ...

Thursday 30 June[35]

... I have returned from Fogg's;[36] so far, little temptation, but two large bottles, rather beautiful seagreen with faint white, like those of the deceased *bambostiere,*[37] perfect, pretty straight and with beautiful stoppers; price 140—cursèd pest of a Jew. The Saxon ware very so-so; other pieces of seagreen and seacoal, cleverly made (?) if you like and fine, but Pompadourised enough to make one vomit.

The Velasquez is a Pope,[38] white and red, stupendous but without that harmony which bids me buy imprudently; as I am always singing "O divine Harmony" I have escaped that fleecing ...

Monday 4 July[39]

... So Chardin is alive, vivacious and energetic. How this news consoles me! Happy he, if his happiness depends on me. There is nobody like myself at looking out for the grandest and most beautiful things, nobody so disposed to throw from the arena all the other athletes—the infamous Edwards, the terrific Spencer, the idiotic Devonshire etc.

... This morning I fell right into Fogg's net. Alas, I was seduced by certain little Saxon tazza, certain seagreen bottles incredibly decorated with bronze, gilded in hell-fire—so bright and strong their colours. Two words breathed in my ear would have made me buy two fantastic Buhl armoire-like cabinets, magnificent, of a Solomonian richness, 400 the pair, and not dear at that. I cannot say that the other things are very attractive (?), but dear or cheap, here they are in this house, being packed up for Fonthill.

According to your letter from Paris it seems that the English weather has followed the cursèd English who flock into France; anyway, fogs, cold and devilish winds etc seem to have abandoned this Island; for five or six days we have had sun, breezes and the cuckoo etc as in spring. It is ten o'clock at night and I am writing with all the windows open, dying of heat …

So you are at the Hotel d'Empire, where the nocturnal visits of the staff almost gave me a consumption; but I would rather die like that than live as I am living. "Oh memories still delightful of one's first fleeting youth!" Poor creature that I am! "And yet I am alive", old <for?>[40] the streets, but fresh as a rose and as hard as a Carmelite[41] …

Sunday 17 July

… The two most sublime seagreen bottles with vine twigs etc, transparent, luminous and perfect, of a colour—of a colour to rest and enchant the eyes, have come from Fogg and are now in the Yellow Room in all their divine, calm and gay splendour, where they make the most harmonious effect possible. They cost 140, but what was I to do—exasperated by the sermons of Rottier, I have acted rather like youths who, scolded by their parents for whoring, rush to a brothel as soon as the sermon is over! …

Sad indeed is your intelligence about the boy situation, sad for Barzabà who is more compassionate and slobbering than ever. John Fowkes' lot is detestable[42]—none of them are in the least promising; all this is enough to make me despair. Mother most pure, mother without stain, Mabusian mother,[43] so divine, so pious, but too spiritual for a poor sinner like me; so many cries, so many prayers to heaven in vain—no one attractive (?), nothing of the right kind. All this would make the holiest of spirits fit for damnation. I cannot exist on agates, china and crystal; I need some nutriment more suitable to the human body.

I cannot continue on this spongy paper—curse Lubazio, curse all of them except my 'family'. To the devil with them!

P.S. This paper bought from Mr Lubazio at Salisbury is a regular sponge—like him, it drinks up everything.

<Friday> 22 July

... "A copy of the Farnese vase by Fiammingo"[44]—don't know if that's very
likely. Judging in a vacuum is ridiculous, but I doubt whether the ivories
are orthodox, I doubt it—we shall see. I thought Denon[45] had acquired a
lot of lacquer after May 1803, but according to your letter the same trifles
left aside by us at the Julliot sale are there. For drawings you must have a
sure nose, extremely sure; as far as Parmigianos and Rembrandts etc are
concerned, Denon has the best in the world, the flower of the thefts—I
know it for certain, and if I could snatch them it would be blissful good
fortune. I will fell an immense amount of wood for this, and you know well
enough that the more one fells here, the more beautiful, picturesque and
healthy Fonthill becomes. This is a truth which daily experience confirms.
Confirma hoc Deus[46] etc I sing morning and evening.

Bravo Chardin, bravo indeed! Here is a letter from him of the 14th July
which is epoch-making—good sound sense; method in answering, clause
by clause; clear, original and enthusiastic as in first youth; and as cordial
as I am myself when I am friendly with people. This Chardin is the best
consolation left to me, and for my part I shall know how to give him all
the proofs of friendship and trust he can want ...

The price of sugar is going to the devil and with it all Rottier's hopes.
Well, one must fell and fell again. In any case, Father Bestorum will make
me detest firs, and buyers abound—divine buyers vastly in need of fir and
with much money; they offer to pay *cash down* (some the lot, and some
half), and I will not remain deaf to such devout prayers. Notwithstanding
my poverty and Rottier's Gorgon-like face, I am always disposed to do
prodigies with dear Chardin ...

I must certainly pass the winter in Paris, Congress or no Congress, but
taking with me as small a train as possible. I do not want the Hotel d'Avoust
or the Hotel Kinski or velvet or gold fringes. I want some agreeable and
not too large hole where one can Chardinise in the morning and have boys
in the evening ...

I am a little disappointed with your harvest of lacquer—I thought it was
more important; this is miserable stuff. So Poland has taken it all. I thought
I heard you enumerate some delightful pieces of china—but nothing,
nothing; I did well to embrace Fogg closely. And tapestries, arras—all
gone too, and the Ecouen glass[47]—that's a mortal blow. About buhl I have
spoken already: I adore the true, capital buhl, but it must be the best. To

be condemned to the mediocre after such toil and such expense, so many miserable little details and minutiae, makes one scream with rage. So the superlative is not for me but for vermin like Simon and Roger! Oh shame! What use is Sir Isaac Heard in this respect! If I could, I would leave myself neither a fir nor a quartering—all would be sold to delight Chardin and to appease cruel fate, which does not leave poor Barzaba (as strong as a Turk) the wherewithal to renew his green old age.

Saturday 6 August

... This is what White writes in his last letter: "I have found it quite impossible to take up Mr H. Wildman's affair,[48] which must be managed with great discretion and attention to make it productive to you." Mark well! We are at sea, with no shore in sight. To write thus—after so many promises, so many assurances, etc! But already it is almost over with me. I no longer find respect or recognition or anything worth finding. Formerly one word sufficed—they all trembled at me. But then I had what I no longer have—lands in Somerset, Gloucester, Hertford, Buckingham, Bedford, London and Jamaica—provinces now lost, sold and gone to the Devil or to people worse than he. And what remains to me? Egg shell,[49] old Japan, old Sèvres! If with this closed the sad catalogue of old age, happy Barzabà! But I am wretched, pitiably wretched, and if I am alive it is clearly a miracle ...

Tuesday 30 August

Rottier on one side of me and Boletus on the other, the books in a heap on the floor, Figley fidgeting to go out and the dwarf to go for a ride—all this takes up my time for writing ...

The last books brought down by Boletus are masterpieces of good taste and exquisitely bound, but I don't know where to place them—it will be necessary to put a line of bookcases, instead of cabinets, in the Edward III Gallery, between the windows, with portraits over them ...

Monday 12 September

Well, we have been to Longleat, and Longleat is indeed clean and comfortable and as fine as a great house can be without that touch of good taste, the lack of which one notices at every step. But there is a succession of apartments, some of them approaching the palatial—noble and spacious, with commodious corridors, and bedrooms in the best economical style of the latest and most up-to-date furnished lodgings. There are some miserable cabinets, a deal of daubs enough to make one spit, and only two pieces of china to envy. They are this shape,[50] over two feet high, light, slim, delicate and harmonious; they have purple mosaic with cartouches in gold cameo and a little bistre painted with exquisite and delicious fineness. I have never seen anything of this sort—a pity I have never met them. Throughout the building one recognises the hall-mark of Bagasse[51]—his poor lazy methods, his eternal vulgar architraves and his false arches etc—a plague of Wyattiana. That infamous style will corrupt all England and like mice and bugs will riddle beds, tables, roofs, walls etc, etc. *Libera me, Domine, di questa morte aeterna*[53]...

Wednesday 14 September

... Believe me, the terrace at Stourton[53] is no longer comparable to that at Fonthill: the lines too straight, the ground not undulating, a repetition of pyramids, larches planted regularly everywhere like the fleurs-de-lis on the royal robe which used to be at St Denis. I don't like it, I can't admire it.

Sixtus the Fifth's cabinet[54] is divine, I know—the bronzes are of extreme delicacy and elegance, and those lovely agates, alabasters and cornelians, mingled with the glittering mother-of-pearl, produce a rich effect, agree able and grateful to the eye. It will be difficult to surpass, but we must try, and produce something to make people doff their hats, whether they will or no ...[55]

... A sad catastrophe, that of poor Gaspar—that's what German eating and drinking leads to. Coxone will follow him 'ere long—his ritual of pickled pork, beer and rum is best calculated to suffocate anyone not too strong in the head or the legs ...

Sunday 9 October[56]

I felt, my dear Gregory, a strong repugnance at leaving the Island, notwithstanding that it is, to me, a thousand times cursèd. And it was not without reason that I had such feelings: we were in mortal peril—four or five "somersaults" on the sands at the harbour entrance threatened to send us to the bottom, but the invisible hand, the benign and powerful hand of my Glorious Protector was not stretched over me in vain ... I'm going to the feet of the Saint—his image is the first object that meets one's eye on entering the church here.

Paris, Sunday 16 October

I've no time to write or to do anything except complain of the horrid din in this cloaca. Already that precious M. Clermont[57] has deafened me with recommendations of this and that; already they've announced the Marquis of Marialva[58] (called The Ambassador etc); already they've suggested to me hotels, cooks, boxes at the theatre, dancers etc. I want to fly like lightning, but I've not yet decided ...

Wednesday 26 October

... The Marquis of Marialva having called here three times in one morning, I admitted him; he seemed very happy to see me again; he dines with me today. He is very depressed at the prospect of going to St Petersburg, Vienna, and finally Brazil—he is so charged with official duties as to disturb his beloved 'scientific' tranquillity. I did not find him as changed in appearance as I had expected, and certainly he is not changed in his feelings towards me. On seeing me he seemed to see his Fatherland, his father, his sister[59] and all the happy serene days of his youth—irrevocable and for ever departed ...

Monday 31 October

I'm still here!—carrying on as best I can. I'm like gunpowder. I explode.
I stupefy. I give kicks in the arse. I make myself obeyed as if I were the
Grand Turk. D. Pedro is all over me (even more than his family was) and
shows me an excess of friendship worthy of what my poor Marquis had
for me. Today I was at the Royal Library. Since all the past flooded into
my memory as vividly as the present, I thundered Greek, Persian, Arabic
etc like the Law, and all that I said was received by the professors as Law.
You cannot imagine the effect produced by the little I know. Méon[60] who
was showing the MSS, and Langlès[61] the oriental books, stood with their
mouths open, almost in fits. Everything came like Divine illumination,
like the gift of tongues to the apostles—it had to be seen to be believed.
They say that the pronunciation of Arabic and Persian was never more
authentic. The immense catalogue of Fathers, geographers and historians
that I named and asked for more than astonished them. Certain books of
which I made a kind of analysis they have not got! Imagine their surprise!
The Saint seems to have inspired me.

... The weeks here, counting the loss on the exchange and the rapacity
of the hotel in a thousand cheating ways, cost much more than double
what they do in London ... Angels large and small abound here, but I see
them from afar, as it were in the clouds. A certain object seemed to pass
like summer lightning at the Marquis'. What a pity! What a pity! Such
expense, so much money gone and nothing to console me (in the supreme
way, I mean). Bion always counts for something.

The Museum[62] is in confusion with preparations for the exhibition. But
I have been there and observed, alas, that the principal pictures hardly
exist any more—the *Transfiguration*, the *Martyrdom of St Peter*, Correggio's
St Jerome, the lovely Raphaels ete, etc[63]—all coloured like the rainbow,
enough to give one the horrors and make one weep. My God what a
shame! I am not at all content with the gallery itself—bad lighting, false
day light, no harmony or effect or mystery (I mean in proportion to the
immense space). Denon led me into a room he had arranged in the best
cinquecento style; this was certainly rich and fine and royal and in the best
taste. The majority of the pictures before Raphael are miseries, re-gilded
and re-painted, without value and without apparent authenticity ...

<Monday> 7 November[64]

No, my very dear friend, I cannot marvel at Paris … Everywhere one discovers a sham style—false Roman of the false Empire which I no longer respect and which I like no better than Birmingham gold or Pinchbeck's masterpieces.[65] As for *chefs d'oeuvre* of cuisine, My Lord Sefton[66] was only too correct: they are no longer to be found. His Most Christian Majesty is not orthodoxly served, but he has one of my former *maîtres d'hôtel* as *chef d'office*, a man of some talent. Chromatically, and for piercing and often discordant shrieks, the opera surpasses anything imaginable in Limbo or Purgatory—one's ears are in penance, if not in Hell. But the setting is unrivalled—down to the last figurant, the scenery, costume and ballet are ravishing and perfect.

I never saw anything which threw me into such an ecstasy as the pantomime *L'Enfant Prodigue*.[67] You are transported into the period of the Patriarchs in the Syrian mountains, and thence you descend to the shores of the Nile, to Memphis in all its splendour, when Sesostris had filled it with his glory, prosperity and power. In the midst of all the seductions of this august and brilliant capital, the young and ingenuous son of a too indulgent father gives himself up to "the triple delight of love, gaming and wine". The hurly-burly of an imperial and commercial city, the processions sacred and profane, the vibration of cithers, the stamping of a thousand neat and graceful feet, the entwining of arms—it is enough to turn your head. Then follows ruin and remorse, the howling desert, repentance and almost death. But no transgression is without pardon (save the sin against Sir Isaac Heard, which is without forgiveness). Since by chance he has married neither a scold nor an Egyptian, he returns, he falls at the feet of a good old man (in appearance at least the most venerable old man in the world) and he is folded in the paternal arms …

Sunday 13 November

… I haven't been round all the shows yet, but they act with a grace, ease and gaiety unknown in the foggy *rosbifish* Island. The vaudeville is divine with its life-like caricatures of the *Milords* and *Miladies,* enough to make one collapse with laughter. At the opera they make a noise like a door on rusty hinges, but they really can dance. *L'Enfant Prodigue* is the triumph of all the Arts together. Lays[68] sings better than ever—the other evening in *Oedipus*[69] he pleased me greatly. Oh how clear and fine this music is—light if you like, but conducted with so much harmonious grace that it goes to the heart.

... If I did not flee from buying temptations I'd be down to my last farthing; for this reason I've left M. Denon in peace—I haven't taken a step in his direction, and since he hasn't given himself the trouble to come galloping to me, he's off my list. I can't help marvelling at this because when I last saw him he seemed to be afire with the liveliest enthusiasm for my accomplishments, and talked about his drawings, prints and pictures etc with those fervent encomiums which were obviously born of a great inclination to cede the said treasures to a dear friend, *for money of course*. As his supremacy at the Museum is on the verge of collapse I rather suspect that he nurses little projects of visiting London and putting in the bank there certain sums (the product of wonderful thefts) which he thinks are no longer safe here. In this respect he isn't wrong—he isn't much *à l'ordre du jour* here, he passes for what he is—one of the most zealous and fond Bonapartists whom the Devil still allows to insult the Royal presence; it's a shame to leave him in his position, but little by little thieves, rogues, Durand,[70] Grivaud,[71] Jacobins, Republicans, heretics, atheists etc will be hurled into the abyss of everlasting perdition. So be it.

Up to now I've not seen a picture comparable to the Vaɪkenborch[72] or the Luke of Holland—only false, infamous and wretched impostures have been shown to me. And what prices! Ah my God—impracticable. Today I'm going to see something which sounds passable. The modern French school has some merit in certain semi-gothic little pictures of interiors, but at prices (10,000, 5,000, 3,000) to make one flee and to extinguish any desire to buy ... I see that £3,000 instead of £2,000 will be paid out from Philpot Lane[73] on the first of January, but not without sobs and tears from poor Rottier, who doesn't paint Jamaica, to me anyway, in so much blue and gold ... It would have been better for me to have fled from Paris according to my first inclination before I knew the excellence of the heavenly truffles, the divine foie-gras, the ortolan, chickens, partridges, etc which are to be found here. M. Buffetaut's art, seconded by supreme Nature, is no longer to be despised. Dear Bion makes me delicate and agreeable bread, so that *la bouche va en carrosse* as that Fleming de Cort[74] (half-beast, half-knave) used to say. Bion behaves well in every respect, but the pompous nullity of St Ambrose[75] always being in the way, I hardly ever profit from the good disposition towards me that this fat, blonde and chaste creature might have.

Monday 14 November

I'm about to see pictures with Constantin, who, you see, isn't dead (as I think you had told me).[76] He's a gentleman and a good connoisseur. I expect I'll do some good business with him; perhaps I'll escape Collot's Leonardo[77] ... Yesterday in General Sébastiani's[78] house I leapt back with horror on seeing the infamies that they call Andrea del Sarto, Giorgione, Domenichino, Wouvermans etc; thinking to make a great impression, these rogues have loaded themselves with objects inferior to those one can see on the *quais*; now that their star is paling, they're selling and leasing, and will learn how foolish they've been. Constantin, being custodian of the pictures etc of the deceased Josephine, has begged me to go and see them at Malmaison—a journey I shan't fail to make. They'll be sold shortly and then I'll be ruined for certain ...

<Monday> 21 November

... Constantin has discovered me a Gaspar Poussin equal in the purity and beauty of its brushwork to my famous one and superior as regards the figures[79]—a great bargain! A great bargain! And also a little picture by Lorenzo Lotto[80] (not Father Lot of Sodom)—divine, divine, acquired in Spain ... I am certain that what is asked is not half what they are worth, yet it is too large a sum for me, too large for a beast who is throwing away £300 a week for apartments, firewood, board-wages etc, etc.

Poor me, without a doctor, without a private counsellor, and, worst of all, without an object of the kind I prefer above all others. I have no spirit for anything. I am a wretched impotent old man, with all the benignity that distinguished Barzaba—sighing, looking round, slobbering etc, but sighing, looking round and slobbering in vain. Ambrose being corpsified with God knows what kind of rheumatism, Bion has been undertaking his duties. He gives me nothing, he is icy, Richardsonian, impracticable and good for nothing, he gives me constipation, he is not the least consolation to me. Game is not lacking here if one knew how to catch it ... The lack of lively and lovely objects, of cheerful, pretty faces and comely forms, afflicts and saddens me ...

I like the gallery at Malmaison well enough and am pleased by the vault, the general colouring and the not too great height of the walls; it is Imperial-like, italianate and comfortable. The pictures make a tolerably fine and harmonious effect. I do not say that they are of the first or second rank—many are copies, clean and good ones, and there are many originals of masters of the third class; but there are a few well-preserved little pictures—an exquisite Garofalo and a tolerably pure van de Velde. The marble columns at each end of the room give an air of grandeur, and the perspective discovered through them of another apartment beyond is enchanting. The *Paris*—Oh heavens, never has Canova[81] produced such a delightful object—what delicate flesh and what quality marble! Most of the pictures come from Germany and discover clearly enough their German origin—false Claudes, false Andrea del Sartos, false Domenichinos and mighty false Holbeins. Constantin's Gaspar Poussin is worth more than the lot of them

Every hour I improve in knowledge and taste. The Abbé will tell you, when you see him, what I am and to what pitch of Frenchiness and flowery Parisian manner of speaking I have attained. In spite of my face and dress they take me for a Frenchman; if you had heard me this morning discoursing in various quarters on politics, military and naval matters, Greek, the court, cooking, botany, astronomy and bigotry, you would have thought yourself in the Senate, the University, the theatre, the chapel and the brothel. How strange my make-up is! The working of my brain is enough to perplex anyone wanting to know about the composition of the human spirit! The weather itself is not more variable than my disposition—one minute sunshine, the next darkness. In nothing am I fixed save in my sincere love for you. With these sentiments, believe me, my dear Gregory, your constant and true friend and Protector.

Wednesday 23 November

I could make stupendous purchases, but I do not dare: the Gaspar Poussin of which I spoke in my last letter is the most perfect, pure, pellucid, poetic and pastoral picture ever executed by mortal hands—the figures are like the style and more excellent brush of the great Nicolas Poussin. I could also buy the Lorenzo Lotto, an onyx for its colour, an evangeliary for its purity of preservation, and a Leonardo da Vinci for the grace and sweetness of its boys—oh what melting eyes the *putti* have, ah, oh!

... *P.S.* The two pictures are mine. Unhappy me!

Monday 5 December

... From there I passed into a kind of cut-throat quarter, God knows where—I think in the Montfaucon district or that of Mon Cu;[82] there I discovered and disenchanted the famous, stupendous and purest Gerard Dou, formerly old Dupré's![83] The same for which I offered at various periods of my sad life 30,000 and 36,000 *lire*.[84] Ah my God, what torment! What a cruel and bitter fate! Without Mr White and his neglect over Henry Wildman I would have bought it and carried it in triumph to London. After *The Dropsical Woman* in the Louvre Museum, which they value at 300,000, it is the principal work of this most rare and costly master ...

Wednesday 7 December

... I would sooner have a little external gout than suffer from a kind of detestable I don't know what; probably I've got internal gout, and certainly bad humours—what would put me in a good humour would be to be visited like yourself by a sweet and amiable sailor; cultivate that plant, I beg you, get it used to frequenting you and then, with divine help, it will frequent me ...

I have had a great fling. I have (Oh! Ho!),[85] I have bought the Gerard Dou. There is nothing for it now; consequently I am overthrown—here

I am on the ground, and without the administration of some cordial, of some of those sums promised by the infamous traitor White, I shall die of melancholy. I do not know where to turn—tempted on this side, robbed on that; sighing and groaning to buy at one moment, and at having bought the next—it's the most delirious and feverish existence imaginable. Ah, what a Gerard Dou! Oh what a price! Ah! Oh! Better the mortal repose of the great Fool-jam,[86] who is with God, than this fatal, expensive, ruinous, perfidious, cursèd activity.

To calm my remorse I see no other remedy than to invent a confessional in the office in Lincoln's Inn, made by the Bald-headed Fool,[87] and, of course, paid for by me (I am Sir Pay-Well). There every day Rottier will be obliged to come and listen (well shut in) to all my laments, my sins, my financial scruples repeated and re-repeated like the echo in the Casa Simonetti at Milan which repeats things thirty-six and a half times. What will be my penance before absolution I do not pretend to guess; but Rottier's will be to hear a rondo like eternity—it will not be a trifling penance, I swear to you ...

Saturday 24 December[88]

Yes—still at Dover for my sins and perdition. The Customs, with so many articles to inspect, have taken the whole day, despite much agreeable rapidity ... I cannot but praise the Customs. I have a lacquer cabinet with a silver key, and on this key a Persian engraved plate which runs 'Saheb-Nadir-Pad Chah'.[89] The lacquer is at least as fine as Maria van Diemen's.[90] Blessed be the Glorious One for so much favour. Here I am with the Gerard Dou safe.

Until tomorrow, until tomorrow, dear Gregory. Farewell. The postillion goes Express—didn't want to let you languish in doubt and uncertainty.

1.　To Douglas in French.
2.　Oscar I of Sweden, son of Napoleon's former Marshal, Bernadotte, who became Charles XIV of Sweden.

3.   Princess Charlotte Augusta (1796–1817), next in succession to the Prince Regent, had been engaged against her will to the Prince of Orange, but soon after this broke it off.

4.   Nickname for one of the staff.

5.   Benjamin Dean Wyatt (1775–1850), eldest son of James; architect of Drury Lane Theatre and Crockford's. "Bitterness" presumably refers to his character, as "Sweetness" does to his younger brother Philip.

6.   This picture by "Velvet" Jan Brueghel the Elder (1568–1625) and Johann Rottenhammer (1564–1625), a German, although in *Phillips*, is more fully described in *Bath* (1841), 1st Day, Lot 16: an allegorical portrayal of the Four Elements in terms of fowls, fishes, insects and animals in a rich landscape with fruit and flowers, and classical figures of nymphs and cupids, 42½" x 25"; it fetched 140 guineas, having cost Beckford £50.

7.   Giovanni Beffini's *Doge Loredan*, sold by Beckford to the National Gallery, 1844. He also had the *Doge Vendramin*, a lesser picture now in the Frick Gallery, New York; but its frame is not striking or so suited to the picture, and it seems most likely that B. is describing the National Gallery picture.

8.   Urbino Pizzetta of Foley Place was a dealer in and restorer of Old Masters. His pictures etc were sold at Christie's in April 1825, after his death.

9.   Henry Constantine Jennings (1731–1819), known as "Dog" Jennings after his purchase of the marble figure of Alcibiades' dog. He spent most of his life in debt and died within the rules of the King's Bench. His collection included stuffed birds and shells, and he was one of the great eccentrics of the age.

10.   Horace Walpole.

11.   To Douglas in French.

12.   Sir William Drummond's privately printed and very rare *Oedipus Judaicus*, 1811, the most daring of his speculative works, attempting to prove that many parts of the Old Testament were allegories.

13.   Portuguese Bucellas.

14.   Pieter Brueghel (1564?–1638) the Younger, known as "Hell" Brueghel from the subjects of his pictures.

15.   In 1795 John Willis is mentioned as Beckford's *valet de chambre*.

16.   David Teniers the Elder (1582–1649), or his son David the Younger (1610–90).

17.   Paolo Veronese (1528–88) worked in Venice.

18.   From London to Susan in French.

19.   Presumably a corruption of *Gujputty*, meaning "Lord of the Elephants", the traditional title of the Kings of Orissa, and in Buddhist legend one

of the four Great Kings who divided the earth. Later Beckford gave this nickname to the purchaser of Fonthill, Farquhar, who had made his fortune in India.

20.   Beckford's dogs. Hayter is "Coxone". Bouffetaut is the chef.

21.   Elizabeth (1750–1828), sixth Baroness Craven by her first marriage, and Margravine of Anspach by her second. She was a playwright and had put herself outside society by her immorality. She had large, expressive eyes.

22.   An old, ugly and mischievous fairy of childhood tales, who troubles everybody by her presence; her name was probably derived from her being *bossue à 36 carats.*

23.   *One O'Clock! or the Knight and the Wood Daemon* by "Monk" Lewis was long one of the most popular of the "gothick terror" melodramas. In 1811 Beckford saw at Sadler's Wells *The Wood Daemon or the Grotto of Venice*, almost certainly an unauthorised adaptation or burlesque of this.

24.   Baron von Thondertentronck is a character in Voltaire's *Candide.*

25.   A.F.F. von Kotzebue (1761–1819), German dramatist.

26.   *Coglione* is a very vulgar word, often used by Beckford.

27.   Here, I presume Louis XVIII.

28.   Douglas was a convinced Bonapartist.

29.   Beckford was writing on Easter Monday.

30.   Franchi in London in French to Douglas.

31.   From London, to Franchi in Paris.

32.   Paul Colnaghi (1751–1833), founder of the firm of art-dealers still in existence; or his son and partner Dominic Paul Colnaghi (1790–1879).

33.   George John, second Earl Spencer (1758–1834), who made his library at Althorp the finest private library in Europe, and retired early from a brilliant political career to devote himself to books and collecting. The spoils of Europe since the French Revolution were now on sale in Paris.

34.   James Edwards (1757–1816), the leading bookseller of his day and himself a great collector; he is supposed to have retired from business about 1804, but evidently still carried out private commissions.

35.   From London.

36.   Robert Fogg of Warwick Street, Golden Square, a long-established dealer in china (a "China Man"). His nephew joined him later; served B., and acted as George IV's agent at important sales.

37.   I do not know the meaning of this word, which is quite clearly written.

38.   Benjamin West offered this to Beckford in his letter of June 29 (in *H.P.*); the seller was asking 400 guineas and West advised 300 or more. Beckford

bought it, and his *Inventory* shows that it was a portrait of Innocent X. (*H.P.S.* 1136, sold for £110 5s.)

39. From London.

40. A word has been torn away with the seal.

41. A vulgar French phrase still current.

42. *i.e.* the stable boys—Fowkes being head groom.

43. Mme Bion, the valet Richardson.

44. François Duquesnoy (1594–1642), considered at the time the finest sculptor of his age. He settled in Italy, where he was called *Il Fiammingo* (the Fleming) because Brussels was his native town.

45. Baron Denon (1747–1825), protégé of Mme de Pompadour; Napoleon's Director-General of Museums; accompanied him on his campaigns to advise him on the foreign art treasures worth filching.

46. The opening phrase of the Offertory prayer of the Mass for Whitsunday.

47. The Château of Ecouen, 19 kilometres north of Paris, was famous for its stained glass executed after Raphael's designs. *Phillips*, Day 18, Lot 845, is three panels with cypher, etc of Diane de Poitiers, mistress of Henri II.

48. The lawsuit which Beckford so gaily embarked on in 1807 and in which he placed so much financial hope.

49. Transparent precious porcelain.

50. Beckford drew a poor sketch here.

51. Jeffry Wyatt (later Wyatville) was working here.

52. From the Absolution in the Mass of Interment (Beckford has italianised the Latin).

53. The original name of the property which the Hoares changed to Stourhead when they bought it in 1720; the fine "terrace" ran for several miles to Alfred's Tower.

54. It is still in the Cabinet Room at Stourhead.

55. Beckford was going to try to rival this Renaissance cabinet (Sixtus V was Pope from 1585 to 1590) with one made to his own design; he already has in mind the great Ebony Cabinet made in 1815 by Hume (see p.176, note 50).

56. From Calais. Beckford was on his way to Paris, from which all subsequent letters up to *Wednesday 7 December* inclusive were written.

57. Beckford's Parisian banker, a partner of Laffitte.

58. Pedro de Menezes (1774–1823), last Marquis of Marialva; the D. Pedro of the *Journal,* and now Portuguese Ambassador in Paris. He was going to Vienna as proxy for the marriage of Archduchess Maria Leopoldina to the Portuguese heir Pedro, and was going to escort her to her husband in Brazil.

59. The Marquis and D. Henriqueta of the *Journal,* both now dead.

60. D.M. Méon, mediævalist and Conservator at the Royal Library (now the Bibliothéque Nationale).

61. L.M. Langlès, orientalist and Keeper of Oriental MSS at the Library.

62. The Louvre.

63. These pictures were looted by Napoleon from Italy, to which they were restored in 1816. They are Raphael's *Transfiguration,* now in the Vatican; Correggio's *Il Giorno,* now at Parma, showing the Madonna with St Jerome and the Magdalen; and Titian's *Martyrdom of St Peter,* which was in the Church of SS Giovanni e Paolo at Venice, until destroyed by fire in 1867. One of the other Raphaels admired by Beckford was *The Madonna di Poligno,* now in the Vatican. He was complaining about their be-daubing by French picture restorers in thick and brilliant colours.

64. To Douglas in French.

65. The elder Christopher Pinchbeck (d. 1782) invented the copper and zinc alloy called after him.

66. Second Earl of Sefton, son-in-law of Beckford's friend the Margravine of Anspach (Lady Craven).

67. A ballet-pantomine by Henri Montan (*dit* Berton), written in 1812. Beckford saw the performance on November 2nd at the Opera.

68. François Lays, a famous baritone, sang at the Opera 1779–1822, and was a constant favourite.

69. Sacchini's *Oedipe à Colone,* his masterpiece, which was consistently performed at the Opera from his death in 1787 until 1844 (583 performances). It was Marie Antoinette's refusal to have it put on immediately in Paris (in deference to the jealousy of French composers) that broke Sacchini's heart and caused his death.

70. Chevalier E. Durand, whose famous collection of antiquities was described in 1836, after his death.

71. C.M. Grivaud de la Vincelle, archaeologist.

72. *Bath* (1845), 328, shows this to be his *Building of the Tower of Babel,* a landscape with many figures, animals, ships, etc; on copper, 13½" x 20", from Charles I's Collection; it fetched £101 17s. It was therefore by Marten van Valkenborch (1542 to after 1602), a Fleming born in Malines.

73. *i.e.* by Messrs Plummer, whose office was there.

74. Hendrick de Cort (1742–1810), Flemish landscape painter who settled in England *c.*1790, exhibited at the Royal Academy, and was patronised by Beckford.

75. Ambrose—on the staff at Fonthill.

76. Guillaume-Jean Constantin (1755–December 1816), picture dealer; a member of the Commission entrusted by Napoleon with the organisation of the Louvre as a museum; appointed *Garde des Tableaux* of Josephine's picture gallery at Malmaison, December 1807.

77. *i.e.* that had been in the collection of one Collot.

78. One of Napoleon's generals. His collection is described in Buchanan *Memoirs of Painting*, 1824, ii. 263–6.

79. It is possible that this is Gaspar Poussin's *Calling of Abraham*, now in the National Gallery. That picture is known to have left Italy at some date after the French Revolution, and to have been sold privately by Beckford to Hart Davis, who sold it to Miles of Leigh Court. The way Constantin sold this picture to Beckford suggests that it had been despoiled by the French from Italy. Waagen's description of the *Abraham* is very like Beckford's remarks in his next letter (including the suggestion that the figures were by Nicolas Poussin). And finally, B. mentions the private sale of his G. Poussin <to Hart Davis> in his letter of 12 May 1817. Since *Abraham* was a shepherd and the *Abraham* is a rural scene, B.'s adjective *pastoral* in the next letter does not rule out the picture being the *Abraham*. Poussin's real name was Gaspar Dughet (1618–75), and he was brother-in-law of the more famous Nicolas Poussin.

80. *c.*1480–*c.*1554; pupil in Venice of Giorgione and G. Bellini.

81. Antonio Canova (1757–1822), the Italian sculptor.

82. *i.e.* my arse—a favourite joke of Beckford's, which Franchi here heavily underlined and marked in pencil.

83. *The Poulterer's Shop* by Gerard Dou (1613–75) the Dutch painter, pupil of Rembrandt; it was in some of the most famous French picture sales, including that of J.F. Coupry Dupré, and is now in the National Gallery.

84. Perhaps he meant *livres* (in French currency).

85. *Oh! Ho!* is inserted by Beckford as a pun on the Italian *Io ho* (I have).

86. *i.e.* Foljambe, somebody who had recently died.

87. Foxhall

88. From Dover.

89. Nadir Shah ruled in Persia 1736–47.

90. A manuscript box made, probably as a wedding present, for Maria van Aalst, who in 1630 married van Diemen, Governor of the Dutch East Indies; Van Diemen's Land (Tasmania) was called after him. *Phillips,* Day 31, Lot 1365; *H.P.S.* 146; now in the Victoria and Albert Museum; see p.166.

1815–1816

LITTLE special comment is called for, but we cannot help noting Beckford's extravagance. As soon as any money is received from the sale of timber, Hayter (Coxone) is despatched to buy copper and seasoned timber for the roofing of the Eastern Transept, and Franchi is sent money to pay for pictures and *objets d'art*. All this is against a sombre economic background of universal depression in England, with wheat prices being more than halved since 1813 and farmers hanging themselves when unable to pay their rents. The short-lived boom of 1814 in sugar had collapsed, the British market was glutted, and the price began that sharp decline from which it never recovered.

In the letters of September 22 and October 3 1816 we glimpse a bizarre piece of social history—the execution of a sodomite, John Attwood Eglerton. He was a waiter with a wife and children to support, and his accuser was a stable-boy. The attitude of the average Englishman of those days to such offences was typified by the jury, who took only ten minutes to return their verdict of "Guilty—Death", upon which the poor man "fell into tears, and begged the Judge to recommend him to mercy on account of his family".[1] The large crowd ("among whom were a great many women") who witnessed his execution at the Old Bailey were no better:

> "the detestable nature of his crime appeared to avert, in the minds
> of the crowd, that sympathy usually shown to culprits undergoing
> the vengeance of the law".[2]

Beckford got his curious information about Eglerton's end from the *News* of Sunday, September 29 (he pasted the account in his special album). On the night before his execution, Eglerton handed a document to the prison chaplain of Newgate (the Reverend Horace Salusbury Cotton) "which disclosed many important facts relative to the extent of these abominable practices". Further, "on his ascending the steps of the scaffold, he bowed to the populace and expressed a desire to address them. Mr Cotton, however, prevailed on him not to attempt it; and upon giving the fatal signal, he was launched into eternity." One of those on Eglerton's list was a Portuguese, who hastily left for Paris, where boys were easier and safer to find.

1815

Tuesday 7 February

... The dampness of this sublime abode is so great that everything will rot. Today, visiting the tabernacles or cribs[3] in the Lancaster Gallery with wretched Rottier, I found them all covered with lichen and stalactites like Fingal's cave;[4] the lacquer was covered with a white beard and verdant like Armida's uncle[5] when he was played by M. Moreau,[6] etc. I don't speak of the gilt stuff—this is already ash-colour like on the first day of Lent. Coxone says he is going to remedy it, but who can trust him—the remedy will be the breaking of ten or twelve pieces of china in the confusion of withdrawing the semi-putrid objects ...

<Friday 10 February>

Certainly, my dear Gregory, I don't mean to stay here to be blown about like bodies (and not holy ones) hanging from a gibbet. I must tell you that this place makes your flesh creep as soon as night falls. Yesterday I thought that everything was coming down. My tower swayed so that at three o'clock in the morning the dwarf awoke with a terrific "God-damn!" (according to Ambrose's story), flew down the staircase and ran for safety. Where? In the closet? No—worse! In the coal-hole? No—worse! In the common shore?[7] No—worse! Then where? In Bush's litter! You can imagine the fresh and charming appearance he had this morning after such a delightful vapour-bath! ...

Thursday 13 April

... I send you some true anecdotes of the famous sale ...;[8] you'll see the Marquis' extravagances—it would be better for him and his blind Signora to buy less useless rubbish and spend more on the decencies and comforts of daily life. According to the enclosed from Boletus, that rogue Forster isn't content with little—is a long way off from £37.16.0, but patience—the object is singular and sufficiently gothic to please me;[9] since I hope to fell the finest pine I have at five guineas or pounds for every forty feet, I'll take it and I'll pay when you judge it time. £40 was good enough; observe how the rogue favours me—those two pounds extra are by special grace for *me*—and yet you aren't convinced of the cheerful, sweet and smiling roguery of the ever so simple, ever so candid Forster ...

... I'm glad the missal[10] hasn't fallen into dirty plebeian hands—would that the *Office of the Blessed Virgin* had not been profaned—according to Boletus' gospel, a certain North, a corn merchant (atrocious extortioner)[11] has gained possession of this delicate work, the best for good taste that I've ever seen in my life.[12] I feel it deeply—above all now that I see the possibility of selling pine. The Turk and Diamond[13] are already waiting at the door—farewell, dear Gregory.

Friday 14 April

Lightning, thunder, icy cold, sleet—in short, all the delights of this celestial climate *à la* Rembrandt, so famous for effects of black and white and light and shade. I don't wonder at your gout, seeing the weather, but I do wonder that neither Shepherd nor Shepherdess have shewn any sign of life. I'm sure they're glad to be free of my visits in Grosvenor Place—a strange race for whom I have no more feelings than they for me.

The splendid vision of the felling of so much pine has passed like the sun's rays—I can't do it without destroying a great deal of beauty. There is no lack of buyers, of big prices and ready money, but I lack the courage to take away one of the most obvious marvels of the place. The oak will fall—for nine guineas or ten pounds. One will economise—that's all one can do; one will have two meals instead of four; one will do like the Dutch and take lessons in economy where one can (not, however, from Grosvenor Place—that would stink too much of niggardliness and Scottishness). At least one won't buy putrid yellow parchments of Psalms and Gospels without any merit whatever;[14] but one will buy the fine little book with the shells ...

Saturday 15 April

... It will cost me something to fell the pines—it will be a shame, even though they offer more than five guineas each for them. They're the finest in England—neither Stourton nor Longleat have ever had anything comparable for quality and cleanness of wood. There are twenty dogs after this bone—that's why they're offering so much. Each tree contains 95 clear feet without defect or knot—Norway has produced nothing superior.

Wednesday 19 April

... It's fortunate that Fausterina's spouse[15] hasn't more spirit—if he had, he'd be a famous rogue—it isn't the will he lacks, only the knowledge and impudence. The cursèd liar—one can't trust the least syllable that falls from his pallid and porcelainish lips, where not Cupid but some little bastard of Satan, the Father of Lies, has made his nest ...

Thursday 20 April

... The horrible atmosphere, icy and foggy, is killing me—just like other mortals: I'm quite unwell, but what use is it writing about my illnesses to a Professor of your rank—it's as if one introduced Robin Adair[16] to Cherubini, thinking to inspire respect and veneration! Anyway, I know that you neither have nor wish to have the smallest compassion for my sufferings.

In mine of yesterday you'll have doubtless observed my remarks on the Pimlico neighbourhood. I don't wonder at those people because already (in good time) I've become familiar with their narrowness of heart and of intellect. The path that they follow isn't calculated to bring them to a good end; accompanied by all the disdain that their nullity, negligence, indifference and petty hypocrisies arouse in me, they'll be once for all exiled from my memory and from the annals of Rottier, vulgarly called a Will.

Saturday 22 April

... I've given orders to Randall to send you Jeronimo Tedesco's book[17]—a thing I wouldn't do for any other person in the world, and which I don't like doing, it being totally against my rules; to take books from here and make them travel is novel to me and not worth the trouble ...

Tuesday 20 June

... According to the news from Arcadia, the Lady Shepherdess is too happy with her Shepherd to think again of this hermitage. As Her Delicious Excellency likes and thinks fit! I'm so much accustomed to this sort of courtesy that it no longer affects me. At first I thought that her heart or her head would dispose her to profit by the smallest invitatory sign I could give. But I'm wrong, and God will give me the courage to support these woes and a thousand others ...

Wednesday 21 June

I don't doubt, my dear Gregory, that the Saint will have pity on us. It is certain that in many respects Providence smiles on what surrounds me. I'm doing wonders with my timber—payments are being made with admirable swiftness. Today Coxone has received £300 and is off to London and Southampton etc to buy copper and seasoned timber for the great roof—an operation that will make everything safe in that part of the building.[18]

This morning I'm sending a little note to the Marchioness, full of all those exquisite expressions that please Shepherdesses who are accustomed to the sweet murmur ing of their Shepherds. I've almost given the final touch to the *Story of Motassem*;[19] it will make an impression on many people, as much as *Vathek* ...

The 43rd Regiment cut in pieces etc isn't of good augury, nor yet the slowness of the Russians. But Wellington's luck is something—that very astute Mazarin always asked of any general proposed to him *s'il étoit*

William Beckford, aged about forty, by John Hoppner
© Salford Museum & Art Gallery

Fonthill Abbey from the south-west, by John Martin, 1822 (from J. Britton's *Illustrations of Fonthill Abbey*)
© Beckford Tower Trust

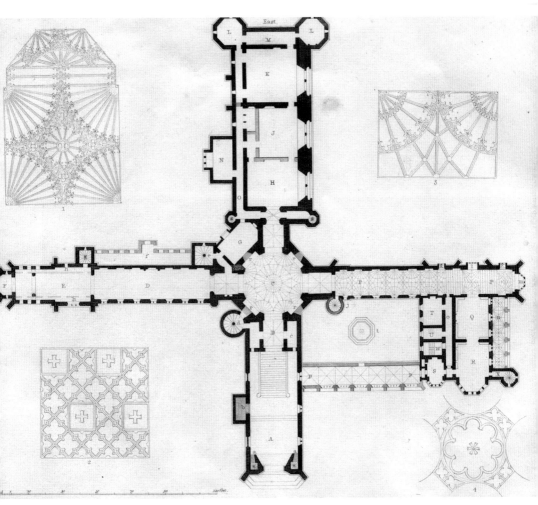

Plan of the main floor of Fonthill (from J. Britton's *Illustrations of Fonthill Abbey*)
© Beckford Tower Trust

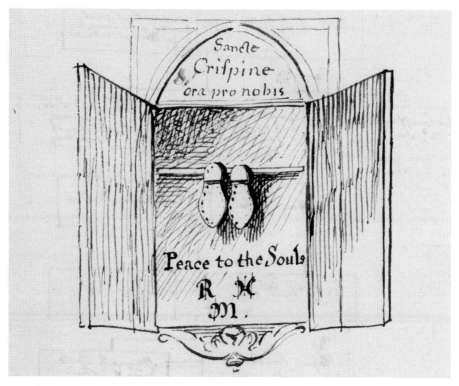

Beckford's design for a wall-cupboard at Fonthill
The Bodleian Library, University of Oxford, MS Beckford c. 19, fol. 42r

Viscount Fartleberry (Beckford's dog),
by Abbé Macquin
The Bodleian Library, University of Oxford,
MS Beckford c. 84, fol. 143r

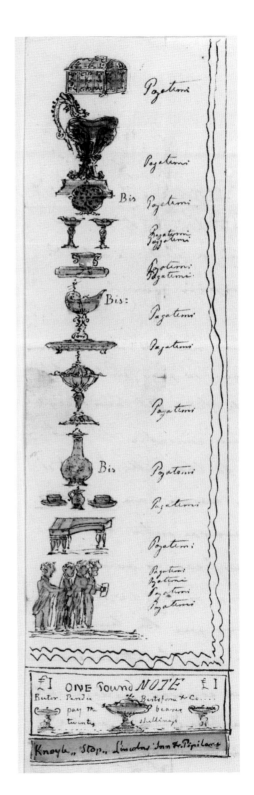

The Millionaire's Nightmare:
"Pay Me", by Chevalier Franchi
The Bodleian Library, University of
Oxford, MS Beckford c. 12, fol. 57v

Beckford with his bookseller Clarke (Boletus), by W. Behnes, 1817
By permission of The British Library, 1466.i.22(2)

Oriel window, Fonthill, by G. Cattermole (from J. Britton's *Illustrations of Fonthill Abbey*)

Perro, Beckford's Dwarf
By kind permission of Bath Library & Information Centre

houroux,[20] and Mazarin knew what he was about—would that our own Puritans had half the brains of that b—r ...

Friday 23 June

Jesu, what gotho-barbaric rejoicing—like alleluias of the Druids chanting round the great idol of dry straw, full of victims.[21] What horrors, what slaughter, what a terrible judgement of God on the blind and brutal fury of the French! How many arms and legs off, how many brains scattered on the ground, what a catalogue of martyrs, dead or cut to pieces whilst yet alive! Never have such important and strong tidings come to my ears; all the other victories pale before it—it is a Trafalgar on land which, one cannot deny, raises Wellington in a colossal manner.

Have you seen the Shepherd? He'll do well to change his flute—his accustomed melody is now only good for making asses bray—neither goats nor sheep nor shepherdesses will leap for him now[22] ...

My yesterday's letter was hardly off before the weather, as if to mock my praises, changed from fair to black and from serene, delicious and summery to stormy, cold and ash-colour. Torrents of rain fell and the whistling wind seemed to bear on bats' wings the sobs of those dying and on the point of death in Flanders. I can't express how a season so changeable makes one hate the putrid yellowish green of this Island. I hope to God that the return of peace and good sense in France will open the way to emigration ... There'll be no hay, no fruit, no flowers—the sky is leaden and laden as in the gloomiest November, as if it were ill with constipation of snow—a strange and horrid sickness for the month of June! Farewell, my dear Gregory, I'm going to digest the great banquet of news which you've sent me with the *Morning Post* ...

Saturday 24 June

... I have a Shepherdly letter just a little despairing but still hoping to see his Beloved[23] turn fresher than ever to the attack; another such attack would fill all England with glory, tears, bankruptcy, monuments in the worst taste and sculpture in Westminster Abbey and St Paul's Cathedral.

... Advise Fiume, or rather Mr Storr,[24] not to let the candelabra languish too long—the four extra are badly needed now that the other eight are all in a row. Don't forget to send back the Jeronimo Tedesco—I don't ever want books from the Abbey to be transported elsewhere. Where is a volume of Berain?[25] I can't find it in its place.

The new gardener hasn't yet arrived.[26] Rottier has done very badly to make him come on a Sunday (instead of this Saturday as he had written to me), when the terribly pious church-going assiduity of the Great Dolt doesn't permit him to come to consecrate him; much depends on this first Mass ... There is a very mild warmth, accompanied by a damp mist everywhere—if it doesn't end in a deluge, I'm going tomorrow to Stourton.

<Sunday> 25 June[27]

I came here wrapped up in the clouds like Prince Agib[28] when he was on the enchanted steed. From time to time there were gleams of sunshine which gilded the verdure of this spot—already sufficiently gilt by the semi-putrid effect of the dampness. Oh God, what a summer, what a June—if this really is June and summer! Last night the voice of November was heard unceasingly in all the chimneys; lucky he who didn't have it in his room. Let him who wants remain in this climate—*I'm* resolved to escape, the moment that two or three more victories *à la* Wellington have obliged England to leave the Continent in peace. I'll give orders for your room, but in that case I won't know where to put the Abbé—I don't want him in Boletus' room on any account—it would be too near me ...

Monday 26 June

The Brueghels have arrived in perfect health and aren't too bad (but not entirely good) in their frames. God knows where to place them. The Lancaster Gallery is a real tumulus for pictures, which doesn't matter when they're in the style of Peter Neeffs,[29] but when they're of the beauty of the Brueghels the sacrifice is pitiful … Yesterday poor Tittup finished his long career, not so much through old age as through the epidemic which is running through all the stables[30] …

Sunday 2 July
(From *The Glove*, a kind of rustic brothel at the foot of the *hill* ridiculously called Salisbury Plain.)

… I'm quite sorry not to be in London to profit from the spoils of the odious Jennings.[31] Keep an eye on them with redoubled vigilance. I doubt if he'll sell the best shells—he's so used to all this and has so much practice and experience in roguery that I doubt if his creditors will have good sport with him, the damned soul. I really do feel about not seeing the shells; what will become of the Brueghel? Probably the books have already been ransacked by Spencer, Greenhorn and other blockheads or birds of prey of this sort. But, anyway, it deserves attention—I'm sure you'll give it the sharpest possible attention. £300 will come to me from the oak on the sixth of the month, and if from the den of the infamous Jennings some object appears cheap and of real value, here is a ready sum …

Yesterday there was Bengal heat, today there is Nova Zembla coolness, a sad leaden sky, a great deal of dust, and a general stink of burnt-up grass to make one vomit. I'm working on the *Story of the Three Mountains*—it will be simple but fine.[32] Boletus, still the King of Fools, has asked me for permission to copy the fine miniature of Francis I—which I don't *at all* like.[33] Instead of saying 'God-dam' I say *José-Street-Arriaga-Brrrrrum da-Silveira*[34] and spit like an incorrigible consumptive …

Tuesday 4 July

… I think that the *Episode of the Story of Motassem* the Father of Vathek will amuse the Abbé. More than any of my sketches it has something of the historic, of the paederastic (?), and of the simplicity of Arabian tales;

and much of the grandiose, the graceful, the whorish (?) and the holy (*secundum ordinem Melchisedek*).[35] What a strange beast or savage I am!

... I don't wonder at the Marchioness being so vexed. Who the devil would like to be mistress of the house in such a household under such a shepherd and with such a flock etc! Since they won't change their system, they'll change their servants, and by dint of changing they won't find a soul left to be changed. The poor reputation of the Marquess in the servant world of London is almost as considerable as that of Wellington in the military sphere.

Sunday 17 September

... The craze for seeing the Abbey grows like the tower itself—every day and well-nigh every hour they twist and turn to corrupt my dragoons—so far in vain. This resistance to the power of gold is a miracle—let us thank the Glorious Saint and put all our hopes in him.

Tuesday 26 September

... After the heat of the last few days we now have an icy, cold rain that bites like a mad dog, and winds which every instant threaten to reduce to dust Porca, Porco, Patty and Porcellana—with every sound I imagine a pinnacle or at least a crocket is down ...

Ah, what a divine celebration was the auto-da-fé of November 1707— how charming and modest it must have been in its holy but gay simplicity. What a fine mixture of fireworks and of flames from burning Jews, of torments below and dancing above ground, of opera in the Rossio and Alleluia in the Church of S. Domingos.[34] These effects of light and shade please me. I'd like to go where one can enjoy them, where heretics are abhorred, where I'll not hear the blockheads of this Island spoken of except in the terms they deserve (according to my gospel). Ah, happy times, if only they could return ...

Thursday 28 September

It seems impossible that Towneley's collection of prints should be sold at a time when not even the Old Clothes Man remains in London; if it has the misfortune to be in Harley Street at this solitary season, whose fault is it? Not mine—wasn't I bored by its presence?[37]

... When I allow any animal (however much of a great beast or brute or fool he may be) to pasture in my fields I don't like offering him nettles instead of clover—I don't want to buy *vin ordinaire* to give to anyone—I like all to drink what I've already found to be good ... I'm for ever condemned to eat the worst British potatoes, the most mediocre puddings, the most villainous fricassées, the least tasty cutlets and the most detestable rice. And I'm condemned to all this though paying as nobody else does! ...

Sunday 1 October

Everything depends, my dear Gregory, where things are placed. An object which looks like nothing on earth in the Brown Parlour is transformed when placed in the Lancaster Gallery, where I've put the strange candle sticks, which produce a wonderful effect there ...

Sunday 15 October

... The moment of your return here will be time enough to try out the marvellous fireplaces (if they really are marvellous); to send them now would only cause a fresh occasion for complaints: they would remain rusting in a corner without the Beasts here, young and old, having the slightest idea what to do with them ...

<Wednesday 18 October>[38]

Today the 18th of October at 11 o'clock, the heavens being serene, the sun bright and the whole of Nature jubilant, there alighted from his now triumphal chariot the heroic Hayter. I rushed out to receive him, and still more, the thousand pounds that I was sure he carried. His reception was like that which (in the opera *Ezio,*[39] anyway) Caesar gives to his illustrious General.

After showing his teeth and his tail, shouting one moment and crying the next; after creeping about like Satan in the Garden of Eden, fleeing hither and thither, hunted, pursued, terrified and at last tamed by our swinish Hercules, the enemy has written a few lines to his bankers, and (Oh miracle worthy of better times!) the bankers have read and obeyed. Great was the confusion, tremendous the struggle. But who can resist Mighty Hayter when accompanied by Divine Justice (like Telemachus by Minerva), revealing herself beautiful, splendid and severe here on earth, and not among the clouds.

Now that I am enjoying the fruits of this victory I can think, without inflaming my brain, about what we must do to relieve somewhat the weight that is suffocating me. Here is £100 for the ivory; tomorrow I will send you the same again for Pizzetta and what you will. The expenditure on the cursèd works flows like a river: I've already given £200 for copper and £135 for dry pine, as well as £100 to the workmen, Westmacott etc.[40] So that if I don't sell some more wood, in a fortnight's time I shan't have a penny left of all the receipts from the oak! ...

No lady of the old or new world has ever been a better judge of the rare, the beautiful and the fine than Mme de Pompadour. My Maria van Diemen was presented to her by the Prince de Conti and bought at her sale by the Duc de Bouillon. The most beautiful lacquer which the Queen[41] had was formerly hers, but for ages now all these treasures have been either moving about or lost sight of in Vienna, Russia and Poland; I doubt whether genuine pieces will ever come to light, but I can assure you that Mme de Pompadour was the finest connoisseur of *objets d'art* and curiosities in the whole of Europe ...

Friday 20 October

I have no hope of a Bassano[42] that has been Pizzettared etc, nor have I the slightest faith in the Pizzettatiser. When I walked round Phillips'[43] with him last year I became convinced that he was either no connoisseur or pretended to be ignorant to see if I was … Since harmonious objects please your eye, the picture probably has some merit, but Pizzetta is not sufficiently capable or honest to be trusted; his face isn't orthodox, and what he says about the genuineness of a picture doesn't count with me: Besides, I detest pictures transferred from wood to canvas and made "the most brilliant of the Master". Too little of the oak payment remains for me to throw away £24 without examining the picture three, four and five times …

You did well to write as you have to Crépin;[44] for him to come here would be madness—if you haven't stated this sufficiently strongly, write again. If it were Grenet,[45] it would be better, but Crépin! Ah, my God, I would not find £10 for the best picture he is capable of painting.

… This very day Mr Still is going to receive what is possible of my Fonthill rents—I doubt if it will be half. Everything is lowered, everything falls except my domestic expenses, which are much the same as last year …

Saturday 11 November

… I haven't failed to perceive and feel the horror of the loss of Foxhall; I'm sure Rottier was counting on him. Spring, summer and autumn passed without the necessary steps being taken in time to flee from the gulph of ruin. Now we're on its verge. Rottier should have perceived in the face and in the looks of the poor deceased the great likelihood of his journey to the everlasting Vale of Adorna; this event has grieved but not surprised me. The object now of my chief terrors is Mr White's own health—I'll do all I can to reassure him and console him.

… I think the enclosed merits attention. Despite our misery it is necessary, according to the Gospel and Bonaparte, to *live,* and in order to live it's necessary to eat and drink—so, my dear Gregory, do me the favour of tasting or getting tasted the Madeira, the Shiraz[46] and the Constantia;[47] we just have time, since the sale isn't till Thursday. I don't well recollect ever having tried Shiraz, but I have an idea that it's like Florentine wine. Kloet is the well-known name for good Constantia; we'll see. The real, superior Constantia is great balm for an afflicted heart (?)—so is Madeira, so is Shiraz, so are all good things, not forgetting the *pâtés de foix gras* so sweetly recommended by the amiable *Pig*-ault.[48] I don't know the auctioneer Burrel or what kind of rogue he is (like Phillips or Squibb?), but to allow the wine to be tried three days in advance is a good sign. He lives a good way off, at No 3 Throgmorton Street, but the wines are to be sold "on the premises, No 102 Gloucester Place, Portman Square."

Monday 13 November

I'm almost stunned, not only by the deplorable impotence of Rottier but by the horrible din of the winds last night. I didn't sleep a half-hour in succession—I thought I heard sobs and lamentations, cannon shots, bomb explosions, and all the delights of the battles of Borodino or Waterloo. Really, this habitation is deathly in the stormy season—this morning I'm more yellow, rent and wretched than a dry leaf.

Coxone hasn't brought me enough balm in the way of money from timber to do me much good but, still, he has brought me £45 in torn and dirty notes, which are already in the putrid hands of putrid Leonard—oh what a face he has! Like the Matron, it seems that he has drunk "mortal bad Rum".

Now I must ask you the menu of the banquet to which Rottier is going to invite me—what does he propose? What does he counsel? To abandon the London house or Fonthill Abbey? To remain here or go away for years? Something drastic is inevitable, and I want to know what it is—as I've already said, I prefer to prostrate myself respectfully on the ground than to remain suspended by the hair from the highest balcony of my proud towers. At the moment I'm doing all I can; to reduce my establishment is more difficult than to reduce the works, which are going to stop the moment the tower is finished. Serjeant, Westmacott and all the masons are departing; I'm only keeping the Obern as carpenters and the two Beckets as woodcutters. I hope this news will give joy and hope to Rottier …

As I write the air is full of leaves, branches and peacocks fleeing from the force of the wind, which threatens to reduce everything to dust. I've never experienced it more terrific or raging—I can't understand how the Tower and the trees are resisting—it seems miraculous. If you have the same weather in London, not a chimney will remain in position. Tomorrow, my dear Gregory, I expect to receive your remarks on the wines. I reel and suffer as if I was on board the Packet. I wouldn't have taken my pen in hand for any other object in the world save that of assuring you how much I am, at every hour of my life, your affectionate and true-hearted friend ...

Tuesday 14 November[49]

All three Madeiras are good without being remarkable: the Culloden seems to me tolerably true; Hall's has fragrance and taste; the Madras was already dry when it arrived, but it's not bad. The Constantia is so-so—certainly much inferior to mine. The Shiraz is strange stuff—I thought this wine was dry and red, but perhaps it's found in various colours; this is light, malmsey-like and delicate—whether or not it's genuine, I won't guarantee. I don't want to give sublime prices for any of these wines. I don't know how many dozen there are in a Lot—let's take one lot of Culloden, one of Hall's and one of Shiraz—that's enough. If on trying it yourself you think it worth buying more, operate accordingly.

Saturday 18 November

Only the final stage of ruin will make me abandon the great Ebony Cabinet.[50] It's better to pay tribute[51] than to allow to go far from the Abbey a piece of furniture so august and colossal—an object calculated to bestow, of its own accord, splendour on any apartment, however imperial. I'm convinced of this without having seen it. This being so, it'll cost me something to deprive this place for ever of an object of this rank, planned for the Abbey, decorated for the Abbey, conceived with all Hume's genius and ardour.[52]

Purgatory isn't the same as Hell: for three years, maybe, the building may have to rest or slumber in the darkness, but who knows if at the end of that period its awakening may not be lively and splendid—neither in good matters nor bad can anyone calculate.

Monday. The above was written but not sent off—it was delayed because fresh tributes are not of the order of my sad days. I'd say nothing if the

Marquis of Buckingham had paid handsomely and promptly—I have Hume's interest too much at heart to embarrass such a negotiation.[53] But to sell it on credit to the miserable, wrinkled Shepherd would be painful, cruelly painful to me. Since, my dear Gregory, you are close to the oracle, the mouth of truth, Mr White in short, who ought to know the state of affairs, you can judge for me in this matter a hundred times better than I ...

Wednesday 22 November

... The porcelain collections of Sudley, Lascelles and Essex surpass a hundred times everything here. Sainte-Foix [54] had some outstanding china, but almost every thing of this quality, acquired from the famous cabinets of Gaignat, Conti, Pompadour and Mazarin, went to Vienna, Russia and Poland. But patience! In matters of true taste and real art there is sufficient consolation for the man who plans cabinets like my ebony and Florentine ones and towers like that which already stands perfect and without blemish before my eyes. You can't imagine the perfection and grace, the slenderness and beauty of this tower.[55] They are now putting into position the fifth angle of its battlements. And what battlements! Grace, elegance, and just proportions! Enchanting! Marvellous! A work like this will bring to his knees, even in mud and ice, anyone who can recognize and feel the triumph of architecture (in this style at least).

Here is Coxone passing by, all illumined by the sun and followed by his most trusted satellites and by a procession of purchasers of timber as fat and shining as himself. From a thousand directions can be heard the noise of chopping; here carts pass; there the men run to load them. "What sweet music ! What joyful harmony! ..."

1816

Wednesday 11 September

Already it's late—for more than half an hour the Turk, Pendu, Spotty and Caroline have been jumping up to make me go out; this impatience, gilded by a few rays of passable sunshine, consoles me ...

The Abbé is occupied with Bouchardon's triumph[56] and at the same time singing a sort of *Stabat*

> *Quis est Homo qui non fleret*
> *Patrem nostrum si vederet*
> *In suo Cubiculo*[57]

(for our poor Father Bestorum has been stinking there for the last three days).

You are divine with ... your imperturbable philosophy—you are a strange but very amiable being. How are Plummer's going on? A certain whisper of almost general bankruptcy runs through all the newspapers— "damned awkward if it should be true!" (Old Q.)[58]

Sunday 22 September

... The Father no longer has diarrhoea but *dolorea*—enough to fill one with pity and horror. He suffers from his eyes worse than usual, and it looks to me as if he is rapidly going blind. Here is the dwarf's reasoning on the said Father:

Beckford.	Comment se porte le Père?
Pierrot.	Que sçais-je, moi—assez mal, je crois.
Beckford.	J'ai peur qu'il ne devient aveugle.
Pierrot.	Et si il devient aveugle, est ce qu'il reviendra ici?
Beckford.	Non.
Pierrot.	Et bien donc, laissez-le devenir aveugle.

This dwarfish logic is worth six foot in stature!

Tomorrow (according to the papers) they are going to hang a poor honest sodomite. I should like to know what kind of deity they fancy they are placating with these shocking human sacrifices. In a numerous list of thieves, assassins, housebreakers, violators ("a man for a rape") etc, he was the only one to be sent to the gallows; all the others were "respited during pleasure". The danger must be great indeed and everyone in the country must be running the risk of having his arse exposed to fire and slaughter.

Thursday 3 October[59]

… Until I see the money from the oak down on the table and can touch it, I fear expenses—as I would the society of the deceased boy-fancier, the Newgate-bird. You may or may not know that this man of honour, before his end, put in the hands of his Anglican confessor, the most Reverend Mister Cotton, Grand-Almoner of Newgate, a tremendous list of the gentlemen affiliated or associated with him! He wanted to inform the populace *viva voce*, but Father Cotton said with evangelical sweetness, "My dear Sir, better not, better not." The stupid, hypocritical, bloodthirsty vermin! The day will come when their infamous vices and stinking hypocrisies will be revealed to the eyes of all Europe … The Portuguese did well to set sail in time before the annals of Father Cotton.

Monday 25 November[60]

… I am very occupied in making myself a kind of farm in the very interior of the sacred Enclosure; I will have grain in abundance and admirable pastures. I begin to see that one can ally the useful with all that is most singular and piquant in garden landscape. My gardener is excellent: we eat grapes worthy of Fontainebleau and cardoons like those at the Palais-Royal; despite the rottenness of our odious climate they bring me sound and flavoured truffles. All very fine!—but not to me since your departure. A hundred times a day the Abbé and I exclaim "Ah, if the Marquis was here, how he would love these perspectives through the woods, terminated by the now truly imposing mass of the Abbey with all its towers, and its clouds of pheasants which whizz up like rockets."

1. *The Public Ledger*, 15 July 1816.
2. *Ibid*, 24 September 1816
3. *Objets d'art.*
4. On Staffa Island. It was discovered and first described by Sir Joseph Banks after his 1772 visit, in T. Pennant's *Tour in Scotland*, 1774, of which B. had a copy with his notes.
5. In Beckford's youth several composers wrote operas called *Armida*, but the most likely is Sacchini's, which was called *Armida* when produced at Milan, *Rinaldo* in London, and *Rinaldo ed Armida* in Paris.
6. Moreau (1772–1822), famous French singer, who made his debut in 1796.
7. Cess-pool.
8. Sixth day of sale of James Edwards' library (see p.150, note 34). Beckford is furious that others are buying lots he cannot afford.
9. Lot 826, duodecimo *Preces Piae*, an early sixteenth century MS on vellum with twelve miniatures and borders of flowers, insects and shells, bound in red morocco. Forster paid £37 16s. for it and resold it to Beckford for £42.
10. The world-famous Bedford Missal (Lot 880), which the Marquess of Blandford wrested from the plebeian North.
11. This reflects contemporary prejudice against the new capitalist class of millers and dealers who were revolutionising the milling and baking trades. The mediæval Assize of Bread was abolished in London in 1815.
12. Lot 829, Italian sixteenth-century duodecimo illuminated MS on vellum, bought by John North, of East Acton, for £120.
13. The Turk was a youth on the Fonthill staff and his name was Ali-dru, an Albanian name (the Albanians were Moslems ruled by the Turks, and so were thought of as Turks). *Diamond* was a dog.
14. Lots 822 and 824, fine ninth and tenth-century MSS on vellum.
15. Colonel Orde.
16. A love song composed about 1750, addressed to a young Irish surgeon of that name.
17. Hieronymus of Braunschweig wrote medical books in German printed around 1500 and translated into English in 1525.

18. The Eastern Transept.

19. *The Episode of the Story of Motassem*, the Father of Vathek, must have been intended as an appendage to *Vathek*, but it is not in *H.P.*; it must have been the *Episode* which Beckford destroyed as being too wild. Motassem was an historic personage, a Caliph, son of Haroun-al-Raschid, whereas Beckford's other *Episodes* were about imaginary Princes.

20. Beckford is giving Mazarin's pronunciation as recorded in some memoir. Although Waterloo was fought on Sunday the 18th, the result did not appear in the English papers until Thursday the 22nd (Beckford's next letter comments on it).

21. It was widely believed, following a statement by Diodorus Siculus, that the Druids burned their human sacrifices alive in wicker cages. This is illustrated in Sammes' *Britannia Antiqua Illustrata*, 1676.

22. Referring to Douglas' Bonapartism.

23. Napoleon.

24. Paul Storr (1771–1844), the greatest goldsmith of the period, who at this date executed orders received by Rundell & Bridge the Royal goldsmiths; *Fiume* is Edmund Rundell.

25. Jean Berain the Elder (1640–1711), French painter, who designed scenery and costume for Court fêtes and ballets. *H.P.S.* gives the very rare *Ornemens: desseins de cheminées et autres sujets*, two imperial folio volumes, Paris, undated (*c.*1711), 150 plates covering an enormous range of designs.

26. He was replacing Milne, who had been with Beckford at least since 1807.

27. From Stourton (Stourhead).

28. A character in the *Arabian Nights* ("The Third Calendar").

29. Pieter Neeffs the Elder (1578–1661), Flemish painter from Antwerp, who specialised in church interiors, as did also his son of the same name. Beckford's *Inventory* has several of them.

30. This horse died aged 30. A tittup is a spring or prance; Beckford elsewhere comments on his spirits.

31. H.C. Jennings (see p.149, note 9). Lugt's *Repertoire des Ventes* gives no sale at this period. Beckford was still after his Brueghel in his sale of 22–23 July 1818, but the only copy of the sale catalogue recorded by Lugt has subsequently been destroyed.

32. *Histoire de Zinan et des Trois Montagnes*, an Arabian tale in French, in MS in *H.P.*

33. Clarke was after all allowed to reproduce it at p.214 of his *Repertorium Bibliographicum*, where the precious MS and miniature are fully described.

34. A Portuguese friend of Beckford's who features in the *Journal* (see there under *Street Arriaga*). The name would be pronounced with great élan that sounded like spitting.

35. *i.e.* "holy in a Meichisedekian way". The Latin phrase occurs several times in the Roman Service books, e.g. in the Mass of Our Lord Jesus Christ the Eternal High Priest, and in the Epistle of the Mass for the Election of a Pope. But Beckford may also be recalling the use of the strange and enigmatic figure of Melchisedek in Black Magic. The 19th-century French magicians Vintras and the Abbé Boullan celebrated a "White Mass of the Glory of Melchisedek".

36. The burning of Jews and heretics frequently took place in the Rossio (Lisbon's principal square), where the Inquisition had a palace, and in the neighbouring Church of S. Domingos.

37. John Towneley's collection was auctioned in May 1816 for £1,400; it looks as if it had been sent *en bloc* on approval to Beckford's house in Harley Street.

38. A timber-merchant who owed Beckford £1,000 for his oak had just gone bankrupt and disappeared. But Hayter (Coxone), Clerk of the Works at Fonthill, pursued him all over Wiltshire and managed to extract the money.

39. By Sacchini.

40. Probably Henry Westmacott (1784–1861), who had already worked as a mason at Kensington Palace, on Nelson's tomb in St Paul's, at Somerset House and Greenwich Palace. But it might have been his elder brother, Sir Richard Westmacott (1775–1856), who sometimes executed designs by James Wyatt and who is best known for his bronze Achilles in Hyde Park. Sir Richard executed a statue at Fonthill in 1799, and from 1815 to 1823 was working on statues at Ashridge. He was a big man with massive features, large nose and side whiskers, a John Bull type, which accords well with Beckford's nickname *Rhinoceros* (of course, his brother Henry may have been of similar physique and appearance).

41. *i.e.* the French Queen—presumably Marie Antoinette. For Van Diemen, see p.153, note 90.

42. Jacopo da Ponte (1510–92), called "Il Bassano" after his birth place, where he resided all his life except for some years in Venice. Painted portraits and Biblical scenes.

43. The auctioneer who conducted the 1823 Fonthill sale. For Pizzetta, the picture restorer and dealer, see p.149, note 8.

44. Louis Philippe Crépin (1772–1851), marine painter taught by Robert and by Joseph Vernet.

45. Presumably Anthelme François Lagrenée (1774–1832), historical, genre, portrait and miniature painter, later patronised by Czar Alexander I. There was also an historical painter, J.B. Lagrenée, who exhibited at the 1814 Paris Salon, but about whom nothing seems to be known.

46. Persian white wine.

47. S. African wine. *Kloet* is for *Cloete*, a South African family of wine-merchants for many generations.

48. G.C.A. Pigault-Lebrun (1753–1885), playwright and very prolific novelist with a great vogue for twenty-five years until about 1816. Having lost his money, he entered the Customs service at Calais in 1806, and also acted as a wine-merchant.

49. Second letter.

50. The great Ebony Cabinet, often referred to, is the one that Rogers professed to admire, which had *vases at the foot* (13 October 1817); in other words, it is *Phillips,* Day 28, 1045, an ebony cabinet of architectural form, eight feet high, whose doors were carved with two scenes from Roman history, viz the example of Mutius Scaevola and Q. Curtius leaping into the gulf; it had friezes of Bacchanalians and allegorical subjects, and three carved ebony columns; it was "supported by six vases". In the next letter B. claims credit for conceiving it. Its interior was later crammed with some of the choicest cups of agate and sardonyx, etc, in the Abbey, e.g. Cellini's Cornaro vase and the Rubens vase. It stood in the Cabinet Room.

51. *i.e.* pay for it.

52. Robert Hume, carver, gilder and cabinet-maker; he had a succession of addresses, but later was for many years at 65 Berners Street. He was buying for Beckford at important art sales from at least 1811, and seems to have taken all Beckford's business from Foxhall (*The Blockhead*), who had just died.

53. Richard Temple N.B.C. Grenville (1776–1839) of Stowe, first Duke of Buckingham (the only Duke created by George IV), extravagant collector of books and works of art. It looks as if Beckford, unable to pay without embarrassment for the ebony cabinet which he had ordered from Hume, was willing for Buckingham to take it off his hands provided he paid cash for it, but Buckingham was notorious for his debts, and Douglas wasn't ready to pay cash for it either.

54. *Sudley* is George Pitt, second Baron Rivers of Sudley (Sudeley) Castle, Gloucestershire, brother of Beckford's cousin by marriage, Louisa. Lascelles is the second Earl of Harewood. The fifth Earl of Essex was patron of Turner and Wilkie. The Sainte-Foix sale may be that of 22–24 April 1782 in Paris.

55. B. must have been writing this in the Chintz Boudoir in the morning, looking east across to the south-east octagonal tower of the Eastern Transept. This turret and its companion were the most ornate and delicately carved of all the Abbey towers.

56. Edme Bouchardon (1698–1762), sculptor, architect and engraver; Sculptor-in-Ordinary to Louis XV. For his ebony Jewel Cabinet, see *Phillips,* Day 29, 1195.

57. A parody of the *Stabat Mater* which is sung at the Mass of the Seven Sorrows of Our Lady on Friday in Passion Week:

> *Quis est homo qui non fleret*
> *Matrem Christi si vederet*
> *In tanto supplicio?*

58. *Old Q.* was the notorious fourth Duke of Queensberry (1724–1810).

59. For this whole letter and the same execution referred to above, see pp.155–6.

60. To Douglas in French.

1817

IMPELLED by the depression of 1815–16, Beckford sold some of his books at Sotheby's on the 6th–8th May, and then, from the 8th–12th, the contents of his London house, No 6 Upper Harley Street, the lease of which he could no longer afford. He remained without a London house for the rest of his Fonthill days. Most of the treasures were sent up from the Abbey and included pictures attributed to Giorgione, Ghirlandaio, Holbein, Rubens, Brueghel, Metzu and Turner, besides the three pictures he mentions below—Salvator Rosa's *Job*, Lodovico Carracci's *Sibyl* and West's *Abraham and Isaac*. The Queen, Prince Regent and Princesses came to view the contents the evening before the sale, so there would have been some things worth seeing. But it was a bad time to sell anything and at least the last three pictures were bought in. On the last day of the sale Dou's *Poulterer's Shop*, which Beckford had bought in Paris in 1814, was sent up by coach from Fonthill to Carlton House so that the Regent could make an offer (he had perhaps mentioned the subject at the private view).

It is extraordinary that this shortage of money did not prevent Beckford undertaking major constructional work at Fonthill—the fitting out of the interior of the Eastern Transept as living-rooms. It will be remembered that the erection of the shell of this arm or wing of the Abbey had only been begun in 1812. It remained unfinished, partly because Beckford lost heart after Wyatt's death, and partly because he was so busy making good Wyatt's botches in other parts of the building job upon which he was still engaged.

But the year is most notable for the visit of Samuel Rogers—the only distinguished man who came to the Abbey to see Beckford whilst he was in residence. He had achieved instantaneous fame as a poet by his publication in 1792 of *The Pleasures of Memory,* which reached fifteen editions in fourteen years. The poem which Rogers himself preferred, and which some regard as superior, is *Human Life,* on which Beckford so sarcastically commented at its appearance in February 1819.[3] Beckford mentions[4] the review of it by the *Champion* for 28th February 1819, which contained the following masterly and justified criticism: "the chastity of these <verses> is of rather too negative a character, and the beauty rather too much of the Dolly Cowslip description for our taste ... We do not deny the smoothness and the sweetness, as it is called, of the versification ... It is polished and graceful and gentleman-like, and has the air of having kept good company, as it <is> called; but who does not know, that what is called good company, can, sometimes, be very insipid ... The common touch of these smooth nothing-writers is oblivion; from which fashion can, only for a day, preserve them." This was the poet who was offered the Laureateship on Wordsworth's death!

Rogers was chiefly noted for his venomous tongue, for which he was universally feared, and for his churchyard-like countenance, which Byron described in some terrible lines:

> "Mouth which marks the envious scorner,
> With a scorpion at the corner,
>
>   .   .   .   .
>
> Eyes of lead-like hue and gummy,
> Carcase picked up from some mummy,
> Bowels—but they were soon forgotten
> (Save the liver, and that's rotten),
> Skin all sallow, flesh all sodden"[5]

It was for these two characteristics that Beckford dubbed him "the Yellow Poet", an idea which he borrowed from the description of Rogers in Lady Caroline Lamb's satirical novel *Glenarvon*.[6]

Wednesday 29 January[7]

My very dear Friend ... everything here is at 'Stormy'—the political barometer makes one tremble, and the state of crisis which you have expected for years is approaching. Yesterday I was next to the Speaker and his little stool opposite H.H. the Regent. He looked distressed rather than frightened; a most melancholy expression gave to his features and face an air lugubrious and fatal and yet noble and even majestic in the midst of his melancholy. His voice was low, almost sepulchral, yet it did not tremble. Hardly had he left the Parliamentary chamber than he was very nearly assassinated: they threw themselves on him like famished wolves as he was entering his coach; further on, its windows were shattered by stones (some even say bullets). He took refuge in St James' Palace and from there at Carlton House, but shewed courage and resolution. Consternation, agitation, fears, doubts, the hopes of some, the panicky terror of others are at their height—it is almost impossible for them not to come to blows before long—I doubt whether it can be put off much longer ...

I am very truly, my dear D., your most affectionate and most devoted friend Guillaume de Beckford ...

Wednesday 2 April

All my happiness at the moment is centred on Boletus and the harvest which he is reaping—a copious and rich one. We are selling the whole of Polier's *Natural History*,[8] valued in the list sent by Scholl[9] at 8,000 and some hundred scudi—I would not refuse shillings ... Boletus is calling me—farewell.

Thursday 3 April

I haven't a moment to write; I would only write to you, my dear Gregory, and to no one else; it costs me something to tear myself away from the books, which are all my care. We have much labour—comparing, examining, deciding whether this or that copy is preferable, etc, etc.

Notwithstanding the fineness of the weather, I can hardly find a moment to go out. If happiness consists in employment, I have certainly found it! Advise Mr Bestifownes not to lose sight of the impossibility of my existing on £2,000 <quarterly> ...

Sunday 27 April

What days of melancholy and nothingness these Anglican Sundays are for me! No Vincent,[10] no Coxone, no Mass and today no Figley. The poor dear creature is getting better under the auspices of the old man; she was devoured by vermin, and yesterday I thought I would become mad with grief and fear on her account.

I have this moment returned from a visit to the Cabinet room,[11] the first I have made since your departure. All is well except that the pictures badly need a good dusting with a silk handkerchief—an article which the Ghoul does not possess and which it is essential to send him. Seeing the beautiful agates there, it costs me something to refuse that rogue Davison's, mounted in gold ...

I am ill and unhappy; the weather doubtless contributes to this—always the same baleful and wintry colour in the clouds, the same sterility, a sickly yellow on the young leaves, a wind which puts a stop even to one's thoughts, a frost which lays waste all vegetation; and in the midst of all this the larches display the loveliest resplendent green, and the beastly cuckoo sings his song.

Thursday 1 May

... I am reminded of the virtuoso who, seeing the crucifix held up to him at the moment of death, said "That Christ is not too well made."[12] Similarly Brandoin,[13] at the moment of deepest anguish (?) and real terror of the devil, was so dominated by his gluttony that he said "Ah, Father, what good omelettes you have!" It is the same with me. Half dead with grief, anxiety and melancholy, I think of little agate vases and little eggshell ... tazza!

What do you want me to tell you about the Turk? He is an excellent boy, attentive, respectful and obedient, but he says little and comes and goes in a flash ...

Sunday 4 May[14]

Still some fever (if not a great deal); no doubt the weather has much to do with it, but it is not the weather only. The lack of the consolations of friendship and society, the utter black monotony of my life acts on my system in my present state of weakness in such a fatal manner that if there is no change soon I will not answer for my existence. I have not sent for Fowler or any other chattering doctor in the neighbourhood to come and see that I am dying of melancholy. Those who love me and desire my preservation ought to see what can be done for me, and act energetically.

I do not think Mrs Hervey is insincere.[15] She says what she thinks, at the top of her voice. If she gave you such a reception it is because she wants to be on good terms with you. What she has said in the past (if she really did say all that) and what she says now are two different things ... Mrs Hervey is excellent company, and if you wish to frequent her I shall not prevent you.

... Remembering that I shall have to travel, I do not know whether it would be wise to refuse, let us say, 400 for the Salvator and 600 for the *Sibyl*.[16] *Think for me.* In this moment of weariness (between the most horrible attacks of nervous fever) I am not very well able to *think for myself* ...

Poor Abbé, I am sorry that he is so pillulating (and with very good reason, I am sure); a singular kind of egoist of the lower order, this Abbé! ...

Wednesday 7 May

This morning I received by the divine and convenient subscription coach the learned Christie's fine catalogue—a poor affair, my dear Gregory, a very poor affair. The Salvator and the *Sibyl* announced in the most vulgar style;

the little Edward III coffer "with the arms of Great Britain". They are not the arms of Great Britain! They did not speak of "Great Britain" in those days. Anachronisms, vulgarity etc; it stinks. But what does all this matter? Nothing. But it is disgusting for me to read these platitudes worthy of the Philippine Islands[17] in a catalogue where my name is so conspicuous ...

There has been a total change in the wind since yesterday. A slight frost followed by straw-coloured sunshine and the most penetrating, keen and unhealthy wind imaginable. In consequence, torments and irritation etc are coming back galore. This has not prevented me from oaking and confirming the order to convert the lake into meadows[18] ...

"Job and his Friends"[19]—What a style! "Admit Chevalier Job and friends to view the pictures. Christie." Where are the "Three capital leaved screens scarcely to be matched"? "Lot 109, 2 doz. and 4 soup plates;" if I remember, these are attractive and in good taste and should not go for nothing. Farewell ...

Friday 9 May[20]

The cursèd post not yet having arrived, I am writing in darkness. A thousand times a day I chafe at being chained down here without having had the pleasure of seeing what so many unworthy idiots have seen—the spectacle of the house[21] arranged by you ... My dear Gregory, how difficult and how long is the path of true taste! One should thank heaven when one arrives in port (if one ever does)—I have not done so in the *Bouchardon!*[22] The more I see it, the less I admire it. I shall never be content with its false magnificence ...

Saturday <10 May>, 5.30 p.m.

I have hardly a moment, my dear Gregory, to assure you that considering the state of the silver market I do not think the basin sold too badly. I hope the candlesticks will be a success with the Earl of Shrewsbury (not Shoesbury),[23] a gentleman of absolute perfection in the eyes of Sir Isaac Heard.

... My ideas about the Prince have always been like those which His Royal Highness has inspired in you. I do not wonder at your enthusiasm. I only wish that some occasion would offer of frequenting and admiring him—it will be his mistake if it does not happen; he ought to send for you to Carlton House.

The Jewish Apelles,[24] with the malice natural to him, will take care to do all he can to prevent a triumphant sale of my pictures, so that I expect to receive news that both the Salvator and the Ludovico <Carracci> remain in the house. They are too fine to be sacrificed. I must stop or the letter will not go. A thousand, and again a thousand embraces, dearest Gregory ...

Sunday 11 May, midday

... I have said nothing about the Royal visits, about the Queen and the Princesses.[25] As a matter of fact, they matter no more to me than I to them. The occasion of these visits is melancholy, not happy—mortifying, not honourable. They are bitter fruits of the Upas[26] or Tree of Death, so well cultivated for me in the past by those gardeners Wildman and Williams[27] and in the present by two good botanists White and Zineke ... Assuredly, my dear Gregory, I am not more insensible than anyone of good taste to the fine accomplishments and most gracious manners of the Prince; but I doubt whether these visits will do the least solid good to the sale. I do not think that the presence of such a saint is worth the wax one has burned in his honour ...

<Monday 12 May>

... From what quarter did the offer of 550 *guineas* for the *Sibyl* come? Do you think that one might get 600 pounds? My most fervent wish being to go to the Continent for years, what does the *Sibyl* matter to me? It is too big for travelling. I think the same about the *Job* now. Consequently I regret more than ever the Prince's lack of taste. 5,000 guineas would have been worthy of us both; in this way he would have acquired two pure and noble pictures for nothing, the Gerard Dou[29] alone being worth more than that.

This is my ultimatum: 3,000 guineas—the pounds for me, the shillings for the *Mater non dolorosa* Christie. The sum must be paid cash down, either in bank notes, or by a draft at sight convertible into bank notes. This is how I was paid for the Claudes and the Gaspar Poussins, and this is how I shall be paid for the Gerard Dou; otherwise it must come back. On this understanding, upon this *sacred trust*, I send it, and I conjure you not to part with it in any other fashion. Neither etiquette nor excuses of any kind matter. And no bargaining: either the cash in hand or the picture at Fonthill. You can see that true taste does not count; I can live without the Gerard Dou, but I swear to you that 3,000 guineas is nothing for the first Flemish painting in the world (according to the gospel of sots, fools and false connoisseurs).

Here then is the Gerard Dou and a little Charter confirming to Christie once and for all the royal Edict or Decree communicated to you. I don't want the picture to be left at Carlton House to become an object of exhibition: Christie must take it there and back; let them see it, take it and pay for it, or see it and send it back. Before you give the picture or the enclosed Charter to Christie, I beg you, my dear Gregory, to establish the clearest understanding on this point. I bleed after plucking this plume and allowing such a capital object to leave this Vale of Adorna. The balm for my wound will be conformity to my decree; otherwise I shall go mad with grief and rage ...

Friday 16 May

Nothing is more contrary to my will, so clearly expressed to Christie, than the retention of the Gerard Dou at Carlton House to be examined and re-examined, recomended or advised against by all the traffickers of that royal den. I believe and trust that this would not have come to pass were it not for your gout. In the midst of a thousand other anxieties this counts for a million. This way of carrying on suits Mr Christie but not me; he wants his shillings if he can get them, I am less interested in my pounds than in obedience to my decrees. In your hands the picture would have been safe. I bitterly repent having sent it and only did so in accordance with your advice and reflections ... This is the last piece of business which Mr Christie will ever do for me or with me.

I shall now answer your questions about the Ebony Cabinet, the West, and the Buhl table at Squibb's ... I do not wish to let the West go for a penny under £200 ... My reason for not sacrificing the West for £100 is its grandeur and feeling of grandeur and feeling of movement (?) ...[30] Every grand historical picture of any merit is important, and some merit the *Abraham* certainly has: there is something grandiose in its landscape, and the whole is pervaded with a certain solemnity and harmony. £200, yes, but anything less would be a shame ...

Friday <23 May>

... I thought that today was the day for Bestifowning, but on re-examining (always in spite of myself) this animal's letters, I find that it is tomorrow (Saturday morning) I am to see this place profaned by his odious and abhorrent presence ...

The wallpapers they despatched certainly do not please me—they are so very scarlet; but what has most decided me against having them is the smell and difficulty involved in putting them nicely in place without sending for a paper-hanger—there is no one in Salisbury capable of doing the job. No, I have decided to use moreen; eighty yards will be enough, there being no necessity to moreen behind the great cabinet and the two Buhl.

5 o'clock. I have returned from my walk, and fortunately for the repose of my stomach I see no other letter on the harpsichord except your own ...

Saturday <24 May>, 3 o'clock

The Beast was vomited forth last night by the Subscription Coach, and I am expecting him any moment. He is only coming here to see how he can "touch" me for money and seize it, no matter how. He will find a powder-barrel, a smell of fire, and he will be blown up ...

Here is the Beast. I have begun a tolerably good wail, and I do not think that he will dare to mention the debts to Lincoln's Inn. *He* shows every disposition to remain here as long as I want, but not I to have him stay; I hope that he will go on Tuesday. He must stay until Monday to see the Great Dolt. He has already made me an offer of £4,000 a year if I will go to the Continent and leave a certain faithful Mr John Plummer to Member-ify in my place.[31] We shall soon have an opportunity, my dear Gregory, to talk this important matter over between ourselves. I have not yet decided.

I am back from the Lancaster Room. He looked at everything in a covetous way, devoured everything with his eyes, and would like to see it all sold to pay himself and his firm. *But, But*—I looked at him with Vathek eyes,[32] and I believe that, with his tail between his legs, he will not come here again looking for payment. He didn't penetrate to the Cabinet room and never will, at least under my auspices[33] ...

Sunday 25 May

Presence of Bestifownes and absence of your news, north-east wind and rain that is half snow—that's the news from here, and you can imagine how I feel in consequence. Every moment new details of debts (Wyatt), of demands (Dr Lambert)[34] and of schemes, open or masked, to get my last farthing ... If I remain with my eyes always fixed on the corpse of my affairs it is impossible that I should not become equally putrid. And with poor Bestifownes' face like a miserable anatomist's, it is impossible not to feel the redoubled horror of the operation. Not every surgeon knows how to mitigate the sharpness of his knife and they have not all as light a touch as your Almeida.

5.15 p.m. ... Bestifownes, seeing that on certain things he was making no progress with me (except towards his total bankruptcy) has wisely decided to be thoroughly obedient to the laws of this place and the etiquette of this Court. He is a real gourmand, a regular Thondertentronck, and at last full of zeal for increasing my miserable income by at least £1,000. Tomorrow will be a full day Grand Dolting, Tuesday he goes, Wednesday I console myself for his departure and Thursday at five in the morning I hope to set out for Staines ... Bestifownes has seen Board of Works, the small octagon and the ivory cabinet in my tower, but was too much occupied with the genealogical table to notice the existence of any other objects whatever. Of the existence of Buhl armoires, the great Leonardo da Vinci cabinet etc, I hope he remains in the most total darkness.

Don't forget that the Sieur d'Assoucy needs a lute as well as a page, so a pianoforte is inevitable[36] ...

Monday 26 May

... When I am in Brunet's bagnio I will put aside the prophet Jeremiah and with fearless front follow the example of the *Conservador da nacao Brittanica*,[37] who gave the Abbade[38] all the champagne he wanted and shouted "f—". This, together with a little attention to the oriental "treasure" given to me by Mafoma,[39] a little of the opera (I am desperately anxious to see Mozart's *Don Giovanni*) and a good deal of hackney coach, will help me to pass the time at least in a different way, if not with much delight and triumph.

... Be good enough, my dear Gregory, to ask Morlands if they have received and paid the last demand from Perregaux, Laffitte & Co.,[40] viz £24 and some shillings for Chardin's quarterly.[41] At the same time tell them that when the account for the MacCarthy sale arrives, 10,000 livres more or less, they are to pay at once.[42] Thank heaven it is not more. The Beast, for a nice consideration, has doubtless "ceded" many items to Payne[43] and others, after having nominally "bought" them for me[44] ...

Tuesday <27 May>

Bestifownes is as alive as gunpowder, ardent, persevering (not to say obstinate) and indefatigable. This morning before six he was already at work examining the very *suspicious* accounts of the Farmer[45] and the Great Dolt. After breakfast, at Coxone's hour, dear Bestifownes wanted to touch the Ark, even if only with the tip of his finger; but he was not able. Suddenly a flash of lightning, as red as the blood of the martyrs, streaked forth and threw him to the ground. He asked a thousand pardons and promised never again to approach within a hundred steps of the sacred threshold; he received absolution and a tolerably mild and gracious farewell ...

Thursday 26 June

The heat has made me bleed at the nose like a fountain. You cannot imagine how suffocating my cursèd tower is ... This morning the mist was universal and refreshing. Never has the vegetation here looked more beautiful; new foliage and flowers, in place of the infamous stinking shreds of last spring, are making the air balsamic. The Brown Parlour is a floral triumph with ranunculi as in Portugal and roses such as are certainly not to be found in my neighbourhood in London

Poor Barzabà is not at all well—everything is like the Valley of Jehoshaphat[46] for him most of the time. But every now and then certain lightning flashes (which do not come from the clouds) illuminate the passage, and in less than the beating of a heart, all becomes sunny and blue[47] ...

I have practically destroyed my nails in a vain effort to open the Bouchardon cabinet. Curse it! This is the last of these gimcrackeries that I shall ever endure ...

Friday 27 June[48]

Sweet, refreshing, blessed rain that makes me a little less diabolical than usual but makes that milksop Vernon despair on account of his strawberries and the Deputy-Dolt Drysdale on account of his hay. I have profited by the lack of sun to bathe with the Turk, who is what Naïs would give all his bronzes to be.[49]

The little bluish marble columns look divine in the Tower—good proportions, fine, delicate and Gothic like Westminster Abbey; one large and two small windows are finished with their bases and capitals; that is all. Here things move at a tortoise pace—patience! ... The ivory cabinet is enchanting with its splendid hinges etc.[50] It is a pity to let the mosaic table, bought years ago from Fogg, remain buried. I must have it made capable of bearing the ivory cabinet—black with few or no bronzes; it will do well in my room ... What I most want is to see again my dear Gregory, whose sincerest friend I always am. Farewell.

If the fir sells, I want Jaunay[51] to send me

4 doz. La Tour Medoc

2 doz. of the fine Sillery Champagne

and 6 Lunel; [52]

as soon as they arrive, I will pay.

Saturday <28 June>, 5.30 p.m.

I return to my old extravagance and send this note by Subscription Coach, vomiting up as quickly as possible dear Francillon's ridiculous little notes—a fine proposition indeed! He also has a Correggio, the *Christ in the Garden*, a copy of copies, at £500 (that's all!); Albani's *Toilet of Venus* for £400.[53] Fine prices—let him get them if he can, but not from me …

Tuesday 1 July [54]

… The day before yesterday, when I was at Stourton, Mr Dwarf's pony threw him to the ground; he fell on his face, his nose and lips were horribly torn and bled. Yesterday he was in bed all day; he is up today, but I have not yet seen him. I only marvel that this is the first accident that has befallen this cavalier! …

Thursday 3 July

… The more I reflect on the Correggio, the less I trust in the hope of its authenticity. The grace of the artist can be communicated in copies, but a certain colouring that he had, a celestial light, cannot be copied. Last year's picture had that light, but I doubt whether this will. No one is more indulgent towards pictures than Signor Pizzetta—too much, much too much. But I am not. If I was, the wall decorations of the Abbey would have been copious but detestable—a Pizzettarish refuge for daubs …

Saturday 5 JULY!!

I spend my sorrowful existence under an *umbrella*, walking, walking, walking, with Vincent, whose face is worthy of a San Benito,[54] Caroline with her tail between her legs, and Diamond dripping water. From time to time a pheasant appears, thin, very thin, and glossy, so glossy, like the flowing cassock of a beastly Jesuit. Everything in view is deathly lugubrious: only when one looks behind does one see a little something that consoles. One no longer sees the lovely verd-antique—the most squalid yellow-green covers the whole countryside, revealing lost crops and foreshadowing famine and pestilence.

... I fully sympathise with the poor Abbé's sad state. I do not know what to counsel him. Fonthill, without Poney[55] at his command or the adored bitch Maria etc, will not be an earthly paradise for him, especially with his holy terror of me. Besides his 'humour' (his cursèd bile), there is his fear of dying (which is only too likely to occur if between his bouts of low company and tippling he does not show more decision and virility—self-indulgence is destroying him body and soul).

... A little more patience, yes my dear Gregory, have patience rather than expose yourself to an attack of gout on the road to the delights of Hackwood Park,[56] where you will hear the cries of souls not in Purgatory but in Hell, into which the damnable Ordures will be cast *in saecula saeculorum* without any hope of grace or salvation (as we confess, now that there no longer exists a beast like White to swindle us).[58] A fine company will be found at Bolton Hall—Lady Dorchester[59] almost in her dotage, a bit of a beast, practically insane, and a termagant too; and several boys and girls of the same set. Let's pass a sponge over all this and turn our backs, shrugging up our shoulders. I spit and am done with them, oh, eh! ...

Monday 18 August (a deluge and icy wind!)

Horrible weather—the earth greenish-yellow and the sky leaden-coloured; you can imagine the effect of such a combination. Yesterday was more tolerable, and I travelled down here fast and without incident.

I find the new room magnificent—the traversing-wall well made, solid and perfectly symmetrical, the proportion of the doors and of the great

niche noble and spacious.[60] The Oriel rooms are getting on wonderfully—
they are light and comfortable; the chimney of the anteroom is in place
etc. Coxone has not lost time in spending, but in selling timber—yes; it
needed my touch to hurry things on. I raged—if they do not pay, *rasibus*
all timber-merchants.

The Bernini cabinet[61] in the Nunneries will not do without a picture, so
see if the genuine Brueghel can be had. In that case the Mantegna[62] will
hang above the cabinet ... The zeal and animation of the workmen both
in the quarry and on the building are beyond praise. Rhinoceros is on
scaffolding carving the ornaments of the Oriel divinely, incomparably ...

Friday 22 August, 5 p.m.

The MacCarthy books are already in St Michael's Gallery, above the
cinquefoils. Compared to many copies here, they are miserable, inferior
in size and beauty etc (I speak of the duplicates, of which there are
several) ...

I have shown that fine drawing to the Calf,[63] who collapsed with hee-
hees; he recognised it at the first glance. The dwarf, more solemn than a
Calvinist Minister, turns his back, gives a little shrug and looks out of
the window, keeping the most stony silence; the dwarfish law, like that of
Mafoma, does not tolerate the representation of living beings ... I have an
idyll from the Shepherd amazingly full of sentiment. The little Count has
been ill with measles but is better; the Shepherd was on thorns and the
Shepherdess absolutely devoured by sensibility! Rome (on the 26th July)
was a sublime solitude, etc. Randall has entered to tell me that hardly
a moment is left for me to assure you, dearest Gregory, of my sincere
affection. Farewell.

<Sunday> 24 August[64]

... Franchi is almost always crippled with gout and rheumatism, suffering
like a damned soul but finding in the midst of his sufferings that there is
nothing like England. I doubt whether anglomania has ever been carried

further. The most amiable of Abbés ... does not share Franchi's fine feelings to the same extent, but he dreads the two or three daily Masses which await him if he returns to Meaux, his beloved homeland. As for me, I have a great longing for devotions, I breathe only the wish to wallow on the threshold of the Saint's chapel at Padua. The miserable Fonthill sanctuary does not satisfy me. In vain they tell me, and think, that it is fine—I don't believe a word of it. On your return from Rome you will find it all just as I say—pitiable. But at any rate you will find here (and wherever I am) a heart devoted to you. Be thoroughly persuaded, my dear Douglas, that in you and all that is dearest to you are concentrated all the affections of my being.

Wednesday 27 August

... Boletus, with the help of the books recently arrived [65] has done prodigies in St Michael's Gallery. The cabinets contain some six hundred volumes of the greatest beauty, interest and curiosity. All the other bookcases have been cleaned and polished up. A fine spectacle, to make the Dotard tremble if he could see them. The rarest and finest travel books (those of the fifteenth and sixteenth centuries) are now in full view and available: in short, 'tis a marvel. An intelligent connoisseur could not take a step in this gallery without exclaiming "Indeed, there is nothing like this in the world!"

... The Bucellas is nothing much; all that charlatan Pigault's wines are mediocre, to give them no worse a name; they may satisfy the drunks of Carlton House but not me. Randall gets all the names mixed up ...

Sunday 31 August, 5 p.m.

I am very sad and very anxious, my dear Gregory, full of the terror of this eternally recurring gout of yours, and none too well myself. Every instant the weather seems to get worse—one moment cold, the next hot, always damp and nearly always windy; never any sun, never anything that reminds one of Summer—neither butterflies nor mushrooms. It is not surprising that I have a single desire—to leave here. I cannot depict the grief caused me by your trembling lines, all feverish and painful, of the day before yesterday. The extreme and continuous dampness makes me ill and torments my nerves, making me believe that I am threatened with half-a-dozen illnesses at least.

They have this moment brought me the onyx and, what I value much more, your yesterday's note, announcing some sort of improvement. My dear Gregory, be persuaded that you have in me a friend who interests himself with all his heart in every step of yours in this sad life. Nothing that you suffer or enjoy is a matter of indifference to me.

Coxone was a little less cadaverous yesterday; today, being Fool's Day, I know nothing. Tomorrow the buyers of my timber are coming to pay for a small part of their last purchase, mounting up to nearly £200—enough to finance the building operations to the end of the week. Nevertheless, I'm ruined, I'm ruined …

Tuesday 2 September

Yesterday, my dear Gregory, although it rained less than usual, was a damnable day for me:

1. No news of you.
2. Partridges few and bad.
3. One of the infamous Bouffetaut's kidney omelettes, which made Caroline and her Uncle hiccup.[65]
4. A sermon by the Great Dolt on debts and building operations, enough to make one weep.
5. 'Balls' from Coxone for the hundredth time, with his false promises and talk of timber bankruptcies.

You can imagine my state of mind. At once I stopped some of the building, giving up the idea of the Great Entrance etc for the time being. I see no remedy for such an accumulation of torments but to shut up shop here and withdraw to the Arcadia of Rome or Pisa.

Saturday 13 September

... The large window is tremendous[66]—the quantity of pine, elm, ash, plane etc which has been used in the various sections from top to bottom and side to side ete, etc is immense and could have been sold for £800. You can't imagine the torments we've undergone to prevent the whole Basilica and the great roof from falling on the heads of the workmen, and over channels here for smoke, channels there for water and dirt, dry closets and water closets. 'Twas a mad and diabolic undertaking. What has been done passes belief and seems more than anything else to be the result of some pact and wager with Satan. Never has so much brick been used except at Babylon—not a little, I swear to you ...

Monday 15 September

I do not know what kind of key can be invented to prevent Dido[68] seeing the full horror of the extravagances here, so diametrically opposed to the economy he commends. Poor Dido! My remorse already avenges him. On arriving here, the first object that will leap to his eye will be the great window; the second, the Oriel in all its glory, carved and decorated by the hand of Rhinoceros with self-evident fineness and mastery. On entering he will find new rooms and new corridors. Looking up, he will perceive beams and joists. A smell of fresh paint and varnish etc will prove to his intelligent and suspicious nose that the crime of *lèse-économie* has been committed. In short, one cannot conceal the half of what has been done, not even the quarter; and to have done all this is a horror ...

Tuesday 16 September

The effect of the two doors with so little space between them and the niche is so poor, so ill-proportioned and feeble that I am going to change them. The niche will become a big door corresponding with the one opposite and the side doors will disappear. The communication between dining room and drawing room will become worthier and the perspective nobler. As soon as your cataplasms permit you to return <here>, order young Hume to come down and ascertain what changes will be necessary in consequence of this plan, a plan upon which I have finally decided after a great deal of reflection. Meanwhile, the general appearance of the first apartment (at least as regards the niche or alcove) will be the same. The ebony cabinet will go where planned. Instead of doors I shall be obliged to have four sideboards, two where you know and two in front of them. The *Sibyl* in this case can be put elsewhere.

... On Friday they are paying for twenty tons of plane at £2 15 a ton—a very poor price, but one has to give way or stop everything. Coxone is better and is climbing up and down the building like a young goat. Bouffetaut has spoken to Randall of retiring to Paris in the near future, being unable to exist here with the reduction of his wages.

Monday 22 September[70]

... But Bath does not please me. After the great spectacle of the Abbey it seems to me incredibly dingy and wretched; and the infamous old men and youths carried in chairs and mechanical carriages round the smoking baths horrify me—a horror not softened by the tender glances of certain old women clad in flounces supremely *à la mode*, who come and go eternally in this paradise of idlers and corpses.

... Nephew is with me and will not leave me an instant in order to go out out with the horses or wherever it may be. He does not seem tired and smiles and licks, the dear little animal ...

Tuesday 23 September[71]

I am this moment returned from Corsham[72] and have found your yesterday's letter on the table ... The evening was delightful, with a celestial calm in the deep green valleys where sheep and cattle cast their placid shadows on the grass beside the river. I won't speak of the daubs in general at Corsham, but a portrait by Van dyke, the Elsheimer and two sketches by Tintoretto merit the highest praise;[73] the porcelain isn't much; the little coffers are fine, rich and harmonious in the highest degree—

their shagreen background pleases me immensely; except for two or three intaglios (one black with green flowers), there is nothing at Corsham to make one envious. The house is spacious and tolerably commodious and indeed fine—with taste (if they had it) it could become really noble; but doors the colour of quick-lime instead of oak, and certain walls eighteen inches thick and no more are pitiful.

... It is five o'clock and the post goes—so I must stop, embracing you in the most affectionate manner.

Tuesday 7 October[74]

... I am this instant returned from the Cathedral, which I like more than ever; it is as finished as St Michael's Gallery, and I am confirmed in my belief that nowhere else is there any Gothic of form less barbarous or colour more suave; the placid majesty of that beautiful nave enchants and consoles me—great repose, great purity ...

Wednesday 8 October

... The progress with the building works has not been marvellous—far from it. The excuses offered are two-fold. Firstly, a lack of stone, the good stuff being finished, and time having been lost in looking for a new quarry. Secondly, a decrease of workmen etc. This last excuse is so good that I shall embrace it and diminish them still further. The Entrance will not be ready this year; we shall enter in winding fashion and not directly, that's all.[75] But I am slightly consoled with the hope of receiving in a few days a decent sum (at least £200) for the timber now being sold ...

Monday <13 October>

... The ride yesterday was divine and did me much good. Frome is ridiculously and abhorrently Presbyterian; its church is deathly pompous—

truly a house of the Devil—not a church at all but a *house*, of a kind of Queen Anne-ish cinquecento. Out of it came forth a hundred thousand fanatics in straight rows like cypresses and with cemetery-ish faces—the cursèd tripe and viscera of this infamous church (a corpse well calculated to produce maggots). The morning was mournful, like the scene, but the evening was soft, radiant and *turkish*;[76] we ate like wolves and drank like Canons of the only true Faith.

Rogers[78] in person is being announced ... Rogers, after three hours' indigestion of pines, pheasants, sheep, Pendu, woods, thickets, cliffs, slopes etc outside, and of lacquer cabinets, onyx, Leonardo da Vinci, the great Octagon (not the small one, for I did not show him Board of Works etc), has returned to Maiden Bradley to the arms of the siren Duchess of Somerset.[79] He said the finest and most poetic things in the world to me on his own behalf and on that of Byron, to whom he is going to scribble down in verse everything he has just swallowed. He says he has already put into verse much of my prose etc, etc ... Rogers thinks the big ebony cabinet better than anything else, especially the talisman vases at the foot—these he declares to be truly sublime ...

Wednesday 15 October[80]

... My present intention is to abandon the Great Entrance, cover the passage with pine and red baize, and finish the first room as best as I can, at least sufficiently to house the ebony cabinet etc and make the room available; this is very important because as things are at present I have nowhere to accommmodate a living soul. For the dead there is room enough—the Octagon and the Great Hall with the statue of the Commendatore[81] on high etc suits them to perfection. So says the Abbé, and so thinks that wretched gaper Bestorum, shivering with cold. Oh what a climate! Oh what a fatal abode! Never doubt the fervour of my prayers to the Saint to make you capable of following me to Italy ... Here it smokes, there the wind blows in (and so would the rain if it were raining); every tower is a conveyor[82] of rheumatism. God and the Saint, if they have pity on me, will not leave me without intimations in dreams and visions to make me emigrate. There are moments when the Abbé becomes animated at the idea of seeing Rome, Florence and Arcadia. But they are only moments. They pass. He turns again to the coddelation of Bermondsey and the delights of his adorable bitch Fan ...

Friday 17 October

... My resolution to abandon the theatre of so much useless labour is fortified every hour that I stay here, experiencing blasts of wind, blasts of cold, blasts of rheum and financial blasts in this uninhabitable place—uninhabitable for more than six months of the year at least. Notwithstanding all that Coxone has sworn, the Ghoul etc assures me that the part of the building next to the Board of Works is still in the greatest danger and threatens to fall when least expected. To prevent the extravasation of the smoke, we have been forced to remove all the wainscoting of the Board of Works in order to re-wall, re-groove and mortar afresh, an operation which has lasted three days and made me die of cold and of the most detestable smell.

How glad I shall be to get away at the end of March ... It is not worth discussing the Father accompanying me; deaf, roguish and gaping, he would be a drag on me and on all my surroundings; a fellow hardly presentable, in Arcadia he would be a disgrace and not an object of admiration ...

Travelling is a less expensive occupation than arranging and furnishing palatial halls forty foot square; the quantity of pine already consumed in the new building, in joists, roofs, partitions, stairs, etc, etc exceeds 360 tons. More than £600 worth of dry oak and pine have been bought or exchanged (which comes to the same thing). Mortaring for fifteen days has been vastly expensive; eight sawyers are sawing wood morning and evening to supply the carpenters and plasterers, and they are hardly enough. They promise that all now in hand will be finished in seven or eight days ...

Saturday 18 October

I shall probably hear some news of Arcadia tomorrow, for the Yellow One knows more of what is passing than us or the Ordures—and he has a viper's tongue. He gave us vaguely to understand that the Shepherd has a passion for Naples—"his *heart* is at Naples." Perhaps some other shepherdess than his own occupies his tender moments[83] ... Since the climate pleases the Marchioness, who trembles at the thought of Scotland's inclemency, and the Neapolitan shepherdesses please the Shepherd, it is not so likely to be a hurried return ...

Monday 20 October

It cost something to set alight the Yellow One, but at last he is on fire. He says that the Abbey is pure Milan as far as the Octagon is concerned and like Vallombrosa outside, with its immense mantle of pines and its immense forests—a holy hermitage. What indeed does he not say! He is in a delirium. He reads, he sees, he swears that *Kalilah* is better than anything of Byron's, that *Barkiarokh*—etc;[84] in short, it would not be decent or possible for me to write down the half of what he says and will without doubt go away saying.

Amongst various bibliomaniac anecdotes, he told me that the hateful Woodburn bought in Paris a wonderful manuscript about Charles V which he <Rogers> wanted to possess but found too dear. Woodburn paid eighty louis for it and sold it the other day to Thomas Grenville for 350.[86] Watch that knave Woodburn, murder him ... do all you can in any way you can (oh ruin! oh Dido!)—anything to hinder that infamous brute Woodburn in his triumphal progress ... The Abbé is calling me to see the *vera effigies*[87] of today's Saint—the incomparable Yellow One. Farewell, dearest Gregory.

<Tuesday 21 October>

... The Yellow One is still here—it seems to cost him something to leave me. Here too is that highly ridiculous, highly impertinent Britton, the Cathedral fellow[88] ...

5.30 p.m. The Yellow One has left in a state of enchantment which I cannot convey and which only poetic souls, by the special grace of God, can understand. Nothing, I think, was lacking on my part—poetry, prose,

music and good food—to fan so divine a flame. I have no doubt that
he will pay you a visit in Harley Street to relieve his feelings … It seems
that everyone becomes amiable after being here. Britton does not displease
me.

Wednesday 22 October

No one in the world has remained so content, so honoured and so
enthusiastic as poor Britton. His Britannia,[89] with the Abbé as Neptune,
has sailed through the Abbey with zephyrs and cupids playing round. I
have not yet seen him because I was in the woods at my daily occupation,
but they all tell me that he is the most agreeable, lively, continentalish and
knowing (?) little personage in the world. Even the Abbé was carried up
into the seventh heaven, like St Paul, and finds that the Abbey begins to
be rose-coloured, and that in a short time here we will have a good life in
every respect.

I will leave the Yellow One the sweet employment of telling you all he
thinks of what he has seen and heard here: doubtless he will knock at your
door in Harley St in a few days. I have not shewn him the great plate or
the inside of the ebony cabinet or a thousand other things. He was too
engulphed in *Kalilah* and *Barkiarokh* etc to bestow a glance or a thought
on other objects.

Very interesting, your story of the most amiable Mary Clarke,[90] but I
am not lucky enough to understand it to the extent it merits … Like a
good soldier, whatever the upshot may be, the General will know how to
conduct himself with prudence and brio. Reply, *s'il vous plait,* it's worth the
trouble—divine, divine! … The authority of a soldier-cook is not sufficient
to make me believe in such barrack-room marvels. Would it were so, but
I'm doubtful. With my continual grief at your cursèd infernal gout, always
returning, always renewing, I have little time for agreeable ideas; certainly
in other days a picture of happiness like that of these interesting amours
would have had its effect on me …

Britton has shewn me some really delightful drawings by a certain
Mackenzie, of a delicacy, a richness of colour, a harmony, a —: in short,
they are celestial … [92]

Thursday 23 October

I hope the oak door is getting on. You can judge of the work that is being done by the following: "since last Friday a hundred tons of wood have been used and 80,000 laths!" Since the beginning of this new and total ruin 482 tons have disappeared, besides the dry pine and the oak which has been bought or exchanged.

Tuesday 28 October, 5 o'clock

Do not expect the window to be so marvellous. The impossibility of my cutting enough timber to meet the heavy expenses which engulf me has compelled me to suspend some of this work. Instead of glass we are using oiled paper; instead of gilding, an ordinary colour simply to prevent rusting. We are suspending everything possible. It was time; Coxone's illness arose from certain debts which he was afraid to declare. So a draft for £150 and another today for £100 has been my lot—a lot I swear by the Saint I no longer mean to tolerate. The rooms will remain unsightly and unfinished until my return from the Continent. Of course the doors must have locks and hinges etc but no ornamental gilding yet—for the time being wooden handles and knobs will do ...

The fine Neeffs with the procession of the Sacrament by Teniers was once mine but vomited up many years ago;[93] at least, I suspect it is the same picture, but probably some worthy Pizzettator has given it a grace it did not have in my time! I will not touch it ...

My last letter to the Marchioness remains unanswered, and a melancholy screed it was, positively crying out for news; since the 31st August last I have not had a line from them. How much all this baffles and afflicts me, you can judge. A thousand suspicions, a thousand fears torment me. The viperisms of the Yellow Poet (between ourselves a wicked tongue) keep running in my head. I know not what to fear or to think. It is easy enough to accuse the post more than it deserves; it is not the post, it is *they* who are to blame for this cruel neglect and forgetfulness of all they owe me ...

If the Yellow One does not knock at your door, so much the better for you. He is a second-rate poet and a first-rate viper. His knowledge is *utterly limited*: Greek he has none; his Latin is slight, very slight; as for his French it is worse than slight, worse than non-existent, being sufficient only for the making of mistakes. I repent indeed of having thrown so many pearls before a castrated *bore* ...

Sunday 2 November

... The Jewish Apelles is f—d and has been kicked out of his fine nest in Pall Mall. Over ten days ago the papers announced that "an occurrence[94] has taken place which prevents the exhibition of Mr W's picture *Death on the Pale Horse*, etc." There is no longer any mention of "Mr West's picture" etc, although he was always Commander-in-Chief of the front page of the newspapers etc[95] ...

Salisbury 4 o'clock. I have ridden through rain—tepid rain and suffocating heat. You cannot imagine the charm of Salisbury on such a day—the soft murmur of streams, the perfume of peat, rural silence, not a soul outside— neither man nor cat. In short, I galloped energetically and I am now much better, as always after violent exercise.

Tuesday 4 November

Since my return from Salisbury (in darkness), almost total obscurity night and day—a damp, biting and dense fog without intermission. So much for the outer world. Within my soul, sadness, fears and uncertainties over your cruel state which makes me ill and has prevented me from sleeping. I awoke two or three times with violent starts and dreams full of ridiculous horrors ...

The proof you give me, my dear Gregory of your true affection by writing to me when you are really not in a condition to write at all, has done me an immense deal of good. There is no feebleness in what you have written; everything is clear and everything breathes zeal and energy on my behalf. Be assured that I would rather be beside you, bereft of everything, halt and maimed, in preference to the most splendid position in the universe amidst the gayest company. Not a moment of my life passes without your being present before my eyes; the Abbé can bear witness how much I occupy myself over you. If my presence can console you I will come: behold me ready. The age I have spent without seeing you here, where everything interests and diverts you, has been leaden to me …

I have this moment returned from a tremendous marking of the finest oaks I have; it will be a sufficiently grave loss, but what can I do? I am writing this by candle-light.

Tenebrae factae sunt in terram Fonthillianam.[96]

All is black, all is drear, save the hope I have in the bottom of my heart of seeing you shortly, better than you have been for a long time. My dear Gregory, it is impossible to be more your friend than I am. I embrace you closely …

Thursday 6 November

Fog so that one cannot see three paces ahead, a June-like heat, and a smell of rotten leaves impossibly odious and unhealthy. It is true, my dear Gregory, that I can get about quickly and nimbly, but my maladies accompany me! I cannot leave them at home. I suffer from certain threats of weakness in the bladder, which is neither agreeable nor of good augury for the future; I think a kind of what in English is called 'stricture'. And then my teeth and gums torment me continually. I am fully aware to whom I am writing all this, and I do so with the modesty and respect owed by such an inferior invalid to a personage of such sublime eminence (alas) of this sort as Your Goutiness. Your Goutiness will pardon me, but I am not too well, not half as well as it pleases you to believe, and indeed you persist in believing …

5 o'clock … The temperature here is tolerably agreeable thanks to the braziers, which are kept well supplied without any ridiculous waste, so that one can be in the Galleries and even in the Octagon as in summertime. They are now making a chimney for use with the braziers—splendid, and safe and useful too … The Pregnac[97] is capital, pure and cordial. I want three dozen sent here. How and when to pay for it I don't know! …

Caroline is more beautiful and lively than ever, and she adores her Uncle more than ever; she catches hares and rabbits every day. This morning I had a near view of the white pheasant; 'twas almost as large as a peacock and red round the head like Rhinoceros. Farewell, dear Gregory.

Saturday 8 November

… I consider her loss pretty great, a sad and dire accident calculated to fill with tears the eyes of almost all the people, a fatal event pregnant with confusion, and, in time, with civil war.[98]

Last night a tremendous breach was opened in the great embankment.[99] The water ran away rapidly, as you can imagine. Now we must have meadows there or incur ruinous expense; the meadows would cost less and be more useful, but it would be cruel to destroy the noble features of Fonthill, especially after the sublime effect produced by the tree-felling and by the particular shape I have given to the shore on a grand scale …

5 o'clock. The Syndic[100] writes to me from Sir Isaac Heard that the poor Princess will be buried at Windsor with little enough ceremony. If they all die in this way, and the illegitimacy of the son of Lady Augusta by the Duke of Sussex continues in force,[101] the Crown will go to the House of Würtemberg, so that it would not be impossible for a descendant of Mlle Wurtemberg and Jérôme Bonaparte to come into the picture.[102] As I have already written, the event is in every respect mournful and from all points of view disastrous. God grant that it be not fatal! …

Tuesday 11 November

I have returned from an oak-marking walk, as usual towards half-past four, and there is hardly a moment left to answer your yesterday's letter. My dear Gregory, I desire nothing in the world so earnestly as to see you here, your sufferings diminished and with a heightened capacity for enjoying what is unfolded at every step in the Galleries. The frame of the Brueghel is ornate and venerable;[103] the Brueghel itself still seems to me so very, very much out of pictorial harmony that I do not bewail the necessity of placing it in the half-light; the balance is enchanting. There in the little Lancaster

Gallery, between the Mantegna and the Van Balen,[104] it must remain the whole time it remains with me ...

I am sending you twenty-five guineas, viz, two pieces of five, two French ones, etc. Alidru, seeing these beautiful *medals* of five pass, thinks they are divine. "A pity to send them away," says he. But I consoled him by telling him that I still had a few more trifles of this sort ... Randall is waiting, I haven't a moment more ...

Tuesday 18 November

... The Abbé goes tomorrow with a provision of flour—and of humours etc fomented and cultivated by pies, truffles, Pregnac, Bordeaux etc. Never have I seen such eating and drinking. He swallows *everything,* he tastes everything, he mixes everything up inside himself: milk, then a collation, then *lonchon,*[105] then dinner, then supper accompanied by a vast deal of rum. If he does not die, if he does not become a fountain of maladies, he must have the special favour not of the Supreme Pontiff but of the Eternal Father Himself.

For God's sake remember that I am now left alone with the Father and his mechanics, paying at least two or three guineas a day. Every little drawing costs two guineas! ...

Absolutely ridiculous, all this fanaticism and hypocrisy about mourning;[106] it's business, business and nothing more—neither politics nor sentiment enter in. The odious race, insular and insolent.

Thursday 20 November

... The Mantegna in the Lancaster Gallery remains where it was and will continue to. The poor Brueghel has gone to the Nunneries, and the fine one, with its rich and excellent frame, looks as noble and harmonious as can be.[107] In this new position it seems to me to gain all that one longed to find in it, and which hitherto was lacking. Now everything is enchanting— composition, colours, effects of light and shade; and for me at least none of the finish is lost—fish, shells, little animals, all can be seen in a half-light, calm and suave.

I no longer mean to furnish the rooms (either the large one or the Oriel) before my departure for the Continent ... It is time, my dear Gregory, that I should breathe again without the everlasting confusion, expenses, false hopes, deceptions, botchings, extravagances, follies etc of the highly disgusting Coxone. Not for a day, not for an hour can one count on him. Today he arranges this and that, tomorrow he is ill, now with a cold, now with an inflamed oyster on the foot,[108] always pissed, always stinking. God deliver me from him! He costs three times what he is worth, and, to tell the truth, he is worth nothing. He does everything through deputies, nothing himself. It is days and weeks since he measured a single tree—five shillings a day are paid to the Hindon man charged with this business. The embankment fares as best it can; everything languishes and wastes under his stinking auspices ...

Monday 24 November
(3 o'clock—so dark that one can hardly see one's nose.)

... Your Beethovenish letter[109] did not please me at all, but words do not matter to me when I consider the integrity of your affection for me. Yesterday there was a big post. Besides Chardin's letter I received one from Mme Bezerra,[110] dated 6th September, very interesting and full of the most fervid friendship for me; I will send it shortly with my reply, which will be long ... and which it is important for Bezerra to receive. So Bezerra is at the top, with all the departments under his dominion—Secretary of State and Chancellor of the Exchequer with all the honours and prerogatives which Ponte di M— had.[111] If a voice from the clouds had announced this to the Marquis of Marialva in the days at Ramalhão,[112] he would have thought that Satan was mocking him ... It is a pity that Palmela is leaving for his abhorred destiny[113] without having seen the Abbey, which is so much spoken about in Rio now that the Bezerrian oracle is the object of everybody's devotion. The Cowpat's letter is tolerably interesting and amusing, and of a truly estimable simplicity, goodness and sincerity. Poor Bezerra in the midst of so much glory, so much solid power. I doubt whether he is still alive—who knows whether the first news from this other world will not announce his death.[114]

... Farewell, dear Gregory, I will always be a Haydn and Sacchini to you, notwithstanding that you may be just a little bit of a Beethoven to me.

1. See p.135.
2. See p.200.
3. See p.251.
4. See p.258.
5. Quoted in Medwin's *Shelley*, 1847, Vol. II, pp.189–190
6. *Glenarvon*, 1816, Vol. I, p. 248. That Beckford took the name from here is shown by the reference in *H.P.S.* (books), III. 1434.
7. From London to Douglas in French. Becklord was attending the opening of Parliament by the Prince Regent. The mob stoned his coach and were said to have fired on him with air-guns.
8. Colonel A.L.H. de Polier (1741–95), a Swiss who served under Warren Hastings, with Indian Princes and under the Mongol Emperor; he became fabulously wealthy and made a wonderful collection of Oriental paintings and manuscripts. In Beckford's sale at Sotheby's, Lots 208–20 are "original Chinese and Hindu drawings <of Natural History> from the Collections of Van Braam, Bradshaw & Polier", but the sources of the individual lots are not assigned; all but one of these lots were bought by White (presumably Beckford's lawyer). Beckford paid the widow Polier £800 for her paintings in 1796.
9. Dr. Abraham Frederic Schöll (*c.*1757–1835) of Vevey, Lausanne and Geneva, physician to Gibbon and Beckford; acted as intermediary in some of Beckford's purchases in Switzerland, e.g. of Gibbon's Library, which he looked after for Beckford.
10. The gardener Vincent, who is usually mentioned in connection with the planting of trees and shrubs. He was gardening for B. in 1796 and outlived him in his service. His nickname *Pendu* is presumably derived from the French, in which case it indicates either that he was as thin as a lath, or that he had a hang-dog expression; the latter seems most likely, since on July 5th B. mentions his "face worthy of a San Benito".
11. In the Eastern Transept; see p.19.
12. Vasari tells this story of Verocchio, but it has also been told of Alonso Cano.

13.   Charles Brandoin (1733–1807), also known as Michel Vincent Brandouin, Swiss artist born at Vevey; exhibited at the Royal Academy, 1770–2.

14.   First letter.

15.   Hervey of Aiton, prolific novelist. Born Elizabeth Marsh, she was Beckford's half-sister; in 1774 she married Colonel William Thomas Hervey of the Guards, natural son of the Hon. Thomas Hervey, a grandson of the first Earl of Bristol.

16.   For this and later references to the forthcoming sale of Beckford's pictures at Christie's, see p.179. In the next letter, Beckford criticises the wording of the sale catalogue.

17.   See p.261.

18.   *i.e.* to drain Bitham Lake because the water threatened to break its banks—an event which happened later.

19.   The title given by Christie to the Salvator Rosa.

20.   First letter.

21.   No. 6 Upper Harley Street, where the sale was to take place.

22.   Bouchardon's cabinet (see p.177, note 56), which Beckford was now selling.

23.   The fifteenth Earl of Shrewsbury, which Franchi misspelt Shoesbury.

24.   West.

25.   They and the Prince Regent attended the private view on the evening of Thursday the 8th, before the sale.

26.   Javanese tree whose sap was used as arrow-poison, and believed to be fatal to whatever came beneath its branches.

27.   Captain Nicholas Williams (died about 1802) was a steward and general factotum at Fonthill, and acted for Beckford in Paris during his peace negotiations in 1797.

28.   Second letter.

29.   *The Poulterer's Shop*, bought in Paris in November 1814 and now in the National Gallery.

30.   West's *Abraham and Isaac* (*Phillips,* Day 25, Lot 199). B. began to alter this last phrase, but did not complete his alteration, which therefore is not translatable as it stands. So I have ignored his alteration.

31.   *i.e.* to occupy Beckford's Parliamentary seat of Hindon in his stead; this he did, in return for substantial monetary concessions, from 1820 to 1826. John Plummer (1780–1839) was the head of the West India merchant house in Philpot Lane, which managed Beckford's sugar affairs

32.   A reference to a passage in the opening paragraph of *Vathek*: "When he was angry one of his eyes became so terrible, that no person could bear to

behold it, and the wretch upon whom it was fixed instantly fell backward, and sometimes expired." Scott took this idea for *Rob Roy.*

33. Beckford managed to keep Fownes out of the new wing (the Eastern Transept), where some of the most costly *objets d'art* were.

34. I think in respect of a local purchase of land made from him.

35. Antonio de Ameida (1761–1822), distinguished Portuguese surgeon, and author of important works on surgery; an exile in London (where he had been a medical student), 1810–14.

36. Charles Coypeau (*c.*1604–74), Sieur d'Assoucy, courtier and burlesque poet, who travelled about with a lute and pages, making enemies by his satires, and several times imprisoned for his perverted morals. Beckford possessed all his works. He is referring to his coming stay in London.

37. Judge J.X. Teles de Sousa, who featured in the *Journal* as a rather equivocal character, although he held several of the highest legal posts in Portugal.

38. The dear old nonagenarian Abbé Xavier, one of the principal characters in the *Journal.*

39. *Mafoma* is always clearly written by Beckford and seems to be equated with Mahomet, but I do not know whence this word derives. Beckford is referring to his Mahometan valet "the Turk".

40. Beckford's Paris bankers. Perregaux died in March 1808. Jacques Laffitte (1767–1844), banker to the House of Bourbon, was later Head of the Government (President of the Council).

41. Tradition runs that Chardin sheltered Beckford secretly in Paris early in 1793, at the time of Louis XVI's execution and the declaration of war against England. Payment of this substantial life-pension by somebody as mean and now straitened as Beckford lends strong support to this tradition.

42. The library of Count Justin de MacCarthy Reagh (*c.*1744–1811) sold in Paris, January to May 1817, was one of the finest ever sold, being especially rich in early printed books on vellum.

43. Thomas Payne the Younger (1752–1831), senior partner in the firm of Payne & Foss of Pall Mall, booksellers.

44. Beckford refers to a common practice of the auction ring, whereby a dealer actually purchases at auction for his client some of the volumes for which the latter gave him commissions, and then after the sale "cedes" them to other dealers in return for their having abstained from opposing purchases of other Lots for the same client. *The Beast* is Chardin.

45. Robert Drysdale, Beckford's first tutor, who had settled down to farm on the Fonthill estate.

46. A reference to Joel iii. 2, 12—an actual or figurative spot near Jerusalem where Jehovah was to judge the Gentiles, "the Valley of Decision".

47. The last paragraph of the letter of May 1st shows that this refers to the Turk.

48. First letter.

49. Naïs is a male Naiad of the fountains. The reference is to some delicate nude statue of a youth in the Fonthill galleries.

50. Probably *Phillips*, Day 15, Lot 545.

51. Francis Jaunay, who succeeded Brunet as hotelier in Leicester Square in 1819.

52. Lunel is near Montpellier in the South of France.

53. These pictures had been offered as Lots 48 and 46 on the second day of Christie's sale of the collection of the Duc d'Alberg (French ambassador at Turin) on June 13th–14th. They were bought in at 350 and 185 guineas. The dealer T. Francillon wrote the Preface of the Sale Catalogue, describing himself as the Duke's curator, etc, and as having been entrusted with their disposal. Albani's *Venus* was surrounded by the Three Graces and several cupids, and Mars was peeping from behind some trees, and it came from the Corsini Gallery. Francesco Albani (1578–1660) was a pupil of the Carracci and a friend of Guido Reni. Correggio's proper name was Antonio Allegri da Correggio (1494–1534), from the village near Mantua, in Lombardy, where he was born.

54. First letter.

55. A San Benito was the cap or robe worn by heretics condemned by the Inquisition and on their way to execution.

56. The pony that drew guests round the grounds in chaises; perhaps this had been discontinued as a measure of economy.

57. Hackwood Park, near Basingstoke, and Bolton Hall in Yorkshire were the seats of the second Lord Bolton (1782–1850), who was really an Orde, his father, Mr Thomas Orde (first Baron Bolton) having added the name Powlett when he inherited the vast estates of the sixth and last Duke of Bolton, after marrying the natural daughter of the fifth Duke. The second Lord Bolton married Maria, daughter of the first Lord Dorchester.

58. *i.e.* to swindle Beckford out of his money by persuading him that his daughter Mrs Orde and her family deserved annuities. Old White was now dead.

59. Wife of the first Lord Dorchester, our last C.-in-C. in America during the War of Independence. She was the daughter of Beckford's aunt, Elizabeth

(née Beckford), second Countess of Effingham. Her younger daughter Frances, now dead, had married the Rev. John Orde, elder brother of B.'s son-in-law.

60   By September 16th, he thought the opposite. He is describing the Cabinet Room (Great Dining Room) in the East Transept. The plan (see insert, room H) makes clear what he is discussing: the traversing-wall runs north to south, dividing this room from the next, and is flanked by the two doors. The recess (niche) was between them, in the middle of the wall. In it was to stand Hume's great Ebony Cabinet, behind crimson damask curtains.

61.   *Bath* (1841), 2nd Day, Lot 20: an ebony cabinet inlaid with agates, jaspers and lapis-lazuli, etc, by Bernini (1598–1680).

62.   Christie, Day 7, Lot 77, the *Agony in the Garden*, then attributed to Mantegna, but now in the National Gallery as G. Bellini; it once belonged to Sir Joshua Reynolds.

63.   One of the brothers Becket.

64.   To Douglas in French.

65.   From the MacCarthy sale. The Dotard is Chardin.

66.   *a far gougle gougle a Carolina*. Her "Uncle" is Beckford.

67.   This must be either the window in Becket's Passage (at the east end of the Eastern Transept) or, more probably, the window of the Cabinet Room on the south side of this transept; it served two floors, the lower of which was 22 feet high. Most of the references that follow are to building in this wing.

68.   Fownes the lawyer. This nickname was derived from the story of Dido and the building of Carthage; perhaps the idea was the ironical one that when B. (Aeneas) was forced to leave Fonthill (Carthage) by selling it, Fownes would die of sorrow and despair.

69.   He is now proposing to alter what on August 18th he had fully approved. He may or may not have carried out these alterations—this Cabinet Room finally remained as originally planned. But the incident shows how extravagant his building was.

70.   From Bath.

71.   From Bath.

72.   Corsham Court, near Bath, seat of the Methuens.

73.   At that date the Collection contained several Vandykes, two Elsheimers and three alleged Tintorettos which might be identified with those Beckford saw. The Elsheimer was either *S. Paul's Shipwreck on Malta* (since sold) or *Apollo and Coronis* (formerly called *The Death of Procris*), which was No. 42 in Wildenstein's "Artists in 17th Century Rome" 1955 Exhibition. The only

remaining Tintoretto is, according to Borenius, a copy after his *Adoration of the Shepherds* in the Escorial. Adam Elsheimer (1578–1610) was a German artist of great originality.

74.   From Winchester, whose Cathedral Beckford is describing.

75.   The Great Entrance mentioned here and on the 15th is that into the Eastern Transept from the Octagon.

76.   A reference to the presence of the Turk.

77.   Samuel Rogers (1763–1855), banker-poet (see p.180).

78.   For the room called *Board of Works*, see p.15.

79.   Douglas' sister, nicknamed the Hyaena; their seat is at Maiden Bradley.

80.   First letter.

81.   S.F. Moore's statue of Alderman Beckford delivering his patriotic reply to the King.

82.   Beckford, living in the Canal Age, wrote *canale*.

83.   This is the first mention of the terrible scandal of Douglas' infatuation for Princess Pauline Borghese, Napoleon's youngest sister (see p.217). The *Yellow One* is Rogers.

84.   Two of the *Episodes of Vathek*, since published.

85.   Samuel Woodburn (1786–1853), the principal art dealer of his day; with his three brothers he had a gallery in St Martin's Lane. His library was sold after his death and Ruskin bought some of his manuscripts.

86.   Thomas Grenville (1755–1846), statesman and book-collector; he left his library to the British Museum (one of the finest accessions it has ever received), where it forms the Grenville Library. *Clarke* 269–70 shows that this manuscript is the miniatures painted by Giulio Clovio for Philip II, representing Charles V's victories; it is the finest of the sixty-four manuscripts in the Grenville Library. In his next letter (in a paragraph not printed here) Beckford corrects his statement by saying that the manuscript was purchased "two years ago" and that it was Durand who sold it to Woodburn.

87.   The original "true effigy" was the imprint of Our Lord's face on St Veronica's veil, when he was on his way to Calvary. Here, the reference is to the Abbé's caricature of Rogers.

88.   Britton (1771–1857), antiquary and topographer, whose many finely illustrated books were most influential in spreading knowledge of Gothic architecture. Beckford is referring to a fresh series he had started in 1814, *Cathedral Antiquities of England.*

89.   Probably a pun on the pronunciation of his name.

90. The original Mary Clarke (1776–1852) had been mistress of the Duke of York, the Commander-in-Chief, so it was appropriate that a pathic batman in barracks who had a similar connection with a general should be so nicknamed. I have omitted a scabrous phrase after *merits* ...

91. All that follows comes from the second letter of the 22nd.

92. Frederick Mackenzie (*c*.1788–1854), water-colour painter and architectural draughtsman of great merit. His plates are in many famous books, e.g. Ackermann's *Oxford and Cambridge* and Pugin's *Specimens of Gothic Architecture*.

93. Lot 609 of the sale at Fonthill House (Splendens) on 22 August 1807 is Neeffs' "Inside of a Church (with figures by Tethers), from the Orleans Collection." Perhaps Beckford bought it back after all, for *Bath* (*1845*), Lot 321 is a similar picture with about fifty figures by David Teniers, a panel 17½" x 25" , signed, 1654.

94. Possibly the last fatal illness of Mrs West, who died on December 6th, and to whom her husband was devoted.

95. This picture, *Death on the Pale Horse, or the Opening of the first Five Seals*, based on Revelation vi, was exhibited at 125 Pall Mall under the Prince Regent's patronage from November 24th. It was the most ambitious and least successful of the series of scriptural subjects on a large scale which West painted. Although his prestige had already begun to decline at his death in 1820, it fetched 2,000 guineas when his pictures were sold in 1829 and is now in the Pennsylvania Academy. For B's probable earlier reference to it, see p.101, note 24.

96. A reflection of the Vulgate (Luke 23. 44 etc), which the English Bible translates "There was a darkness over all the earth until the ninth hour".

97. White *Graves* wine.

98. Refers to the death in child-birth of Princess Charlotte, next in succession to the Prince Regent.

99. The banks of Bitham Lake. Because of the likelihood of this happening, Beckford had already on May 7th agreed to its conversion into water-meadows; but he never brought himself to do it.

100. G.F. Beltz, the Herald.

101. George III's son, Augustus Frederick, Duke of Sussex, married in 1793 Lady Augusta Murray, daughter of the fourth Earl of Dunmore, who was uncle (by marriage) to the Marquess of Douglas and Beckford's deceased wife, Lady Margaret. The marriage was declared void by the Royal Marriage Act of 1772.

102. Napoleon's brother Jérôme married the daughter of the first King of Würtemberg by his first wife, a Brunswick-Wolfenbüttel princess (the King's second wife was George III's eldest daughter).

103. The letter of the 20th shows, I think, that this must be the Brueghel-Rottenhammer already described on p.149, note 6.

104. *Phillips,* Day 24, Lot 79, where it is described as a landscape by Velvet Brueghel and van Balen: a garden scene with the Virgin and Child, and infants presenting flowers; *Inventory* 1.15; *H.P.S. (1919),* Lot 4.

105. Beckford has written *Lonchone* in large, heavy letters, and I suspect is imitating the Abbé's pronunciation.

106. Mourning for Princess Charlotte.

107. See p.149, note 6.

108. Presumably a verruca.

109. Beckford's letter of the 23rd calls this same letter of Franchi's "crude, harsh and resumptuous (?) like one of Beethoven's sonatas".

110. Mrs Bezerra was the elder Miss (Betty) Sill (1753–1835) of the *Journal,* whom Bezerra was then courting and soon after married. For his services to the State she was made Viscondessa de Tagoahi in 1819. She died in Piccadilly. Her nickname "The Cowpat" (Portuguese *poya,* meaning a large flat loaf, or cow-dung) indicates that she had a large, flat, plebeian face (her brother was a Yorkshire business-man in Lisbon), but is also a pun on her name Bezerra (= a young cow).

111. *i.e.* with the same privileges etc, which the first Marquis of Ponte de Lima had when in the same posts (Finance Minister and Chancellor of the Exchequer). Mrs Bezerra's letter is in *H.P.* and makes it clear that it is Ponte de Lima who is being referred to; Beckford is perhaps using a nickname for him. Bezerra was in fact acting Prime Minister in Rio de Janeiro, holding practically every Cabinet portfolio.

112. Ramalhão was the country house near Cintra rented by Beckford in 1787. Evidently old Marialva did not approve of Bezerra, who was not a gentleman of good family and not devout.

113. Palmela had been appointed Secretary of State for Foreign Affairs and War in June, which meant sailing to Rio. But he was cosily ensconced in England as Ambassador, and was unwilling to leave. So he disobeyed orders and remained on in London until May 1820.

114. Mrs. Bezerra's next letter announced his death on November 28th—four days after Beckford wrote this.

1818

NOW there were two causes for real concern—the death of his Clerk of the Works, Hayter (Coxone), and the infatuation of his son-in-law, the Marquess of Douglas, for Napoleon's youngest sister Pauline, Princess Borghese. Douglas was now fifty and crippled with rheumatism; Pauline was thirty-eight, her health shattered by a dissipated life. But Douglas, a Whig in opposition to the Government, and self-styled claimant to the Scottish throne, was an ardent Bonapartist who had corresponded with Napoleon during the war, when it was treasonable to do so, and had visited him on Elba. It was therefore feared that there was some plot between them to further Napoleon's release or escape from St Helena, and their protracted affair caused much interest and concern.

It develops excellently in Beckford's letters. For a long time we are left in ignorance of the temptress' identity. The affair is gradually worked up from a whispering campaign of vague rumours conveyed in Rogers' honeyed tones—"his heart is at Naples".[1] The rumours are taken up by the relatives, including the family romancer, Mrs Hervey. They say that Susan, throwing up the sponge, has fled from her husband and from Rome and is about to embark at Livorno for England. At last a letter comes from Susan—all seems to have been a false alarm—she wanted only to see her sister before she died. Beckford is temporarily triumphant and pictures the gossips left with asses' ears two feet long. But three weeks later an ominous letter from Susan fills him with disquiet and alarm—"I'm afraid, I'm afraid that a horrid mystery is going to be revealed." And revealed it is in 1819, to the whole kingdom, by sneering paragraphs in the newspapers of the Tory

Government, delighted to tilt at a Whig magnifico. Meanwhile, Douglas' father, the old Duke, dies in February 1819, leaving his affairs in a mess, and a legacy of family quarrels. Well-wishers in the House of Commons earnestly desire the heir's return, already long-delayed. But overcome by the charms of Pauline, he dallies on in Rome until the summer.

Such an affair was bound to affect the delicate health of Susan. But the health of the Abbey was no less affected by the death, through over-eating, of the Clerk of the Works, Hayter. The debts he had incurred, the mistakes he had made were now to emerge and torment his master, so that Beckford lost heart, and it seems that no more building was done at the Abbey except necessary repair work.

Saturday 13 June

Up to now I've received no description of the divine packet just arrived from Paris and so well bought by Chardin, but I have the objects themselves, and they are certainly beautiful, really beautiful, and in the best taste. I know of nothing of such Cinquecento purity as this Valerio di Vicenza.[2] What inspiration! What genius! What a divine little piece of enamel, with little rubies and emeralds and a small garland, worthy to form a crown for the nymph victorious in the games and races on Calypso's isle. The jade is superior—in short, everything is good. Judging from these few items, what must the collection as a whole have been like! It does honour to Durand, and Fate was kind to you ... Enclosed you will find an order on Morland for £108. I find this lot a good bargain and the Valerio sublime ...

Wednesday 17 June

Once more there is wind and rain as in springtime, with the usual accompaniment of peacocks, smoke, birds in the chimneys, etc ... For three days I've suffered a good deal in my stomach, so I give myself as much exercise as possible with Boletus—it's lucky he's here—the necessity of mounting and climbing a hundred times a day does me some good[4] ... Today they are Memberifying at Hindon and Shaftesbury and in a hundred other putrid places throughout the realm[5] ...

5.30 p.m. The Great Dolt has returned from the Hindon ceremony, after having been carried in triumph as is customary. The dwarf is there eating and drinking etc; he is president of a table very well supplied—a wonderful dinner according to what the Squirrel tells me ...

Friday 19 June

... Coxone, Marsh, Serjeant and a bevy (?) of the best masons are at work on the Great Entrance. It was impossible to tolerate the wretched door, the cloth covered with cobwebs etc, etc. The balcony is being left without any wall visible, niches or mouldings etc; the Great Portal will be sufficient.

A new serge curtain forty feet or so, and no more, will for the time being cover the whole of the space above the balcony. At least the entrance from the Octagon will now be respectable.[6]

The Dwarf has been eating and drinking like a giant, but without falling from the table or his horse; it's incredible what strength he possesses and how he smells; now one who is beginning to have a delectable little odour is young Hume ...

Saturday 20 June

... The portrait of Edward VI (after the Holbein by Bone) cannot fail to be fine if the Phoenix will give himself the trouble.[7] This original fellow has it in his power to make the six pictures in the Gallery inestimable. An abler artist than he doesn't exist—unlike him, Lawrence[8] and the rest have not got a diploma from Mother Nature and true inspiration, with at the same time the real finish of olden times. Would to God I could afford to animate him in the way he deserves ...

Coxone and I are working, like dragons or birds of prey hunting for treasures in the enchanted mountains, to make the Great Portal worthy, absolutely worthy, of William of Wykeham, which it will be. Tomorrow Rhinoceros arrives, and today there fell from the sky another virtuoso equally important to me, the great Minery, fresh as a rose and quick as a great butterfly—Jesus, what a delivery from the detestable Bouffetaut! ...

The papers continue the most extravagant eulogies of Moore.[9] His birthday is to be celebrated in Dublin as if he were St Francis or St Rose of Viterbo.[10] I would be very glad if he were here receiving all the incense I could offer and arranging my miserable little works to make a little money to forward the arts and buy ladles, crystals and blood-red jasper ...

Monday 29 June

... Here we spend our life putting up and taking down pictures. The Berchem[11] and the Turner (a *View* which escaped the sale)[12] are in the large room, where they are not too bad. The Brueghel looked terrible and is now back where it was in the Lancaster Gallery. The de Cort[13] has replaced the Berchem and is passable above the van Huysum.[14] A great pity not to have more pictures or the money to buy them.

Not having been animated by any letters from you, I'll stop now, as always begging the Saint to protect you.

Friday 24 July

… The little Baur pictures at least are genuine and quite please me, one especially;[15] I'd like to know whether it can be separated from its infamous companion, which is of a disgusting gross obscenity such as only a German or a Swiss could tolerate … Have you ever seen a lady as shameless as the fair Pisseress? She is enough to prevent a sale in a refined and decent country[16] …

My dear Gregory, my Fiammingo is more important, as you know (I've told you so a thousand times), but for the grace and essence of the artist, his very spirit, where can you find a better example than the one which meets the eye of a true connoisseur on the vases of the Margravine?[17] I feel my poverty bitterly, and feeling it to the marrow of my bones I can't give extravagant commissions; £300 is enough and more than enough, particularly as I haven't seen them again—and one can't too often examine an *objet d'art*.

I don't know what kind of thing this Tankard attributed (doubtless falsely) to Benvenuto Cellini will turn out to be,[18] but one must remember, and I beg you to remember, that it is better to give a considerable sum for things of undoubted authenticity, than to buy at a lower price carvings that are uncertain, problematic and second-rate. You'll know what to do, I don't pretend to decide for you at this distance …

Mme de Stael's third volume stinks more than all the others with Neckerish vanity.[19] It deals principally with England—but how? In a way that shows the most impudent ignorance and the wildest adoration of the glory of France. It has obliged me to scribble a little résumé of her perfections, which, if the Devil shows it to her in the next world, will make any other flames and torments unnecessary; she is dealt with as she deserves, in a single page only, but I don't think one could want a line more. The Abbé will enjoy it, and mightily.

... The idea of staying in Rome would please me immensely if I could live there cheaply in the way I like without seeing English people, playing at being devout, churchifying, strolling about the ruins ...

At a reasonable price I might perhaps have taken the miniatures and the Baur, despite the 亦 which appears to me suspect etc.[20] They certainly are of an exquisite delicacy; the altar where Mass is being said, the *Gloria* and the Crucifixion are full of merit and at least approach Lucas van Leyden. There is however in all this a certain intolerable badness of design which is not his. When one is familiar with the genuine works of this artist, such as a pen drawing which I possess and the beautiful Lady in the Lancaster Room,[21] one sees that he knew how to draw; and when one recalls, as I do, that wonderful picture of the Last Judgment which he made for a court-room in Leyden, one can't believe him guilty of such stinking mistakes as one sees in almost all the miniatures in the little book. It is therefore unjust to ask, for the sweet and delicate (but that is all) work of God knows what illuminist, the price due to so great a painter as Lucas. I repeat that the monogram, especially the one on the crystal globe, seems doubtful to me. More doubtful still are certain angels and a Christ on the Cross a league long ...

Thursday 8 October (superb sun)

Yesterday evening I took the two pills, and this morning the little red potion,[22] and I feel *at least* as bad as I did when you last saw me—my stomach is not accustomed to the English system of draughts. During the night I slept passably and the pills worked, but at the moment (midday) I feel melancholy and downcast, with little hope of getting better. To treat me successfully it is necessary to know me, to know the extreme debility and mistrustful sensibility of my system. Anglican methods, gloominess and solemnity will kill me. I feel just as I used to feel on certain days in London, without appetite and with a slight fever, my hands hot and my nerves in a horrible state of anxiety and distress ...

I am tolerably unwell and have, so far, no great faith in the great Anatomist.[23] The Great Dolt tells me that he is not a regular doctor—just a little bit of a charlatan; what was said about Regnault is whispered about him, namely that the doctors have no wish to consult with him in any serious way. God knows; and God knows whither I'm going to be led by what I feel inside me. I doubt whether the Anatomist understands, or is capable of understanding me. I may send the Squirrel to Bath next Sunday to find out your news and pass on some p— and sh— information to Hakim Heïkes;[24] perhaps he will then know about the kind of treatment which since Ehrhart's era has been of some slight benefit to me. I neither perceive nor believe that this new regime suits me. If they irritate me, if they frighten me, I am lost.

Saturday <*10 October*>, *2.30 p.m.*

They've gone—not discontent (I hope) with what they've seen, heard and experienced. Few, however, are the hopes I have of doing great things with them, but what does it matter? A little tranquillity, a little health is all that will be conceded to me, even if Providence remains in a good humour. Sad are my prospects and sad the state of many wheels in the machine which composes me. The poor General was too rich in woes to concern himself with other riches, and Signor Roden too ignorant to understand the half of what was shewn him (including genealogy).[25] I didn't open cabinets and cupboards—God defend me from such demonstrations.

... Up to this moment, not a syllable of news from the Shepherd or his unfortunate Shepherdess, but *horrible* rumours (according to the General) of what is happening in Rome. Where all this is going to end up, God knows! What a fine opportunity for Mrs Hervey to spread her poison— she's in Paris and doubtless will write *volumes* on a theme so suitable to her genius for *romance*.[26]

8p.m. ... I'd like to know why my usual medicine (if it's necessary to purge me) isn't preferable to a draught and two pills. I don't demand a reply in flicks' hand because I detest his jargon, I abhor medical messages and surgical sermons—I won't read anything not communicated in your letters ... Really, I don't know where to turn to enjoy a moment's peace: the idea of your being buried alive in bed in Bath, burning with fever and eating roast-meat instead of cooling things, grieves me beyond expression. Faith is a gift of God, and I can't yet claim that it has been conceded to me in favour of the great scraper Hicks. Almost everything is illusory; the only certainty I have at this moment is of being ill without hope of getting better ... 'Tis in vain to write now, in vain to complain, all is in vain.

Wednesday 21 October

Yesterday a tolerably good gallop of an hour and fifty-five minutes from Bath to Warminster, and from there in fifty-seven minutes to the Amazon's post-house.[27] Despite this exercise, no appetite—there's no doubt that my digestive system is pretty disorganised. Patience and pills. But not *moral* pills, like that of the visit you ultra-persuaded me to receive—a detestable visit, which left a none too agreeable impression on me. What a race! Ouf! The smaller lady was plebeian and common, and the other a kind of Princess of Hesse-*Blank*enbourg-*Stiff*endorf-*Staring*stein with an out-of-tune voice about the least harmonious I've ever heard.[28]

On my arrival here, the first object after Caroline which leapt to my eyes was a letter from Livorno of 29th September from the Marchioness, very charming and almost jubilant. The Shepherd has returned to the Shepherdess, and I shouldn't wonder if they don't think about Dr Thynne.[29] All idea of embarkation is off. "*Quelle agréable surprise pour moi, mon bien-aimé Père, ne voilà-t-il pas, le cher Marquis qui arrive à Livorne.*" Yes, my fine Lady, and he has already persuaded you, it seems, to winter at *Rome*. So much the better. According to this precious document, which I'll shew you next Monday, it was only sister-mania that caused her to travel overland and resolve to entrust herself to the waves. And Mrs Hervey and Mrs Hamilton and that poor fool of a General with his eyes lifted up to Heaven find themselves fooled and inveigled into a false step by our really original Arcadia. A great weight is lifted from my heart.

The letter has two pages of tendernesses for the Shepherd and myself, and compliments to the Abbé on his delightful story about the Pig, the Calf and Pendu, etc; it has whimsicality and spirit, and decent lamentations scattered here and there on the well-nigh certain loss of her poor sister, etc; but all this will pass with the help of the Marquis, who will doubtless begin again to pay delicate, sentimental and suave court to his true Shepherdess. And these charlatanish vermin will be left with ears two feet long, vibrating with calumnies. May the gulf of Satan receive them—the whole lot!

Farewell, dear Gregory, I'm going to profit from the sun, which is shining as at Colares or Porto Brandão ...

<Thursday> 29 October[31]

My God, what evolutions and revolutions! The Rome establishment kicked over, your charming Angelica[32] running about like a heroine in novels, victim of a sensibility so exquisite and subtle that one can barely divine its essence. You have arrived in time to forestall a caprice which makes me shudder to think of it—the fine idea of embarking on the Mediterranean during the equinoctial gales. I hope that after dissolving into tears for at least forty-eight hours on end she will be comforted and will emerge from quarantine at Livorna more charming and original than ever.

I have no use for ultra-sensibilities, I do not understand them. All I know for certain is that I have been practically killed with chagrin, anxiety and conjecture by this precipitate departure from Naples, the journey in the midst of malaria, the flight from Rome as if Herod was at her heels, the gallopede for Paris, and the fine abridgment of the said journey by the embarkation for Marseilles, accompanied by the hissing of those vipers Hervey, Cliftonian Hamilton[33] and the like ...

You may assure the divine Shrew that her inconceivable journey has kept me in a well-nigh mortal state of alarm and torment. She may love her sister *à outrance* if she chooses—but not if it means risking killing her Papa with alarm and his enemies with delight on learning of such a fine prank so well calculated to excite suspicions of every kind. Moreover they have fooled me prettily with the nicest anecdotes—old wives' tales and sinister stories ...

Friday 30 October, 9 p.m.

... I'm none too well; something is not as it ought to be, despite the everlasting pills; it costs me something to take so many without direct orders from the Pillulator; pills all the time, whether they do one good or harm; I can't make it out—neither can they ...

The felling of the pines is on the increase and is producing, it must be said, the finest effect. And even if it weren't so, it would still be necessary to cut them down before Death cuts me down. I hope to hear tomorrow the state of your corpsification. I too am a corpsifier.

Monday 2 November

... Exercise is my salvation—nothing else. The effect of the ride yesterday was magical. I went out and came back, galloping and trotting, on Strawberry Codling (who is as strong as a posting-hackney) and on a quite superb half-arab high-bred which I bought by the luckiest chance in the world at Stourton; a stupendous animal, young, good-tempered and healthy. It was a thirty to forty mile ride, counting the circuit of the Terrace etc ... The horse cost me a hundred guineas and is worth it; my two others won't last another year, consequently this expense was inevitable ...

Tuesday 3 November

Really, I have no idea what kind of throat one is supposed to have in order to swallow such a prolific succession of pills! The moment I feel a little less miserable I have to take broth with laxative salts and pills—pills all the time. That's what comes of having a doctor who is not at hand to judge the state of his patient from day to day! I haven't the honour of quartering doctors' coats-of-arms, but if I had, I would at once eclipse their wretched balls, so much do I hate anything that has the semblance of a pill ...

<Thursday> 5 November[34]

... So today departs the Fountain of Tears. If Signor Samuel Romilly had lamented thus he would not have 'cutato il throato'. No one ever sold justice more than this 'honest' man—this excellent Jacobin, this good Calvinist, this perfect Genevan. *Faustus damnatus est.* The curtain falls, and all is said as far as he is concerned. Then a fresh uproar at Westminster for the election of the new Member[35] ...

Saturday 14 November

The enclosed jeremiad from Arcadia is so leaden and sepulchral in tone that it shrivels my heart. I can't think that the Marquis wants to destroy his wife, dragging her almost by force to this cursèd Rome, destined to become (perhaps) her tomb. Know, then, that I don't at all like the wind that blows from that quarter—"a deathly breeze", as they sing in *Vologeso*.[36] Would to God that you and I had gone there—I don't doubt that one would have been able to change the aspect of affairs, laughing and playing the fool. It seems to me that the Marchioness is consumed with melancholy, vexation and weariness—Italy bores and disgusts her. He must be a miserable Shepherd indeed to make such plans and to vex her after this fashion. God grant that the close of this drama be not fatal—God grant it ... My daughter's state afflicts me cruelly. If so many tears were merely for her sister, well and good. But I'm afraid—after the last letter—I'm afraid that a horrid mystery is going to be revealed.

My God, how long will this privation last of which you speak! When will you be allowed a change of air and objects by this King of putrid bones, this tremendous Scraper, the despotic, anatomic, inflexible Hicks ...

Wednesday 18 November

... 'Tis in vain to think or speak of Arcadia. The languid Shepherdess' lack of character, and the habit of not changing ideas or shirts until they rot to pieces, which distinguishes our Shepherd, makes all that concerns them ashen-colour.

Franchi to Douglas, Thursday 26 November[37]

My Lord, ... Our Pig[38] has just eaten and drunk so much that apoplexy has not failed to serve him as dessert ... This accident is bound to affect M. de Beckford and, above all, everything pertaining to the Abbey—for a long time now Hayter has been architect, seller of timber and a pastime for two hours a day to his master. For a thousand reasons I tremble for the future.

... Several days ago I wrote to the Marchioness to tell her about the purchase of the famous Nuremberg vase. It is truly beautiful and I repeat that it is the finest object in the Abbey—because of its curious work manship, its antiquity and its size, besides which, a sardonyx of this magnitude is a unique object.[39]

... Monseigneur is at the Abbey with Father Bestorum (for what that's worth): what a mess there'll be now that this villainous eater and drinker is perhaps in the next world! I expect to see everything go to the D—v—l and debts emerge on every side, like springs of water from the earth after heavy rain; I expect to see every chimney smoke, walls collapse and water-pipes gush forth everywhere except where they were meant to; I expect to see discovered everything that his negligence and stupidity hid from the eyes and *omniscience* of his master. I assure you that all this will not look rose-coloured! I shall not be at all surprised if M. de Beckford abandons everything out of disgust, not knowing which way to turn. That's what always happens to those who behave like him and who have so perfect an opinion of themselves.

If the Abbé dies, if Randall is finished and poor Franchi follows them, what will happen to him, what will he do? Not a soul round him to counsel him who is worth a thought or good for anything. What a situation! I do not doubt that he will come here soon to see me: since I am his butt he is bound to come and tell me what is passing and *what ought to be done* (which is what he never does!)... He is in good health, at any rate except for a few teeth, but he does not like one saying, knowing or even *thinking* it.

I beg you to say on my behalf to the Marchioness all that your friendship and affection for me can inspire you to say, and affectionate and gay things to the dear, very dear Count of Anguise and My Lady Suzade,[40] and be assured, My Lord, that to my last moment I shall not cease to be your sincerely devoted, attached and obedient Servant, the Chevalier G. Franchi.

Friday 27 November

A very damp day yesterday, and much eating in the carriage by the Abbé and I. My appetite isn't bad and would be better still but for the fanatical continuance of this system of pills and draughts ... One can't open one's mouth to yawn naturally in this solitude without a pill being immediately dropped in. Poor Caroline was waiting for me at the door all trembling and jubilant from an excess of passion. Poor animal, how she loves me! She bared her teeth horribly at Nephew—she can't bear anyone else near me.

The Abbé seems to be getting ready to leave. Never mind! In some respects there is little one can do with him. He is pig-headed and egotistic to a degree. He isn't prepared to lift a finger for anyone or anything outside his *routine.* So I found him in Paris, so I shall find him *in saeculo saeculorum.* He[41] is useless regarding the Yellow One and won't go to him.[42] He is incapable of any intrigue, any subtlety, any finesse; all he is good for is eating and drinking and low company, and now that he is fairly well he is amiable enough in that respect and a precious companion for anyone with little taste and few occupations. He is as much afraid of Hicks as of a Confessor, and on both counts will die (I fear) in a state of final impenitence. In spite of all this and his spiritual defects and lack of talent in painting, I love him with my whole heart and hold him in some esteem ...

My last fine trip to Bath cost me £60, including Hicks' fee of £5 ...

Thursday 3 December

Coxone has shown himself truly worthy of his nickname and has put to good use his withdrawal for the last four days from the business of the Abbey. A weakness in the legs was the pretext for not subjecting himself to any movement but that of the throat. The day before yesterday (Tuesday) he amused himself by eating dried pilchard (red herring) and yesterday by lunching off an enormous suet pudding. The consequence was some kind of stroke. Messrs Lambert and Ames came at once to the attack with blood-lettings, leeches and emetics, with little effect. He is unable to speak and I fancy is going to coxonise in the other world. At the moment he is being given an enema but probably it will be in vain ...

They have come in to tell me that there is little hope. They are putting mustard plasters on his feet. The enema has had some effect but this isn't of much consequence. From his mouth there issues a stink which Ames, who is experienced in stinks, declares to exceed all the stinks in Hell and foretells gangrene.

Friday 4 December

Coxone, pure martyr to the most sublime indigestion, has departed to receive his palm—at 8 o'clock this morning he escaped from the hands of Dr Ames and Dr Lambert and Lawless the scribe.[43] He's finished—a poor honest fellow but a mere stinking brute beast! ...

Tomorrow, and not till tomorrow, arrives the Great Dolt, who, by the way, is not well himself and threatens collapse ... All but the trees and the canine family (Heaven be praised) are dying around me. The Squirrel is a worse than feverish yellow—furious tooth-ache prevents him sleeping. Randall is so-so, more or less limping about and twiddling as usual. The Father is present every morning at the *toilette des fleurs,* exasperating the dwarf with his *Oh, hu, ah, ah, hu*! It only needs the Weeper, the Professor[44] with his music and three or four other persons of similar worth, and three lamps in a row in the Brown Parlour, to compose an Elysium from which I'll be compelled to hurl myself forth—even if into the very abyss of eternal oblivion! ...

Tuesday 8 December

... Something must be done to arrange the immense quantity of books imprisoned in cellars and cupboards, and the best thing to do in this respect is to put six bookcases in a line in the Edward III Gallery as was planned. I've ordered the wood to be prepared. That's all ...

Wednesday 9 December

... The waters of Bath are very powerful, the most sovereign waters in the world. Woe to whoever takes them without being prepared. Like the Body of Our Lord taken without confession and pontifical forgiveness, it carries eternal perdition. But one who believes, as you do, and has confessed and made repentance for weeks and months can take them and be saved.

There really seems to be a mortal pestilence in the air. Yesterday Pendu's son died almost in a flash, and worse, a hundred times worse than this, the Great Dolt has a swollen face and a kind of apoplectic look which frightens me exceedingly—it really would be the *coup de grâce* to my living here. Too much cannot be said in praise of the zeal which this excellent man shows on my behalf and his desire to be of use to me. He has appointed Sampson director of the few works which are planned and remain to be done[45] ...

The yawning sighs of the Father of Beasts (well-named) are in harmony with the sepulchrism of this place and of the weather, which is beyond description. The Turk will tell you when he comes the perfection with which Father Smith repeats ten times running his mournful *heh, hu, hoh, heh,* and the faithfulness with which he is imitated by me. I no longer speak to anyone withou a refrain of *hoh, heh, hu*—so prepare yourself for this music and for finding it divine; I don't practise anything else ...

Thursday 10 December

... I don't welcome Hicks' dominion over you; my faith in so many pills and draughts (so contrary to the system and religion of Ehrhart) is weakening. With the disposition I've always had to internal piles, I can't believe that such a tripish commotion can be a good thing. The Sage is too precipitate in his judgments, too hasty: he lays his eggs (*i.e.* his pills) as flies do and then flies off. He may know anything you like, he may have passed eighteen months underground with corpses, etc, but I'm not absolutely sure that he knows a living being like myself. My system is of a different order; it will be lucky if he doesn't destroy it! ...

Saturday 12 December

... Enough, they're calling me to give them this letter, it being coachtime.
I'm scribbling on the dining table in haste ... You are right—Smollett is
divine (a powerful intellect) and *Candide*[46] is sometimes most insipid.

Friday 18 December

... Yesterday offered the strangest atmospheric effects I've ever seen. I went
with the Father himself by the Rock Passage in those oakwoods which are
so like Genzano[47] and even at certain moments Cintra. The softest and
most luminous vapours covered a landscape that might have been Italian:
the hills transformed into mountains and the valleys into lakes produced
a thousand illusions. Turning Knoyle Point, the whole immense desert of
Hindon etc looked like a boundless sea, varied, however, by splendid shores,
with here and there little wooded islands clad in the gayest green; all this
was on the left hand. On the right, all the Abbey forests were enamelled
by a lurid sun under the loveliest blue sky, and from out these forests rose
the Castle of Atlas with all its windows sparkling like diamonds! Nothing
I've ever seen in my life can equal this unique vision in grandeur of form
or magic of colour. The semblance of water was so life-like and transparent
that one could even see reflections in it. They talk of the mirage in Egypt
and in the great desert: I have now seen it, and seen it at Fonthill; I'm
lucky to have had with me a witness in the person of Smith!

Sunday 20 December

To-day's fine post hasn't brought me a letter from you, but one from the
very pious Marchioness ... I've replied to the poor pig-headed Lady Writer
of the enclosed in the way she deserves. Oh, how I sympathise with the
Marquis! Yesterday the Great Dolt, with a grave face and a cough that
shook the chairs and tables, told me that the debts were raining down, and
not in small drops! ... In cold weather the Octagon is a horror, an inferno
of wind, and has an icy atmosphere: without three or four thousand

pounds to the Marquis of Chabannes it'll never be habitable, and hardly even traversable, for seven months in the year. Since my last return from Bath I haven't gone any further than St Michael's Gallery ...

A little summary of my letter (not a pastoral one) to the Marchioness of Douglas: "With your highly abstract sentiments in religious matters, you must find Rome detestable. I hope, and I don't doubt, that Lausanne will be more to your liking. As (for want of beak and claws) I'm as tolerant as can be, we won't argue about Heavenly doctrine. We'll enjoy trout from the water and grapes from the land and the absurdities of almost all those men and women who are born to consume them" ...

If you so much enjoy Sterne, read *Tristram Shandy*: there you'll find amidst 1000000000 words, bad taste etc, some incomparable little stories— for instance, that of the abbess of Quidlingbourg and of the fellow with the big nose. They are not invented by him, but that doesn't matter, they are so very characteristic and well constructed.

Monday 21 December

What a letter I sent on to you yesterday—poor, colourless and insipid! At one moment it is full of the most stinking Calvinism (*l'Être supreme* etc), at the next of the sweet Marchioness Coutts[49] and her progeny—*sa charmante fille dont la beauté est vraiment ettonnante*. I, who am surprised at nothing, am enchanted by all this. She doesn't sleep, she's consumed by melancholy and tears, but she walks out conjugally with the Marquis—a weary and imbecile existence without taste or spirit or any thing to render it in any way interesting ...

1.   18 October 1817.
2.   More properly called Valerio Belli (1468-1546) of Vicenza, crystal and gem
     cutter, one of the earliest named gem cutters; patronised by Clement VII.
     This was an oblong rock-crystal vase from the pre-Revolution Royal *Garde-
     Meuble* (*Inventory* 2. 35) and was Lot 93 in Durand's Paris sale, May 25th–
     27th, bought by Chardin for 501 *livres*. Part of its decoration consisted of

monsters fighting in the waves, according to Beckford's unpublished letter of June 15th; this proves that the vase is *H.P.S.* 2027 (illustrated), which fetched £1,207.

3.   This is another object from the same sale, Lot 43 "a cup of oriental agate and chalcedony, mammillated and with various arborizations; a garland of leaves and fruit in relief on its surface forms a handle", 220 *livres*. This looks like *Christie,* 2nd Day, Lot 22, "an oval cup and cover of oriental mammillated agate, marked in arborescent mocoa <= chalcedony>, elaborately chased and engraved"; or perhaps 3rd Day, 26, which mentions rubies. B. bought six objects, for which he paid £84 5s.

4.   They were arranging books in the Alcove Library (the Vaulted Library of *Rutter* 17–18).

5.   A General Election was being held; one seat at Hindon was Beckford's.

6.   For the Great Entrance, more properly called the Great or Octagonal Portal, from the Octagon into the Eastern Transept, see *Rutter* 27–8 and his Plate 9 facing his page 20. B. was concentrating on the first (West) doorway from the Octagon, with its parapet or balcony above (forming a Music Gallery). This door led into a porch (Octagonal Portal), at the east end of which rose the Organ Screen and Loft, which B. was leaving for the time being; evidently it was executed very much later, for Rutter, writing in 1822, says "this screen has been recently erected" (p.28). For B.'s temporary measure in 1817, see p.199.

7.   The Phoenix was (Sir) George Hayter (1792–1871), R.A., principal painter in ordinary to Queen Victoria, nephew of Beckford's Clerk of the Works, George Hayter (Coxone)—hence his nickname the Phoenix. He was painting Holbein's Edward VI from the enamel of it painted by Henry Bone (1755–1834), the great enameller.

8.   Sir Thomas Lawrence, P.R.A.

9.   Tom Moore the poet. Through Rogers, Beckford tried unsuccessfully to tempt him to Fonthill and to prepare for the press Beckford's 'travel-letters' (which later appeared as *Italy, Spain and Portugal*); but Moore did not want to risk the displeasure of the society hostesses whom he courted by being linked with Beckford.

10   Obscure thirteenth-century Italian saint.

11.   Nicolaes Berchem (1620–83), Dutch painter. *Phillips*, Day 26, Lot 260; or Day 27, Lot 353.

12.   The May 1817 sale; probably that in *Inventory* 1. 8: "A <water-colour> drawing; View of Fonthill".

13. *Phillips,* Day 26, Lot 117 or 328; for de Cort, see p.152, note 74.

14. *H.P.S.* 1,115, flowers in a terra-cotta vase adorned with bas-reliefs of boys and on a marble table; it fetched £1,228 10s.; Jan van Huysum (1682–1749) was a Dutch painter.

15. Presumably *Phillips,* Day 11, Lot 57, water-colour of sea-port with many figures—which is also the only Baur in *Inventory,* which describes it as an "Italian sea front …" Johann Wilhelm Baur (1600–42) was a German artist, born in Strasbourg, who spent most of his working life in Italy. Beckford was being offered the pair for £40.

16. Later in the letter Beckford writes: "I'd like to seethe Anglican Misses and Mistresses suddenly turning their backs at this apparition, and to hear their 'Oh fie', 'shocking', 'shameful', etc."

17. Phillips' sale at Brandenburgh House of *objets d'art,* etc, belonging to the Margravine of Anspach, 29 July, Lot 89–90 bought by Hume for Beckford at 465 guineas. *Phillips* (*1823*), Day 15, Lot 574–5; *H.P.S.* 872–3 (photo), £719. For Fiammingo, see p.151, note 44.

18. Anspach sale, Lot 79, "small ivory Tankard … sculptured in groups and figures, shells etc by Benvenuto Cellini", bought by Hume for Beckford for 42 guineas; possibly *H.P.S.* 868.

19. Her *Considérations sur… la Révolution Française,* 3 volumes, London 1818. Beckford's note is in *H.P.*

20. The rest of this paragraph discusses a Missal allegedly illuminated by Albert Dürer (whose monogram was 🅐) and Lucas van Leyden; it is described, as an outstanding gem, by *Clarke,* pp.v–vi ("Advertisement"). As soon as he had bought it, Beckford became convinced that it was by those two artists, and a great bargain! It was sold to him by the Abbé Celotti, an Italian priest who collected manuscripts in Italy and sold them in London.

21. See p.102, note 39.

22. Rhubarb.

23. Beckford's new doctor, the Bath surgeon Charles Hicks (died 1842?) of Edgar Buildings. Like Beckford, the Bath *Guide* and *Directory* spell him indifferently Hicks and Hickes, but he is consistently spelt Hicks in the annual printed lists of the Royal College of Surgeons, of which he became a Member in 1808.

24. *Hakim* is Arabic for a physician. A later letter shows that *Heïkes* represents the Arabic *haïck,* a mantle; Beckford is punning on his name in Arabic, and later remarks, "I'm equally consoled by his name in Arabic, being resolved to put myself under his mantle".

25. The second Earl of Roden (1756–1820), K.P., who had a good record as a soldier and was addicted to gambling; but what was his bond with Beckford? (He was the only man in Society, outside the Beckford family circle, who ever stayed at the Abbey.) Beckford nicknamed him 'the Professor,' but what does this refer to? His second wife was a sister of Beckford's son-in-law, General James Orde, and his brother was the notorious Bishop of Clogher (see p.305, note 11). *The General* is James Orde, who is lamenting the death of his wife on September 7th.

26. Mrs Hervey, Beckford's half-sister, wrote romantic Society novels; the reference is to Douglas' affair with Napoleon's sister Pauline (see p.217).

27. Probably at Hindon.

28. The Princess of Hesse was Elizabeth (1770–1840), third daughter of George III; she was called an artist because of her drawings of Cupid and Love, and she established a society at Windsor for giving marriage portions to virtuous girls. She had recently re-emerged into the public eye by marrying, in April, Frederick, later Landgrave of Hesse-Homburg.

29. Dr. Andrew Thynne (died 1818), well-known accoucheur and lecturer on midwifery, and physician to a Lying-in hospital.

30. Naturally, Susan's sudden flight from Rome was interpreted by gossips as her leaving her husband in disgust at his affair with Pauline; in reality, she wanted to see her dying sister in England.

31. In French to Douglas in Rome.

32. See p.124, note 31.

33. *i.e.* Mrs Hamilton of Clifton.

34. First letter.

35. Sir Samuel Romilly, the great law reformer; he cut his throat with a razor on November 2nd, after his wife's death. He was a radical of republican sympathies, austere and puritanical. *Genevan* refers to his friendship with the Genevan preacher Dumont, and also perhaps to his belief in the doctrines of Rousseau, who was born and bred in Geneva. At the time of his suicide, he was M.P. for Westminster. Beckford could not forgive him for being leading counsel on the other side during B.'s appeal in the Campbell case in 1801, and also perhaps for his advocacy of the abolition of slavery. *The Fountain of Tears* is Orde.

36. Sacchini's opera.

37. In French.

38. Coxone (Hayter).

39. This is the famous Rubens Vase, now in the Walters Art Gallery at Baltimore, and is one of the most important gem carvings in the world. It was bought

by Rubens, who drew it. It is described in *Christie,* 5th Day, Lot 46; *H.P.S.* 487 (*Journal of Walters Art Gallery,* Vol. VI, 1943, pp.9–39; and is illustrated on the title-page (bottom right corner) of Britton's *Fonthill,* 1823. Beckford bought it in Holland for £420. It may have been carved about A.D. 400.

40. Douglas' children.

41. Beckford wrote "I" by mistake!

42. Moore having refused to edit Beckford's travel books, Rogers was unwilling to face Beckford at Fonthill and evaded going, and the Abbé Macquin refused to pursue him.

43. An attorney's clerk, who was there to take down Hayter's last will and testament.

44. The Weeper is Orde; the Professor is Lord Roden.

45. Sampson is appointed Clerk of the Works in place of his deceased brother Coxone (Hayter). His nickname is sometimes given in the Italian form *Sansone;* another reference makes it quite clear that he is nicknamed after Sanson, the famous French family of Royal executioners, two of whom executed Louis XVI and Marie Antoinette. *Pendu* is Vincent.

46. By Voltaire; Beckford quotes frequently from it, and often uses one of its characters, Baron von Thondertentronck, as a nickname and phrase.

47. A town above Lake Nemi in the Alban Hills.

48. J.B. Marie-Frédéric, Marquis de Chabannes (1770–1835), inventor and publicist who, whilst an emigré, unsuccessfully undertook the lighting of London and its cleansing from coal effects. Beckford refers to his scheme of ventilating large buildings by using gas chandeliers which caused air currents; these he installed late in 1817 in Covent Garden Theatre and Lloyd's, and described in his book *On conducting air by forced ventilation* …, 1818.

49. The mock or familiar name given to the second daughter of old Thomas Coutts the banker; she married the first Marquis of Bute, son of the Prime Minister; her daughter, born in 1801, married the second Earl of Harrowby.

1819

THE sombre tone of the year (sombre for the whole country) is set by the first letter, written on a pouring winter's night in a deserted coaching-inn at Marlborough, when Beckford found himself quite alone except for the companionship of his dog. He had not been there for fifty years; the contrast between his position then and now was almost too much for him. His affairs were rapidly nearing a crisis. Sugar was approaching its lowest price so far. He had three Chancery suits to cope with, and the lawyers' expenses must have been prodigious, eating into his precious and inadequate income. Everything pointed to a sacrifice which, now that it was at hand, he hardly liked even to name—the sale of Fonthill.

The national situation was even more alarming, and is amply reflected in Beckford's letters. "The revolution advances with giant strides"[1] was no exaggerated phrase, nor the metaphor of a volcano, nor the frequent use of the word "Jacobinical". The country was on the verge of civil war. Both sides were arming and drilling—the workers in despair and anger at their poverty, helplessness and unemployment; the property-owners in alarm for their possessions. This was the year of Peterloo,[2] when armed yeomanry rode down an angry crowd of eighty thousand (a number equal to Napoleon's army at Waterloo), which was well-drilled in mass formation behind revolutionary banners.

But Beckford had a strain of toughness and resilience in him, and responded quickly to outside stimulation—the London theatre, the channel crossing, and midnight confabulations with Fulibus, the great Palmela. So in these letters the sombre mingles with the gay. Incidentally, the Paris trip, begun with such verve and cheerfulness, ended abruptly and sadly. Beckford imagined himself slighted by Fulibus and by the Marquis of Marialva (the Dom Pedro of the *Journal*), who was Portuguese Ambassador there. The dear Marquis was now contemptuously dubbed "Twiddle-alva," and the friendship of a lifetime severed. Beckford consoled himself by emphasising the deference which his money procured from the lower orders—passporteers, Customs officers and the like.

Monday 11 January[3]

From Melksham to Devizes the rain was very sharp and I did not meet a living soul—Sabbath stupidity reigned undisturbed. Between Devizes and Marlborough here and there were discovered Methodists walking piously to their Methoderies—square houses with pointed windows and with an air and style worthy of their builders. From afar the mournful voice of church bells summoned in vain those who disliked that dogma also. One cannot speak severely enough about the lugubriousness of the landscape, both natural and human. Approaching Marlborough, a few intervals in the mist enabled me to see still primitive plains and immense green solitudes worthy of ancient Wiltshire, with depressing tumuli of sad, unknown people.

I found the ducal palace as I had left it fifty years ago—so-so.[4] I recognised everything. The staircase was passably illumined and the fires well lit; the servants in procession with candlesticks still had a feudal air. It was as if the Lord of that place, having lost his last farthing gaming, was now returned to take possession of the little that was left to him—and that lord was I. Dinner was plentiful but mediocre—poor crayfish and detestable butter that tainted everything (according to the English rite). At night I had as the companion of my extreme and almost terrifying solitude the beloved (and truly worthy of being loved) Nephew, snuggling up as always, and from time to time giving a tender sigh or feeble scratching ...

Tuesday 12 January[5]

One can change shirts, places and pills, but not bad health once it has set in with the course of years. Since Hicks has told me to take pills etc only every fifth day, and since last Saturday night was the night of pill-taking, I shan't begin again until next Thursday.

I'm taking rhubarb at the appointed times, and it seems to me that already I've become a root of that plant; I'm aware of an internal stench of rhu*barb* that does not delight me; I detest anything *barbato*, and I see with real dismay Alidru's development in this direction[6]—rhu-*barbe*, rhu-*barbaric*, rhu-God-knows-what; and I've got to taint myself with this every day before dinner. I really don't know what to say about all this giving of physic.

Last night's storm ... has been followed by the finest, clearest, freshest (yet not cold) morning, springlike rather than wintry. The fields round this ever smiling spot are all clothed in the finest green mingled with a cold reddish colour.

Windsor Castle is seen as clearly as if one were in the atmosphere of Naples. There is the great Royal Standard lapping in the breeze, marking the residence of the abandoned and solitary Sovereign.[7] Its towers, which hardly have the dignity of chimneys, recall to my mind the cursèd Bagasse,[8] and hard on this recollection follows an indigestion of vain expenses and fruitless remorse ...

I suppose Bestifownes has already returned to the Sage, but this fellow is so hurried, so devoured by the moribund that he can't see quite clearly what he's at. During my last consultation he seemed to me so hurried as not to be able to make out positively what he wanted one to do or not to do. Farewell, here are the horses and Nephew ...

London,[9] Thursday 14 January

... Last night I went to the theatre to see *Munchausen*[10]—a trifling affair, much inferior to *Gulliver;*[11] a large audience and immense heat notwithstanding M. de Chabannes' artificial breezes[12] (although I returned home without my coach through a fine mire, I feel no evil consequences— at least so far). The music of the pantomime is the worst I've ever heard, and the dances of an insipidity worthy of certain Protestant fraternities at your Seven Dials[13] ... In the scenery of *Munchausen* is discovered here and there a certain imagination—a palace in the Moon has some merit and a lunar cottage still more: through a kind of window one sees snow-white, icy rocks and pyramids full of pale horror, their form and colour inspiring respect! Grimaldi, he's getting old; what would you? One can't do anything else—neither pills nor rhubarb taken at the astrologic, star-predicted, Hicksian hour can impede the fatal progress of the years.

Certainly yesterday Boletus was under the influence of a benign star: the beautiful book fell for four guineas (only half its value)[14] ...

Friday 15 January

Yesterday, my dear Gregory, just at the dinner-hour I had the delight of receiving (to help forward my digestion) a sweet little letter from Mr Scorpion[15] announcing a formidable tempest in Jamaica; he had scented it from certain indications in the papers ten days ago. Since the beginning of the scorpionish letter is in a rather ornate style, I'm taking the trouble to copy it down:

"My dear Sir, I am sorry to be the herald of bad news, but the uncontrollable Elements having occasioned serious mischief upon your Draxhall Estate, I am unwillingly obliged to be so." Enough! And enough to reduce me to all the misery and straitened circumstances imaginable. Poor Bestifownes will be cruelly afflicted, and rightly so: the merchants, in their fine honeyed tones one knows so well, will doubtless beg me "to be so indulgent to them and to my own affairs as to revert to the £750 instead of £1,000" <quarterly> etc, etc. I await a thousand torments reproduced in a thousand forms ...

The Abbé dined here yesterday eating and drinking, and saying all the time that he was none too well; it's certain that his face doesn't look good but his throat is splendid ...

Saturday 16 January

My destiny begins to be clouded more than ever. This last blow is hard and serious and will for a long time totally embarrass me. I don't know where to turn: if one goes to the merchants for the least help one will hear the old shrill song, and even taking this help one is only approaching the moment when the force and accumulation of debts will oblige one to sell Fonthill. And what can I do? My establishment is too necessary to the *little* health that remains to me to be diminished—I say 'little' because I find myself threatened with various illnesses, amongst others a kind of weakness in the bladder which is increasing. Where are the servants, where the horses that I can dismiss? Sedan-chair I have none. House I have none. What remains to me is the gulph of the Abbey and its land, swallowing me up alive.

I've been to see the Missal: it's beautiful and executed by a painter's hand, but it's very German, of the period a little before Holbein, perfect in form, parchment and preservation ... In this nest I've found proof upon proof of Chardin's infamies and knaveries: almost all that this Jarman[16] has acquired comes from MacCarthy—there are the books that I had marked in the sale catalogue and desired, the *Hours* of a Queen of Spain,[17] the Dictys Cretensis, etc[18] ...

Tuesday 19 January

I found Fulibus in his accustomed glory amongst old papers, morocco folders and secretaries, mixing in a queer kind of way the useful and the agreeable, in his new diplomatic palace (Thomas' Hotel). There he was, between two or three fine fat boys, half secretaries, half *valets de chambre*— one or two dough-coloured and another rose-and-lily (after four days' scrubbing, of course), like the acolytes of poor Fuentes y Egmont;[19] there he was, a most disagreeable kind of Misterfluto ... In short, that's Fulibus in London (why he should be there, I can't think), poor man, with his face pretty ugly and old, and yellower than the Yellow Poet has ever been; indignant to the highest degree at not being in South Audley Street,[20] pouring the utmost contempt and hatred on the memory of Bezerra and even bothering to abhor the poor Cowpat, the cause (says he) of an untold amount of beastly gossip about him, etc, etc, etc.

Whilst I was with him there entered a kind of German waiter belonging to the hotel, who said in a low and mysterious voice "Your Exshellence, here is the Watchman"; "*Milles pardons; un moment, je sort pour affaires.*" Fulibus returns and I, with a smile of the tenderest innocence, worthy of yourself or rather of that mental decline upon which I suppose I'm entering, I observe "*C'est apparemment quelque betise de ce sot allemand: c'est votre horloger, je suppose.*" "*Point-du-tout, point-du tout.* It's a night watchman, an excellent fellow, who has brought me the address of a very amiable little person whom I could no longer find; late last night, coming out of Jacquier's, I went in search of a little amusement in an accustomed quarter. I knock. They've gone away. 'Past one, past one';[22] I recognise the voice—it's an *old* acquaintance, this good man. I give him the commission of finding out, and he has found out. *Pardon encore si j'écrit l'adresse.*"

And then he spoke of the Marchioness, lowering his voice to a whisper: all the stories about Pauline are *absolutely* true; it's true about the great friendship with the Marchioness Coutts; it's absolutely true about the table scattered with devotional books; happily the Marchioness is really passably well. Fulibus, constant in all things (as you can see on my previous page), still *adores* her and has the blessing of receiving from her tolerably frequent letters—anyway, longer than those so sparingly and insipidly vouchsafed to me.

Yesterday I went to Elliston's Olympic.[23] How divine he is, and his companion Mrs Edwin;[24] and how divine, amusing, perfectly well *costumé*, and deliciously lively and gay is the comedy called *Rochester*.[24] All the actors and actresses (and they're many) are good; there is some pretty music, the play is lively and full of theatrical effects in the best Parisian style, and its plot is properly complicated and tangled. I went at seven o'clock; there wasn't even room for a pin—what I saw, I saw standing. I don't yet know the beginning or the end, but I'll return before long at six o'clock; I don't want to send to reserve seats or boxes etc—I enjoy my incognito (*à propos* of incognito, Jarman doesn't yet know who was with him). One can't overpraise Elliston. What a pity to see an actor like him, so much the master of the stage, grow old and fat and Scarmanise[26] ...

Friday 22 January

... Fulibus, faithful to all his customs, came to pay me a visit last night at half-past eleven. I was already in bed, but I heard the voice of a punchinello on the stairs, proclaiming "*Fort bien, je reviendrai bientôt*" ...

Enter 'Magnus Berg' Davies[27] with a salver of beaten silver etc—la, la. Exit with ditto, begging a thousand pardons, but without a kick in the arse because I'm too ill to give it (this spoken *sotto voce*) ...

Sunday 24 January

A time of rare insipidity, of damp and foggy cold. Everything dead. No voice in the streets or in the air save that of the melancholy bell calling melancholy Englishmen to their melancholy churches and methoderies.

All this is familiar, but what is strange is how a Government, however feeble, can tolerate a Fulibus living in mortal sin against the Royal commandments. He was nominated for a really important mission at Madrid, but nominated in vain. Now that the poor Infanta-Queen is dead,[28] he says that an Ambassador-Extraordinary isn't necessary and an Envoy is sufficient, but that as Councillor of State he can counsel equally well *here* as *there* (the good soul!). To go and govern in Lisbon—yes, on certain conditions. In short, yesterday was a day of great confidences, half-true and half-false. Nothing changes him or will change him. The Marchioness being ever sovereign of his thoughts, he absolutely wants to go where she is—Lausanne or Paris or wherever you will. Meanwhile he is going to spend eight days at Brighton, having received a great welcome from the Regent (according to him, the Pavilion is magnificent, splendid, divine). Then he'll return here to speak again about the divine Shepherdess and profit by the watch man. If he isn't at least an original, I don't know who is.

Bestifownes' faith in Hicks diminishes visibly. He fears the tributes of Bath and other expenses at least as much as Fulibus the Court of Madrid. He begins to allow himself to be assured by various personages that the Sage is nothing else than a tremendous charlatan (his own words were 'a vain boaster') and often a killer too … so sing all: the moment the London air fills their lungs they make a general chorus of "Quack, quack, quack" …

Monday <25 January>

A melancholy day of wind and rain, but at least I have some zephyrs from Rome (of the 2nd January) full of mildness and perfumes. In the midst of a certain gaiety—"*le cher Marquis, les bijoux d'enfans, les bénédictions de Sa Sainteté qui a l'air de vouloir me pucer et doucer tout comme si j'etois Caroline*"—she laments the poor Queen of Spain ("the most notorious of Royal strumpets" writes the impudent Phipps in his *News*)[29] "*qui avoit tant d'empressement de me voir*", etc, etc, and then she sentimen*teases* on the nullity and uncertainty of this sojourn in the vale of tears. But she confesses to being admirably well—"*Ma santé est beaucoup meilleure*", speaks of Franchi with her usual benignity, and how cruel it will be if he does not come to Rome, accompanying *"le plus cheri des pères"* etc, etc. Then she ends with the usual refrain ... Divine people, divine, my dear Gregory—they and Fulibus are always the same, with the most delightful pig-headedness and originality ... The Shepherdess' anglicanism doesn't prevent her receiving the Margravine to dinner *frequently* or dropping a shimmering tear on the urn of Queen Maria Theresa,[30] that sublime f—r. Oh the dear Shepherdess! Oh the delicious, honest Shepherd! ...

Tuesday 26 January

Yesterday I went to Drury Lane where for the thirtieth time they acted *Brutus* and all his family.[31] There was a great hubbub, a great storm, hail, thunder and lightning, a great trumpeting, great scenery semi-extravagantly Italian and semi-English *à la* Adams, a tumbling down of buildings and of the statue of the tyrant Tarquinius Superbus, the heat of Bengal and of Sadlers Wells, melodramatic music, processions with vestal virgins and censer-swinging boys, in short a regular hotch-potch worthy of the Circus or Sanspareil[32] but not of a national theatre. The adored Kean with the voice of a carrion-crow dying of indigestion, shrieking like a Fury and from time to time sighing and bewailing in a very low contralto. The play itself was poverty-stricken in ideas and poetry, but what does that matter—it pleases our astrologers! It's incredible, this nation's lack of taste. I don't understand it, nurtured as they are on the productions of sublime authors. The full orchestra was good and with the help of some pieces of Haydn and so many mechanical and theatrical effects the people didn't seem bored. But they shouldn't applaud such so-called tragedies, defective in everything which (in combination) inspires and fills the soul. To animate patriotism or draw tears, a single glance at the sublime picture by Lethière[33] is worth more than all the affected agonies of the great Kean masquerading as Consul and sitting in his paltry Tribunal, announced in the playbills etc as the exact imitation of the picture of which I speak. Oh what a miserable imitation!

... The second portion of the Bindley Sale is finished.[34] My purchases mount up to over a hundred pounds—a serious sum for me today; without the abandonment (forced on me by circumstances) of various desirable items, it would have been much more than twice that amount: ... it's cruel when you think that, without house, carriage, or splendour I'm spending £100 a week! ...

Friday 29 January[35]

... I haven't been in Fogg's realm but I met him in the street with the most triumphant and prosperous air I've ever seen, like the ancient Venetian in certain Italian couplets—rich, splendid and seignorial. Would that I had at my disposition half a quarter of what he's thieved, and I wouldn't be long in debt.

The odious Gillow has got it into his head to buy all Father Tettone's picture relics for 11,000 guineas. They were mysteriously conveyed by caravan at dead of night from the garret in young Hume's house to the cellar in Argyll Street under the dominion of the well-known Bard[36] ...

If *Vathek* is making such a furore at Bordeaux, they will do well to send for copies because soon none will be left here and I do not want another edition for the time being. I do not feel the least inclination to give light to the *Episodes* save that of the fire which will consume them ...

Sunday 31 January

... I was at the oratorio celebrated yesterday in the dramatic chapel at Drury Lane, it being the anniversary of that holy Martyr of the Anglicans, Charles I. Signor Ambrogetti sang detestably badly, and Signora Georgi Bellochi, prima donna at the Haymarket, passably well. The music of Paër and of a certain Bonfichi, pretty villainous, was mixed with the eternal *train-train* of Handel and a whole movement of Beethoven that was mediocre and trivial rather than erudite—a thing I didn't expect.

The grandiose effect of the orchestra gave the greatest possible pleasure to the Turk who never (in the manner of his ambassador) uttered the slightest *Ouf!* He seems to like music better than tragedy; you can't imagine how the fine Italian style delights him.[37]

Tuesday 2 February

It's real winter with its accompaniment of thick snow interspersed with sleet, and the colour of Divine Judgement over every object, enough to make one tremble. In perfect harmony with this perspective, one hears the tang-dang-tang of church bells, alternately summoning the living to Anglican prayers at eleven and the dead to the cemetery. At three, Bestifownes, Pandora and Finch[38] will march in sad procession to inter (probably) the little that remains to me and to hear the confirmation of a decree[39] that, in conformity with certain signs, will force me to a sacrifice which, now that it is at hand, I hardly like even to name ...

Thursday 4 February

... Bestifownes and Pandora continue to do their utmost to free me from these cursèd Committees.[40] Today there are two of them in session, which will oblige me to spend three or four hours in succession in St Stephen's Oven. At least one learns a great deal of information there, since there is nothing one can do during the ballot. The Anglicans become Catholics as far as gossiping and confidences are concerned. A good Confessor like myself knows how to spur on the laxer Brethren and induce them to divulge various little stories and anecdotes, all highly curious—political sins already committed or only conceived. I grant or withhold absolution according to the direction of the wind; as it continues to blow from the North-East it doesn't look as if they're going to have much consolation from me this time.

... The Bindley medals are now being sold—a superb collection, especially in its comparatively modern items of the Medici, Louis XIV etc. I looked over them this morning: some of them have a delicacy and an almost imperceptible relief which is enchanting. In days gone by more than fifty of them would have adorned the interiors of the Michael Angelo[41] or Bouchardon cabinets.

Friday 5 February

… According to what I feel inside, my liver is now doing its duty, which was not the case some time ago. Honour then to the Hicksian pills and to the regimen which I continue to observe with tolerable regularity: soup seldom, little wine, no fillets of this or that *à la* Bouffetaut, no cabbage, little or no salad, and large quantities of excellent mutton …

Rhinoceros was here yesterday and said all the bad he could (doubtless with good reason) about Sampson. My tower threatens disaster. It will have to be attended to in the summer, and this means completely rebuilding it—every bit of it!

A painter of the greatest promise has died—Harlow, a true genius.[43] What a pity it was not the Phoenix. I've been three times running to the Exhibition in Pall Mall to admire *The Capture of Babylon* by Martin. He adds the greatest distinction to contemporary art. Oh what a sublime thing![44]

Saturday 6 February

… Bestifownes, who is deep in a thousand other affairs than mine, continues to work ten hours at a time, and (growing paler every moment) devours, when he can, all that a souvenir left by Hicksius enables him to. The time will come, and can't be far off, when he'll repent in vain of having sacrificed the meagre remains of his health to false Gods.

… You cannot imagine what a horror of iniquity this last injustice is.[45] The chief Judge and coryphaeus was in 1801 my own lawyer[46]—zealous, friendly, convinced of the infamy of the lawsuit, and full of the joyful prospect of defending me against such an unjust and base attack. Now that the aforementioned gentleman is an integral part of the Government, he thinks the opposite of what he thought and proved then—worthy of those who have ordered an atrocious decision, which reveals the fine state of our Courts! …

Sunday 7 February

... Rogers' poem (it came into the world yesterday after a good deal of touching up and many second thoughts—a hard confinement, in short) possesses little grace, slight harmony, no originality and no fire. As moral and sentimental syrup it will find many ladies, nurses and mothers and many decided Methodists (and half-hearted ones as well) willing to buy it—perhaps all its cautious, cold-blooded, bankerish, hypocritical author expects.[47]

Fulibus has returned from Brighton. Yesterday at four o'clock he was dropping cards at my door, certain, I think, of not finding me in, but naturally to announce his arrival. The newspapers have latterly taken it into their heads to mingle the poor, religious, chaste Marchioness in highly profane company—here is a tit-bit where she figures as the confidante of the Princess of Wales!

Wednesday 10 February

... Not knowing what to do, I profited from a brief interval in the rain and gloom to visit the Cousin Boltons at their Gordon's Hotel. The said Bolton has visited me so many times in vain that it was time to see him and his consort—the poor consort of a very poor husband ... He looked at me and looked at me like the tailor in the comedy "That's a pretty Spencer"[48]—fearful and half delighted, as if he feared to miss the measure. The Bolton herself, alas, has changed from the pretty smiling fresh girl that she was twenty-eight or thirty years ago! She seemed to be surprised but enchanted at seeing and hearing me, which animated me to give out a thousand flashes of oddity. Beside her was another cousin (I suppose), perhaps one of the Courtenays, who laughed and was amused in the most sincere way. *Not a word* about the sentimental and pious Marchioness—despite all her sisterly piety, *she* doesn't figure or count at this Court; I, yes, and the Chevalier Franchi.

... Father Bestorum is very content at receiving superb news from his son in India, who, at a famous assault on a not too famous fortress, has acquired much glory and still more money, rich spoils, jade, emeralds, rupees and even some rose diamonds.[49]

... The political barometer is at 'stormy', Parliament falling every day in public opinion and the Poor Rates rising. The word *Reform* means *Revolution*, who can doubt it ... In France everything marches to Bonapartism, like Cherubino in Mozart's *Figaro*—"to victory, to military glory".

Thursday 11 February

... According to all that I can learn, in France they talk only of political quarrels, precursors of a civil war that will pass the time and train them for the ardently awaited moment of revenge against the cursèd Island, and the opening of a new path to Glory ...

Friday 12 February

... How many times do I not curse and send to the Devil the fanaticism for Hicks that sways you, the spider's web that has caught you like a fly! Poor dear Gregory, created for better purposes than to serve as a drain-pipe or canal for the experiments of Hicks, a man in no wise extraordinary save for his desperate incisions. He says that nothing coming out of your body is perfect![50] I can well believe it—in the eyes of so tremendous a dilettante: "If thou, Lord, shouldest mark iniquities, who may abide it?"[51] I see no end to the inquisitions of such a *Mesa Censoria*.[52] Who will ever come out alive? Art, art and never Nature. These are mysteries which faith alone can venerate ...

Saturday 13 February

The confidential confabulation with Fulibus continued last night until twelve-fifteen. This faithful worshipper is never tired of talking of the Shepherdess. According to him, the splendour of her beauty increases instead of diminishing. And then in singing she is supreme—no professional or amateur can be compared to her. The lessons she received from Crescentini and the celebrated Pellegrini (a lady of fifty who sings as if she were fifteen)[53] have eradicated the smallest trace of original sin in her prosody and musical tone: her style, totally purified from the poor English taste, has become celestial Catholic; in short, it must be something superior. We'll see. I'm most impatient to hear her.

Another interval in her news. Her strange negligence in writing is truly incredible—after so many promises and so much jargon on her part and so many letters on mine. God knows what's passing in Rome at the moment—chills, illnesses, Bonapartish terrors, Paulinish disgusts, the whole Litany of the Arcadian Church. On account of his love for his false Gods, the Shepherd has conducted himself very badly with regard to Blacas and even Consalvi.[54] So the return to Scotland will be insipid indeed after the pastoral-political life he's leading; apparently his truly great name (seldom lost sight of!) gives him a high place, entirely distinct from his fellow-countrymen. The Marchioness participates not a little in all this homage. And then the children, with their accomplishments and lively grace, are so lovely, prepossessing, vivacious and Roman that they attract and delight every glance; Fulibus speaks of them with enthusiasm—I've never seen him so animated ...

Monday 15 February

I really don't want to keep from you the enclosed masterpiece of Hamiltonism, gibberish, perfidy, eccentricity etc, etc. Oh what a sublime epistle after its fashion! Yesterday, being in Fulibus' house, No. 36 Berkeley Square, at the canonical hour, we laughed for half-an-hour on end. Her chills have once more appeared on the scene; *mais comme on se flatte (vous voyez) que cela ne sera pas grande chose*, one needn't have any fears (and yet these strange people are more or less always calculated to inspire them).

Amongst his other portable curiosities Fulibus shewed me plasters, cameos and intaglios—each a portrait of the Shepherdess—sculptured by Girometti, Pikler and other worthy men, and each one pretty mediocre—I don't in the least covet them.[55]

I doubt whether the Frogmore things will be tempting to a supreme degree, but who knows whether the little lacquer cabinet will come to light.[56] Since young Hume had only just come when Sucribus' appearance caused him to beat a hasty retreat,[57] there was no time to ask him what is happening (that's the only reason), but I don't believe that anything marvellous will turn up; I'd like to believe it, anyway ...

Fulibus' drolleries, as original as can be, are worth more than two hundred pages of *Tristram Shandy*. I've never been able to digest a single volume of that book; it's a piece of mosaic, half original and fine like Pliny's villa, and half like Bonelli or Belfort ...; I don't like it and never have, but you've got a good nose for things[58] ...

Tuesday 16 February

... Whilst twenty or thirty pounds was the usual price being given for books of old English poetry at the Bindley Sale, Boletus and I bought several interesting, curious and agreeable books for four shillings and sixpence! half a crown! two shillings! etc; and for one guinea a book with wood-cuts by the famous Bernard,[59] which was worth six, etc ...

Wednesday 17 February

... Another of Golownin's volumes on Japan has just come out.[60] Genuine, beautiful Japanese porcelain is hardly ever seen; what is called *Japan* is an inferior variety—heavy, coarse, and much more like faience. The Japanese import much of theirs from China, their own products being horribly dear; they have very few makes of the best quality and it takes a long time to manufacture them.

The population of Yeddo is so immense that it is hard to believe: millions and millions, and more than 180,000 houses. The province where Miaco and the *Dairi*[61] are is famous for its lovely boys (real *terre papale!*); from there they come to provide the delights of the theatres, inns and brothels! A strange people, a strange country—the only one which still remains to be known.

Thursday 18 February

As the weather yesterday was a little less wet and stormy than usual I took my chance and went for one of my famous rides through the counties of Surrey and Kent. I was more than four hours on horseback, Nephew running beside me the whole time without ever stopping for a rest. For me the monotony of all these houses which resemble each other like cherries, of all these little gardens and all these little Methodist chapels etc is tiresome in the highest degree. One can no longer find a single field, a single wood or a single green hill which isn't in the act of being transformed into battalions of houses—all built in straight lines, with their everlasting little roads of yellow sand bordered with cypress and laurel. The stupid birds were singing as if it were already May, and all the windows being open made one suspect the presence of solitary 'kept mistresses' and mysterious wet nurses with mysterious offspring. I suppose I must have covered at least thirty miles. I galloped in a straight line to Beckenham, and thence to Croydon, where are to be seen some old buildings of the Archbishops of Canterbury, which show how little magnificence, compared with Toledo and Italy etc, these Gentlemen have ever possessed.

This was written whilst I was awaiting the arrival of your letters. The hour has passed—they haven't arrived. So, my dear Gregory, farewell, I'm going out.

Friday 19 February

... I can't think who has put it into your head that my health is flourishing—certainly not I: were I to say such a thing I would be lying. It would be equally untrue to say that I laugh at the Sage. I'm taking pills and sulphurous powders which put me in mind of my 'Family' and the itch and the Grand Dogs' Minuet, so much beloved and repeated by Sacchini ... This morning I received quite a vivacious and happy letter from the Shepherdess dated the 26th January, ... sending a tiny blest cross for Caroline ... The moment one believes sincerely that Hicksius (without realising it) is acting under the auspices of the Glorious Saint, and that the latter's invisible and benign influence directs every step one takes, everything seems to me consolation and light.

Alidru is becoming outwardly rather too European and is getting fat; but he remains very thin on the intellectual side. I can't see that he is making any progress. He asks after you a great deal ... I suppose you already know that the infamous mad-Dog[1] Jennings died in the King's Bench, probably in a state of final impenitence. The struggle at Westminster isn't being much discussed; it is thought that the Jacobin Hobhouse will be soundly beaten, as he richly deserves.[63] Don't ever revert to this failure to write letters as happened yesterday. Once the habit is lost, and the clock no longer tells the time, it is hung up in the corner, and no one gives it another thought.

Saturday 20 February

Great news! The Most Christian King is dying, if not dead; Sir Francis Burdett is spending £20,000 on organizing a tremendous tumult next Monday;[64] and the quarrelsome Duke has departed to where heretics go when Satan sounds his gong to summon them to the other world[65] a great liberation for Douglas! A genteel little note from Brother Crotchet authorises me to inform you of this event, which will throw the whole of Arcadia into confusion. Will they set out or not? When it pleases them to, they laugh at snow and the Alps. If they get it into their head to travel, neither cold nor winds will prevent the Ducal Caravan from moving. A picturesque and original lot! Strange people, who'll become stranger still with the varnish that Destiny, the Toucher-up, will apply to them. Their Snarling Dog shewed his teeth for the last time last Thursday night ...

I have another note from Archibald: they've contented themselves with sending the great news by post and not by special courier (it's so much cheaper!). I'd love to see the sentimental-jubilant face of the Shepherd-Duke. Farewell, dear Gregory, I'm going to Fulibus, who'll be enchanted, having long promised to salute the Shepherdess with the title of Your Ducal Majesty.

Monday 22 February

... I can see clearly from your letter of the day before yesterday that once one puts oneself entirely in Hicksius' hands there is no way of escape: this is his system, and as long as he can find people to follow it he will put it in action without yielding on any point. I can only compare this form of domination to that which used to be (and still is) exercised by the Father Confessors in the houses of many a good soul in Spain and < > Portugal ...

Friday 26 February

... As I'll get £4,000 from the Merchants and £1,000 from the Great Dolt I can manage to exist, provided, of course, I don't make any big purchases; this regular income will suffice for what is strictly necessary. The Sage is mistaken if he thinks that I'm ever low-spirited. That's not my way. I'm no more like the Anglicans in this respect than in their addiction to Port, beefsteaks, Clubs and brothels ...

Yesterday at the Bindley sale Boletus bought for me a beautiful copy of the Life of the Glorious One, with many engravings which I don't remember having ever seen before; the price was ten and sixpence; the binding, new and in quite good taste, must have cost 18 shillings! It's a real treasure for me and will be full of instruction and interest. I forgot to tell you that the fine portrait by Tintoretto became mine for slightly more than half what it cost Bindley, eight guineas; Bindley had paid Edwards fourteen for it, and this was as a favour.[66]

Monday 1 March

The Phoenix has at last done me the honour of a visit; he was quite foolish, conceited and faltering, but less dandified than usual. Unfortunately for me he is busying himself with the portraits and, having obtained the original of the Edward VI by the grace of the Duke of Bedford, promises to make a real Holbein; the Francis the First will be a Titian, and doubtless all will have merit. It would be impossible to be more pleased with oneself than him; he is come from Woburn (the said Bedford's abbey), crowned with all the laurels that sprout on that Parnassus. He finds the Yellow Poet (the Apollo of the place) delightful and his poem divine, and is going to do the portrait of this great man for that other great man and Maecenas, the Duke of Bedford[67] ... he enjoys his lovely effigy: he finds in that pallid and poisonous beak an enchanting air of sublime ugliness, and I think he's right. But everyone is not of our opinion. Yesterday's *Champion,* overturning the poor poet from his pedestal, p—ss—s and sh—s upon him without mercy;[68] my small gloss on this sublime little work, now written in a corner of the book, is a confection of roses compared with the gall *<amaro>* of this critic. O poor Yellow One *<Amarello>*, what colour must you now become? ... France is a volcano, and so is England: everywhere one hears subterranean rumblings that bode ill. In the Exchange there are horrible fears. Hope, Baring, Rothschild, all are in confusion: they've been forced to sell millions at great loss to face certain bills which the Bank refuses to discount. France is going up, they're all going up![69]

Tuesday 2 March

Poor dear Fulibus, with what difficulty he withdraws from this country; yet at the same time he speaks ill enough of all he hears and sees, eats and drinks over here—the stupidity more block-headed than ever, melancholy and disquiet stamped on every face etc, etc. At Wellington's last great banquet, shabbiness mingled with the most solid splendour, mediocre dishes, unworthy dessert and really weak, muddy and detestable coffee were what leapt to his eyes—and his mouth. Every hour the great Wellington becomes smaller and more insignificant. Not only at the banquet-table but at the council-table too he begins to count for almost nothing. After dinner the abandoned *Mater dolorosa* of his family received all the nymphs of London most *à la mode*: there was Milady Caroline Lamb ('Glenarvon') seeing if she could make use of her well-known eloquence to get help for the election of her brother-in-law, etc. The whole scene was depicted for me yesterday until one in the morning with all the confidential Fulibusian vivacity.[70]

... For twice twenty-four hours it hasn't ceased to rain or snow. You can imagine the fevers, rheumatism, paralysis etc which are spreading round the hustings at Westminster; but what does all this signify? Nothing. Without an open, true and honest pestilence we'll never be free of an excess of population.

A fine situation indeed, that of Greenhorn Marlborough! I don't doubt that it is gospel: the Professor's news is in conformity with all I know.[71] Oh how, how unfortunate I am to be a eunuch in this harem, "Oh, what a pity it is to be without balls"![72] ... White Knights is the name of the place, where the most delightful garden, cultivated by him with all possible intelligence and taste, is going to be the prey of plunderers worse than the most intrepid carrion crows at Waterloo! We'll see issuing from it a torrent of treasures, books, porcelain, bronzes, ivories, agates etc, etc; and there I'll be with my harp in my hand, like the Israelites looking at the waters of Babylon flowing by, weeping and Jeremiah-ifying, but nothing more: it's enough to make me tear out the few hairs I have left!

The Abbé Macquin awaits a paralytic visitation; he has signs and symptoms which smell no better to me than they do to him. It's all this eating and drinking—rum at night and champagne by day: one pays for it to the last farthing; creditors of this sort are as implacable as those of Greenhorn. One recovers, one recovers, but then comes the fatal day and the Gong sounds ...

The Greenhorn has had his reign, he has for many years enjoyed the omnipotence of having all he wanted what ever it cost, no matter what the price. And I? No, I've never had, until recently, brio or courage in these matters. Now that I have, where am I to turn to find a Jewish lender? With £10,000 one would get treasures from this mine. Even with £5,000 one could show a judgment more sound than Paris', and make a choice not only of the purest taste but of the most substantial profit! If Rottier was alive one could have a fling, spitting in the face of caution, as he used to do, blessed soul; but in my Bestifownial position, goodbye hope: for me neither Limbo nor Purgatory, but Hell with all its eternal horrors, where *nulla est redemptio*.[73] Ah, if only! If only! What bargains! What delight: a residence in the neighbourhood of White Knights; every morning at the sale, every evening in conclave with you and Hume; the sweet transports, the precious caresses given to Eggshell, Seagreen, Old Crackle;[74] and then Boletus in permanent session nodding his judicious head: "Twenty pounds—guineas." "Mr Clarke."[75] In the intervals one might read *Le Bachelier de Salamanque*.[76] Everything one could want—gold, blue, red, the most heavenly splendours of the rainbow will surround me; and having become heavenly myself from the joy and balm of humours no longer mortal, I'd shed on all around contentment and peace ...

One can't imagine (especially in the matter of books and curious pamphlets in *my* own style)[77] the enormous quantity of objects that will be revealed, relics of Baldock, of Mme Decaix etc, thousands and thousands of things forgotten by their owners, things accumulated in the dawn of the French Revolution and in the course of twenty or thirty years. Ah, Professor, Professor, what a talisman you have touched to make my brain seethe and make me call to my aid Satan and all his devils!

Saturday 6 March

A fine idea indeed that I should buy White Knights! All the shaving[78] I could do at Fonthill would barely give lather enough to enter into such a business! White Knights won't go cheap, for it is at a distance from London suitable for many buyers. The climate is nothing, the views nothing, it's all nothing to me, but altogether a greater affair for many others who like a smiling, populated neighbourhood, fashionable Society, packs of hounds etc.

Doubtless certain little trips to Blenheim and another place have diminished its treasures, which are for ever sparkling and scintillating in the memory and imagination of Boletus; but still, an immense quantity of beautiful and finely bound books should come to light the moment the sale begins ...

The weekly expenses continue as usual—£100 more or less, including certain bills for boots, shoes, breeches etc. From time to time there are large accounts, for example £42 for sheets, £38 for wax candles, £21 to Morell for bacon oil, etc, etc[80] ...

Wednesday 10 March

... Yesterday the Calf ushered into my room, when I least expected it, Sweetness in person—more hirsute, bearded and baboon-like than the fantastic faces one can see on coconuts; very amiable, very thin, pretty poor I don't doubt, but bursting with sublime plans. He has been in Paris and goes back there the day after tomorrow under the orders of a new *Fortunate Youth*[81] worth £800,000, who bears the illustrious name of Ball, or something of the kind, the heir and bastard of a Lady Hughes, widow of an admiral (despoiler of the Indies) of that name.[82] This Philipine gem[83] has bought treasures of the most capital Buhl, ebony carvings after your own heart and heaven knows what marvels; and there still remains many a mine of sublime things and artistic marvels to be bought in Paris. He is making a *pied-à-terre* for the said Fortunate One (who'll be twenty-one in a month or two) in Brook Street for the modest price of £4,000; meanwhile it is proposed to acquire all the land in Berkeley Square, a front of 169 feet beginning from Thomas' Hotel!

The ostensible object of his call was first of all to ask for news of the Chevalier Franchi and then for my protection with the Duke of Hamilton. On both matters I answered with equal benignity, for the rogue really is a person of taste and is always as alive as quicksilver. I regret not being still young and roguish enough to profit by the *Fortunate Youth* in every respect and way—in front and behind, above and below.

Not a word was breathed about the Abbey, the deceased Bagasse, the quarrel[84] with his infernal brother Benjamin etc. Making a most dandified bow and asking if I had any orders for Paris (I said 'no' with a suave expression) he decamped without knowing a thing more than when he coaxed the simple Calf to let him in ...

Friday 12 March

... I send you the letter received this morning from Rome. What the devil is the matter with this delightful, highly original and despotic sovereign of your Fulibus: "*Je ne suis rien moins qu'en bonne santé*", she writes. My God, what can be the matter—disgust, jealousy or boredom with cardinals and the relics of St Pauline or whatever? By this time they know everything and repent of their dawdling.

Yesterday in Parliament two or three ancient Scotsmen of high lineage and with all Mr Drysdale's age, voice, accent and benevolence, begged me for the love of all that remains of Hamiltonian greatness to make them return at once—and very quickly at that; as if I could do anything serious or solid with them! I replied half Scottishly, "O vary well, vaary well, I will do ale I can"; "Pray do and you will serve the Hoose of Hamilton essentially", they rejoined ...

Saturday 13 March

You can imagine, my dear Gregory, what I feel on seeing before my eyes the sad proof of the state of your hand. How it afflicts me! How it augments the disagreeableness and anguish of my insipid and lugubrious existence! It's in vain to complain, it's like the weather—I know of no machine powerful enough to electrify it, as a certain Williams proposed to do in his book on the climate of England.[85] With a kind of Tower of Babel on Bagshot Heath or Salisbury Plain he promised to send away clouds, fog and frost; the sun was always to shine in the most azure of skies; coughs, colds, rheumatism, consumption etc sent to Hell; pills rendered unnecessary; and all the produce of the earth in such bounty and abundance and so full of living sap that not a single face would appear pinched or deformed. Until this great millennium of triumphant happiness arrives, we pass our time poorly enough!

... No one can resist the progress of the years. To say that I am as well as I used to be, not only in Ehrhart's time but even in Regnault's, would be false. My sleep is no longer so tranquil, and on various nights I'm agitated by the most ridiculous and extravagant dreams of your sort ... It wouldn't be right to leave you with the mistaken thought that you are the only one who has cause for complaint.

Not a ray of sunshine has fallen for five or six days upon this Dominant (so solitary for me).[86] The sameness of a mantle of mourning for ever suspended in the sky is enough to inspire the profoundest melancholy; and the north-east wind is enough to inspire the most torturing and harmful sensations—I feel at every moment as if thousands and thousands of envenomed steel points are entering my veins.

... I pay up when I can. This very day I've sent Randall to pay £24 6s. to the paperer on Ludgate Hill[87] who two or three years ago supplied the paper for the Cabinet Room. Farewell, dear Gregory, I sincerely beg the Glorious One to inspire you for the best.

Monday 15 March

Poor Hume, for the last four years he hasn't stopped writing in vain (now the seventeenth letter) to the Marquis of Buckingham. Doubtless he's in a fairly bad way by reason of many other illustrious unassailable debtors.[88] The thought of owing him so much torments me night and day ...

Tuesday 16 March

... When one thinks that the merchants have disbursed in the conduct of my affairs £1,200 for the Hindon festivities, £2,400 for Linley Farm, and £1,800 for regaling certain friends of Mr Still at Hindon,[89] without counting various tolerably large sums for Bestifownes, and the debts existing even before the deluge of Coxone's etc, etc, one sees the impossibility of going and looking for help from them ... A single *coup* could give me a fine yearly income—but what *coup*? You know what I mean, but I can't bear to mention it ...

Wednesday 17 March

... I'm sorry that Hicks is so afflicted with fasting and fatigue etc, and above all by the loss of such a fine banknote—it seems to me that he is not insensible to that kind of article—no one who wasn't absolutely avid for them would spend his life as he does—a life which in a few years, or even months, will bring him to his death—and then of what use will banknotes be! ...

The heat in the Chamber yesterday surpassed anything I've ever experienced in any theatre whatsoever. Four hundred Members and two ballots (making eight in succession), without me being nominated—a strange and rare thing. I always have a circle round me awaiting every word I let fall, as if they were pearls—that *they* are Swine (at least the greater part) is more certain! If the mephitic atmosphere was not thoroughly bad for me, these retinues of attendants would not bore me—one gets used to anything.

Thursday 18 March

... The Government newspapers do not cease to proclaim Douglas' frequent visits to Signora Borghese. The day before yesterday in the *Courier* one read "The ex-King of Holland lives retired but Princess Borghese most splendidly. The Marquis of Douglas visits there frequently." That's the only celebrity possessed by the Head of two great Houses amongst the most historic and illustrious in all Europe!!! ...

Friday 19 March

... The Quarrelsome Duke has gone as far as the law allowed him in burdening the Lancaster estates in favour of the Somerset Hyaena and her children.[90] I fear that poor Florindo will be neither rich nor potent—save in the favour of Madame Mère[91] and perhaps (though I don't swear to it) of the *infamous* Borghese. According to what is whispered to me in the Chamber, the Duke's conduct at Rome has disgusted all his Party,[92] the Ministry *and the whole Kingdom*. The perspective for the Duchess (who is pitied and bemoaned) is none too smiling, with Brother Crotchet on one side, dying of hunger, avid, desperate and venomous; and *Bouche-de-sucre* on the other, sponging and asking alms; and her husband sighing after Italy, etc. She'll spend sad days on her poor throne at Hamilton. God knows what they'll do or what will become of them.

I know nothing for certain about Ashton except for the general sale of furniture and horses etc which there is going to be. I know nothing of the fate of the house in New Road, where I see people about, birds in their cages, flowers in the windows etc, and no funeral portrait hung up (as is always done).[93]

... Who knows now how long yet is needed to complete the poor boy's pillular education. By this new system everyone, great and small, become (or are already, without knowing or suspecting it) Strasbourg geese.[94] How the great Ehrhart would laugh, and how the great words *Poureau, Pête, Garladan* etc would reverberate in room, stair and street! ...

Saturday 20 March

... Almost every day now I see Hume, and seeing him one sees objects of curiosity, and seeing them one always thinks them desirable; then one gives little commissions, and then one makes little purchases and so piling up debts and deficits one marches towards an abyss as black as Death! The three parts of the Bindley sale that there have so far been have meant more than £200 to me. The delightful collection which in consequence adorns the little Hotel Jaunay is not to be despised, and being composed not only of books to look at but also to read, it has been my entire consolation in the lonely evenings I've been passing. I rarely go to the theatre, and would hardly ever go at all were it not for a desire to amuse the poor Turk, who never stops asking after you and when you are returning.

They say that the Hyaena is hurrying on the Ashton sale with the greatest eagerness; a catalogue is being made: to this end one of Christie's satellites (pretty imbecile and ignorant, according to Hume) has already left. Doubtless they'll take out the fixtures and destroy as much as possible of the house, gardens and stables etc. Such are the thorns produced by the Rose of Arcady![95] ... There were many pictures and prints supplied by the Woodburns etc— nothing superfine (unless accidentally!) but many things—things useful to anyone living there. This house will be treated as if the French had passed by, with hunger, destruction and battle in their train ...

Monday 22 March

I was right in thinking I wouldn't escape a few little purchases. I trusted—I had a look and there already in a tiny corner of my cupboard at Jaunay's are the divine, gold-mounted little chest painted in the Hindu style (formerly at Gwennap's)[96] and the most magnificent piece of engraving in silver I've ever seen (the Margrave's Wildercom—sublime).[97] With all possible honesty and, one might say, friendship, Hume let me have them for what they cost him, by a happy chance, at that rogue Phillips', who, tired of putting up and withdrawing the chest so many times for £22, £24 and £25, let it fall for £18. That's not dear. The Wildercom at £13 (it weighs 16 ounces) was dirt cheap ...

The sun is shining again and a breeze has sprung up. I'm going out to get a breath of air—it's already late—half-past three.

Fonthill, Tuesday 13 April <*10 a.m.*>

I'm better, in spite of having been lashed in the face by cruel rain for an hour on end yesterday, during my ride down from the *French Horn*.[98] To my great delight I've returned to the Brown Parlour and the Sacristy: the Lancaster Room isn't bearable—the staircase, its narrowness, the impossibility of serving at table there etc would have made me despair, shriek and tantrumise. They could have saved me a good deal of inconvenience with a little judgement, but the Sow[99] is the Sow and the Ghoul the Ghoul, and the whole lot dirty beasts or great blockheads; I'm not speaking about Caroline—she has intelligence.

This morning I'm fresh and healthy and my tongue is clear. I don't know whether I'll amuse myself with medicines, but certainly not this evening. With a palisade in front of the windows I don't think the building operations will inconvenience me or that it will be necessary to take the books from St Michael's Gallery.

Yesterday's view of the forests put me in mind of Poligny-les-Rousses etc, and gave me *saudades* of the Lake of Geneva, Gibbon's library and Dr Scholl.[100] I think we'll get some sun. It's ten o'clock and they're coming to hasten this letter to despatch it with some things they're sending you. I embrace you, my dear Gregory.

Midday[101]

... I begin to be well here and to pass in review all the delicious *bimberie* of this poetic and almost uninhabitable place. It's always a joy for anyone who reads to find a treasury of books like the one here. How many beautiful things there are—it surprises one when one returns and sees them after an interval of two or three months.

... Rhinoceros' work seems to me worthy of the times of King Manuel,[102] but the great rose in the middle is just a little large for the surrounding mouldings. The weather finds it difficult to clear up—the sky is still ashen and the peacocks and bantams etc don't yet trust it; they're clucking, preening and shitting in their favourite corner. The flowers they've brought me this morning are stupendous: they might be from Portugal, they're so large, flourishing and clear in colour.

Thursday 15 April

... Alas, Rhinoceros is a beast as beastly as the deceased Coxone (with the added fault of being alive). He has neither taste nor a sense of proportion, and not the least knowledge of the true Gothic style. With a ray of intellect he would have himself abhorred that flat, thick, stupid great rose; it must be done away with, it isn't to be tolerated. Even the frieze contrived by this animal isn't comparable to many in existence, which he would have done well to copy. It wasn't without reason that I recalled King Manuel and his happily unfinished chapels[103] ...

I've only seen the Great Dolt once—the beastly priest's[104] visit was enough to last me for centuries (and hellish ones at that). What a fanatic—but not about music! Tomorrow, after all, I'll take medicine; it seems to me that I have the greatest need of it. Farewell, dear Gregory, would that Monday had already come.[105]

Friday 16 April

... The weather continues absolutely spring-like—little showers interspersed with stray rays of sunshine. The cold having diminished, the atmosphere was favourable enough for operations in honour of the memory of Ehrhart. I sympathise sincerely with the Professor, I sympathise with anyone who comes under the Hicksian rod. This superstition, like many others, does not save from Hell—one conforms, one believes, and after a terribly long pillulation one remains where one was at the beginning.

I wish you could see the Lancaster Room with the Salvator, and under the Salvator the two Poelenburghs and the Patel, all three in the richest old frames; the Wilson on one side of the door, the Berchem on the other; the Mieris in the corner where one of the Poelenburghs was, and the new Brueghel in place of the other.[106] I must needs think about a musical instrument for the Duchess—I think she'll be admirably suited in this room, so independent from her bedroom, watercloset etc …

I doubt if the Ducal Caravan has yet set forth: without a magic flute it's difficult to move such a be-flowered, *italianissimo* Shepherd …

Saturday, 24 April, 1 o'clock[107]

… Without a severe rule about every kind of purchase, great or small, one will certainly fall under the rule of Messrs Plummer, who, refusing to advance a penny more, will force the sale of —. It's horrible to think of, but I see in the air phantoms fit to inspire frenzies, dire and fatal like those of Lady Anne Hamilton …

Yesterday, permission having been given to the great man and his four other followers (all M.P.s) to see the Abbey, they were received by the Great Dolt (I was still at Bath) and magnificently fed by Randall, Bouffetaut and Nicobuze with salad *à l'italienne*, Bologna sausage, fricandean, cinnamon ice and an abundance[108] of extra special wine. They admired, and ate and drank like wolves, and I've had a letter full of devotion, satisfaction and gratitude. When one thinks that such magnificence, such good cheer etc threatens a total eclipse, there's a fresh dagger in one's heart—never was Our Lady more wounded than I.

Monday, pay-day and a North wind, 26 April

I only have a moment to scribble to you, my dear Gregory. The Great Dolt is here with a hundred thousand questions about how this and that is to be paid for. At the same time hammerings and clouds of dust (the tower[109] being already in a state of collapse) are the despair of me …

Dover; Saturday 22 May, 6.30 p.m.

... From Fonthill to here I've had nothing but superb horses and cheerful postillions, riding like the wind. Thanks to six horses, the Calf going on ahead etc (and, I suppose, my great reputation for not being poor), I made the journey to Dover no longer than that to Basingstoke. The most delicious fresh breezes wafted the perfume of a thousand herbs and flowers, and there wasn't an atom of dust; it was truly delightful.

This evening all is the colour of mother-of-pearl and opal; the sea is covered with vessels and fishing barques; the coast of France is as visible as Wardour from Fonthill; there's a slight breeze which crisps the waves like those so delicately sculptured by Valerio di Vicenza; over the Castle I see a faint, pale rainbow; far, far off at ten leagues there are fleeting clouds with their little falls of rain, as transparent as the curtains which are lowered in an opera when small storms are represented.

My coach is being embarked. The Customs are all sweetness and pleasantness. Tomorrow at eight o'clock I go on board; according to the look of things, everything will pass off agreeably provided the wind doesn't get up more in the south. Two packet-boats are approaching: who knows if one of them does not bring Florindo![110]

In London I went with Hume to Christie's tabernacle where the Queen's trumperies were on show. I saw the jade which I detest and the Frogmore cabinet which I still like but not as much as I thought; it is covered with smoky filth. I suppose it will be bought and will go to fulfil its destiny at Fonthill. Who the devil would have ever thought of such a thing? Not I. When one remembers that I had commissioned Bagasse to offer a diamond in exchange![111]

The speed of my journey gave me time to see in detail a thousand objects at Rochester and Canterbury—sculpture and glass that I had not noticed before, certain doorways, certain cloisters, very curious. Having got up at six and not leaving Rochester this morning till nine, I passed an hour and a half in the Cathedral before breakfast. At Canterbury, where I arrived at midday, I made a big tour in the crypt, and in the galleries above and below, always followed by Nephew and Alidru. Both these animals have already profited by the change of air; they are more lively and amiable than at Fonthill.

Sunday 23 May

Nature and Art are all silent on an Anglican Sunday. Not a breath of wind. But they say the tide is sufficient. I hope so. I'm just off.

Charter from Calais

Here I am at last, after three and a half hours of the greatest jubilation and good fortune imaginable at sea. All was enchantment—a sea of diamonds, a sky of the most luminous azure yet powdered with clouds, breezes wafted from Paradise, the coast clad in the softest and most harmonious colours, and all the Divinities of the waves propitiated. But not so those of the land—Quillac served me with a pretty mediocre dinner. But it doesn't matter—the sea has been passed and I hope the dinner will pass too without indigestion. But the one who will have an indigestion of me is the infamous Pigault—I received him like one does a dog on a racecourse. Mouron, who came running the moment he saw, to his surprise, my discharge (for, you know, I landed in a four-oared skiff), has confirmed me in my opinion of Pigault[112] ...

The Customs have been benign—as at Dover, benign, quite benign. They're singing and drumming in every street, all the shops are open, and all the people have a gaiety and primitive Frenchiness, dancing and shitting with zest and talking all the time—nothing Anglican about it ...

Wednesday 26 May[113]

On the road and everywhere my eyes turn, *squalid misery*. Just as certain insects take their colour from the leaves they eat, so the people, who, alas, only have but stones to eat, are the colour of their own dwellings. Everything seems to be falling into ruin, nothing announces a ray of hope or prosperity.

I've just returned from the Cathedral, as always gigantic and imposing in its general mass but ugly enough in detail; for details it doesn't compare with St Wulfran's portal at Abbeville ...

Monday 7 June

… I came like a thunderbolt, having electrified by sheer weight of money the passporteers, Customs-ites, inn and post-house keepers, in short *everybody* along the whole route—of me alone do they talk and think, to me only do they drink …

Friday 25 June

Rain everywhere, penetrating damp—but that's nothing. A fatal illness is going to deprive me of my poor Caroline; this has thrown me into a state of melancholy, anxiety and anguish such as I've never experienced in my whole life. I'm more dead than alive myself. I neither eat nor sleep. Like the victims of Eblis, I seek what I cannot find—nor ever shall find.[115]

Fowkes watches by the poor animal day and night, with all possible attention and, I think, good sense. She is consumed by some internal complaint caused by her damned gestation; she suffers cruelly. You can imagine what I feel, loving thus this faithful companion of my tomb-like solitude. Never more will she appear sleeping at my feet; never more will she console me with those intelligent looks so full of affection for me. I feel as if there was a ball of lead in the pit of my stomach; there are painful constrictions in my forehead. Tears have not yet come to my aid …

Saturday 26 June

Caroline … is still alive but at death's door. This morning she recognised me and licked me most affectionately … Yesterday really was for me the day of the Last Judgment—I thought I was already in Hell. Your letters are full of nothing but gout, rheumatism, hideous dreams, and harsh, cruel reflections. They are not in a style to placate or console me, but are as unsuited as possible to my present state …

What is happening in the case of the Duke of Marlborough shows very clearly the consequence of incurring debts etc in a country which, unlike Portugal, does not enjoy the benign power of royal proclamations, with their paternal advice to people of the lower orders to leave untroubled the repose of the heroes of the upper classes. Never before has a Most Excellent Greenhorn been more humiliated than he: it's pitiful to see such an illustrious title dragged so low. The small books are selling, but the larger items, especially those bought at the Bedlamite Roxburghe Sale, show an immense loss. A Caxton sold then for 351 <pounds> has now fetched only 55; about the Boccaccio you know already; Morlini's *Novellae* fetched 48 at Roxburghe and 19 at Greenhorn's etc. The stupendous Froissart (now mine) which fetched 63 at Roxburghe cost me only 32; but this was due to the passing-by of the Persian Ambassador just as it was on the rostrum: everyone rushed to the door and windows, so Boletus, staying put, carried off the palm. That infamous thief and puppy Jarman gave 105 guineas for the little missal in silver filigree which was brought me, years ago (if you remember) by that rogue Foster[116] ...

Sunday 27 June

... I'm not completely extinct, neither is Caroline—she's alive. The day before yesterday, full of the bitterest pain, I threw myself at the feet of the Saint; after that half-hour passed in the most intimate persuasion of a special protection, I was consoled and the poor animal free from danger ...

Tuesday 29 June

I begin by informing you that my Caroline is better. She has already accompanied me as far as Stone Gate, not yet jumping about but watching me all the time with eyes which (to me at any rate) seemed full of life and grateful affection ... I don't know whether the Duchess will fall upon the Duke, but the Duke, I fear, will not fall any more upon her—"he is too worn out and disordered" (it's impossible to translate what she writes into reasonable language) ...

Now that I recollect that the Methodist has in his keeping the lapis-lazuli and the gold, it wouldn't surprise me if he made off and if one heard no more of him until one read in the American papers: "New York, 21st Sept. 1819—Brother Harris, newly arrived from the Land of perdition, has gladdened our hearts with much spiritual discourse etc, etc"[117] ...

Thursday 15 July

What a fine Court, what a triumphant Court is the Portuguese now that it has had the wit to make the Most Serene Cowpat Viscountess of Tagoa*hy* (it's as if one was sneezing *hy-hy*).[118] I won't keep from you the highly sentimental letter announcing this illustrious favour; here it is ... In a short time, perhaps at the beginning of this autumn, the pathetic Viscountess will arrive to enjoy her distinguished honours on the highest steps of the throne of King Heavisides at Bath. What luck for Don José Sill! But I doubt whether, in effect, he will enjoy the celebrity conferred on him by his sister's great title—it brings too much light to the shade of his cherished parsimony[119] ...

Tuesday 20 July

Thank you, my dear Gregory, for your lively and (I'm sure) true description of Mrs Matthews' museum. You can be quite sure that the Brueghels, along with their fifty-eight companions, are copies. Originals of this artist are extremely rare: they were too few, took too long to make and were too dear to be common. Pictures which he had spoilt and rejected, yes; but fine ones like mine from the Escurial[120] and the last one bought at Panné's sale aren't offered every day ...

The weather, the hideous chorus of the peacocks, the sad condition of my adored Caroline, all inspire me with an almost irresistible wish to flee from here. No one who does not understand my strange composition can guess what is passing within me at this time. It isn't living, but languishing suspended between life and death with bowed head ...

The cupboards etc will be arranged under your supervision. When you are far away I haven't the spirit or the courage to think of anything.

You'll find the great room in disorder because of the repair to the cloth, but I think it has been well done. The rest goes on as best it can, not as one would wish ...

Wednesday 21 July

... I have no news from Paris except some bestialism of the 14th inst. from the incredible Chardin, addressed as usual to "M.P. 6. Upper Harley Square Street London hotel Launai Leicester Angleterre."[121] You can imagine the postmarks and marginal notes on this fine imbroglio; I only wonder at its arrival here—but they know by heart at the Post Office where to send and how to read this long string of incomparable absurdity. It does honour indeed to those who pity this great dotard's corpse. If it was he and not Caroline who was dying, it wouldn't cost me many sighs.

Farewell hay! Farewell flowers! Farewell corn! Hail Comet—you are the only machine capable of liquidating the debts, annoyances, infamies and torments of this Chardinesque globe.[122]

Friday 13 August!
Just as I expected

The fine gallery in my mouth has gone. Originals and copies all fell out this morning at breakfast. I'm left whistling, and creaking like a door not properly shut. My situation is anything but delightful, I can assure you, but if it was miraculously proposed to me to resuscitate either my teeth or Caroline, I would take Caroline, and would bury myself with her no matter where. On Monday I'll leave here and see Scarman and what can be done; but as I've never been passionately fond of the mechanical arts, I doubt whether I shall submit to having my mouth put in harness ... You can't imagine in what a state I am; the change in my voice is horrible.

Saturday 14 August

From time to time, when least expected, I make a whistling, a flute-like note, a transition to another key; ... I have the airiest of spaces in my mouth, and a grace in eating and talking that would be the despair of anyone but myself ...

London, young Hume writes, "is almost as quiet as Salisbury Plain, but not so healthy". That is good news for me, who am more than ever a lover of solitude, and have such evident cause to hide my shame etc. Pray God for the repose of my mouth and the safety of my soul,

Your pitiable *Patron* Saint Splutterer ...

Monday 30 August

... The lacquer box, of a rare and superior quality, was worthy of more careful preservation; it is a fine and curious piece. The tremendous magic baboons, suspended from one of the most luxuriant Japanese trees I have ever seen, are busy fishing with their interminable arms for the moon reflected in the water—some Japanese satire, I suppose ...

Thursday 16 September

... The Abbé is not in bad health. He is singing in his Chapter-house "Lord, open Thou my lips"[123]—that I may yawn—as he reads the *great* tome of the learned Berington,[124] which is nothing to write home about, especially for those who have already swallowed 20,000 volumes of fictitious history ...

Saturday 25 September

... The Abbé eats and drinks with his usual intrepidity, and talks—my God how he talks! Mr. Still's windmill does not go faster on the windiest days of this century ...

Monday 27 September

… One can see from Bestifownes' letter that the Lugubrious One[125] is also feeding himself on the idea that the Duchess is in very poor health. One must have good nerves to endure so *cathedralic* a habitation as mine and the weepings of a guest (when he comes) as *cat-e-drawlic* as he—foreboding whisperings at midnight and lamentations as of devil-possessed cats in the gutters. The Abbé provides at least some sort of counterblast to all this— he laughs and talks, roisters, eats and drinks; and if he does no better, the fault is not his but that of the specimens which adorn this museum …

Wednesday 29 September

… Here is the Duchess' letter. A fine and very short journey, to leave London on Sunday at ten and arrive at Hamilton Palace on Tuesday at three; I would like to imitate it, but for me these 'economical'[126] journeys would be not only a Passion but death as well. With all her ultra-sentiment, she must be pretty strong …

Thursday 30 September

… I trust that you will not be bestially benign enough to go to the Scottish Court in preference to that of Fonthill … The Duchess thinks of herself and not of me. When she really wants to travel here, she does! Everything else about her is jargon and egoism; he who thinks otherwise only deceives himself. Why, the poor General's great compliments about my excellent merit are worth as much or more as all her sentiment and all her rubrics *"le plus cheri des Pères"* etc.

Friday 1 October

Notwithstanding your lively desire to go to the Kingdom of the Cinquefoils,

I still think that from every point of view and for every reason the Fonthill journey will be more salutiferous, even if not more agreeable. Ever since yesterday morning I have suffered less; but even if I was suffering much more, your brazen stubbornness would withstand my 'complaining' communications.

I knew that you were bound to shit on the Inquisition and on a thousand sacred and venerable things after reading the Introduction to the *History of Charles V*; when one reflects that all this was the production of a Calvinist minister, an atheist at bottom, I don't wonder. Such people and such principles I abhor, and I fear that ere long I will have only too much reason to execrate them, curse the lot. It was sane and just—the policy which, until our inauspicious days, prevented the progress of false learning. He paints a sad and insipid picture where all is the same colour, a monotonous plain where one sees neither hills nor mountains! Would that the ideas in this reprobate volume were true, pure and clear like his style and logic. Once you concede that all priests are charlatans and all monarchs tyrants, you can prove, in a mathematical way, what you like; but if you dispute the first step in the argument you find a labyrinth of the most fatal errors. Oh how right Rome was, and he, infamous vermin, stinking heretic, how wrong![128] ...

Saturday 2 October

Yesterday was a day of wind, tempest and smoke, enough to make one despair; not a single chimney was quiet. In consequence of too much heat on one side and too little on the other I have fresh rheumatic pains and feverish tremors. The poor General has departed, not ill-content, I trust, with his reception at this extraordinary Court.

I perfectly understand your indigestion of solitude. My stomach being (and having always been) very strong in this respect, I cannot pretend to feel such a windy vacuum, but still, I desire some society and above all yours. Consequently, if you can find me a passably commodious lair for fifteen days I won't refuse it.

According to the General's politics, the Revolution advances with giant strides. Most of the soldiers—generals, captains and privates—abhor Wellington; this schismatic disposition is of a truly fatal augury. Before everything falls into total disorder I shall begin, I think, to cut down some ash in the Rookery, if I can get a decent price.[129] One can find seventy or eighty tons there without absolutely ruining its picturesque beauties. Once the ash is felled I shall consider the oak—I have no other resource, as you well know.

That the necessity of your journey to London is imperious, I don't doubt, but that the Scottish journey is also, I can't see. And what would you have me do here *alone*—my only music the howling of the winds, my principal occupation the just and bitter sentiment of the loss of my poor, faithful Caroline! Not a day, not a single night passes without my recollection of that terrible 24th July. If you go to Scotland, perforce I must go to London, and if I go to hotelise there for three or four months I shall be obliged to send the picturesque to the Devil and fell the last saleable ash or oak ...

Sunday 3 October

Yes, my dear Gregory, < > I'm ready to sell Wills to whoever will buy them, and for £4,000 down (not three) I'll leave ten to the children of the General or of the Phoenix George Hayter, as you will; but no money, no Will.

... Do not trust that atheistical Calvinist minister Robertson. He knows little and says much, a good equal style without ups and downs, a murmuring well-mannered rivulet of commonplace ideas, little curious research, little reading outside that offered by books already compiled by many others—what a difference between him and Gibbon! ...

Tuesday 5 October

... It does little credit to Mr Joe or the gamekeeper to send you such a villainous old pheasant. Those they have hitherto presented to me merit M. de la Motte's compliment "*Sortez, Monsieur, vous n'est pas presentable.*"

Wednesday 6 October

They have reconsidered the idea of selling the ash: the greater part of these immense old trees are like the papers of the Marquis Tulip—ready to fall to powder. There are hardly forty-five or fifty tons of solid wood, for which they'll give me no more than £5 a ton. It is very sad! Turn in whatever direction I may, I find only difficulty and penury. After my miserable calculations, I fear an establishment other than this one. I don't much like the idea of Pulteney Street, and then, wherever one takes the Abbé one takes a ticket to an expensive hotel! …

Saturday 9 October

… Ah my God, how agonising it is to receive Bestifownes' jeremiads! They never cease. I tremble every time the creaking of the door and the smell of rotten dwarf announces the arrival of letters. A wind as cursèd as any of November's, bearing on bat's wings rheumatic melancholy, renders me doubly sensible of the misery of my position. In the space of a few hours we will lament and splutter[130] together …

Tuesday 12 October

Suffocating heat and a mist one could cut with a knife—that's this morning; at the moment, sun and air as at Collares. Herewith the £50. I hope they will find me a sofa more suitable for my use and Nephew's than the non-electric machine I saw yesterday.[131] The more the cursèd ash of the Rookery is examined, the rottener it is found to be. Sampson wants to use sycamore for the two rooms; this will save a big expense.

I'm thinking that at this perilous political moment it is time to get ready "for the field and to arms." So if you can find the soldier we noticed yesterday I will take some lessons in drilling from him and we'll write to Bestifownes that I'm going to Bath to learn on the cheap how to use a rifle without getting a very expensive drill sergeant to come to Fonthill. In all this I sigh only for

Prudence!

Economy!

Honour!

Country!

and Religion![132]

With such pure and becoming sentiments I pray God, my dear Saint Gregory, to have you in his holy and worthy keeping,

                                          Spluttering Drill-maniac.

Thursday 14 October

… I have news from the Arcadian Palace enough to make anyone weep who interests himself in them—it is so nebulous, so melancholy, so hypochondriacal, so day-bedish …

I'll send everything that I consider indispensable by the Waggon, and two chamber-witches or chamber-whores, or whatever you like to call them; but no kitchen-maid, since I'll entrust myself to the old woman of the house. So there'll be

Bouffetaut and Nicobuze

Randall and Farret

the Calf and the Turk

the Soft Brother with two ponies

and the two female animals;[133]

That's the lot! Isn't it enough? I think so. Enough at any rate to make my expenses accumulate; for this reason, even with the best will in the world, it won't be to my advantage to remain in Bath for more than five or six days …

Friday 15 October

So, my dear Gregory, you have ill-digested your reading from sacred and profane history; from this come bad dreams, base illusions, ridiculous chimeras and jacobinical contempt for everything that has been grand or venerable. When one reads to such purpose, how much better ignorance is!

I approve much more of your plan of the tap-room. Everything must have a beginning, and beginnings are allowed to be rather humble. Let us begin, then, in the grosser style to end up with the purest and highest platonic adoration of *the true beauty*. Oh what a soft and compassionate glance—it will be years (if I live that long) before I forget it[134] ...

Thursday 28 October

On leaving Bath the weather was delicious, but after Warminster the sky became covered with leaden clouds. Sharp cold set in and certain sad drops of frozen rain fell—an all too appropriate accompaniment of the depressing news given by *l'Inforcato*: following the example of sugar, timber fetches barely half what it fetched last year: for the best ash they offer £3 15s. per ton and for first quality oak £7, and not a penny more. At these prices (especially for oak) the sacrifice is terrible.

Cup, goblets, the Queen's salvers, harpsichord, china for sweetmeats, massive objects from Ceylon, Cuttel, Coulson, Aldridge and Fogg—all are crying out "Pay me! Pay me!"[135] And how to pay I no longer know.

If anything could enchant a timid and religious soul, it would be the incredibly rich and sublime effect produced by Cellini's stupendous dragon alongside the conch in the Bouchardon cabinet: diamonds, topaz and enamel—everything glitters in a magical way. The little piece of scarlet leather, on which this sublime *objet d'art* rests, looks so well, and the height of the vase is so correct when it is grouped with the conch, that I see no need to despatch the lapis-lazuli. I've ordered them to send to Bath the lingam[137] and the two tazzas from the Lancaster Gallery ...

Friday 29 October

... On days of this colour and temperature (brown-breadish, as you put it) I find the Abbey like a vault—the moment the Great Portal is closed, the

Octagon becomes a mausoleum, the Ebony Cabinet a royal tomb, and the other coffers tombs and repositories of sacred relics.

You may admire the Zenobia[138] as much as prejudice permits; for my part I prefer the Cornaro—if it is the Cornaro. I've searched in vain so far for any information about this real marvel in the writings of Benvenuto Cellini. In his treatise on the goldsmith's art[139] he talks a good deal about enamelling, but I can't see that he ever quotes this vase as an example. I'll return to this research another day, though it matters little whether or not I find the answer—the object in itself deserves the most wholehearted eulogy. You can't imagine how the Dragon strikes your gaze when opening the Bouchardon …

All I have to pay—it's horrible: £65 to Whitley for flowers and plants etc,[140] £17 to Turner, and then Fogg, and then and then—eviction. In English one would say: I founder—like a horse in a bog …

Thursday 4 November

… I will leave for Bath at seven and I will have a collation at York Hotel between ten and eleven; at half-past one at the latest I will return for dinner at the Abbey; at Warminster I will enter a postchaise to escape the inclemency of the evening breezes. In three hours we will have time to discuss many things which it is troublesome to scribble.

Yesterday the Abbe celebrated his convalescence by eating several copious helpings of a truly delicious *blanquette aux truffes* which did real honour to M. Bouffetaut but which I hardly touched, being ever mindful of the severe but justifiable rules of the Tyrant Hicks …

Farewell, I am going out—awaited by the pony which at present is called by the sweet name of Mousy-Powsy …

1.   Letter of October 2nd.
2.   August 16th.
3.   From Marlborough.

4. The famous coaching Castle Inn, now part of Marlborough College. *Ducal palace* is a scathing reference to the creation of Sir Hugh Smithson as first Duke of Northumberland in 1766 (he acquired the property by marriage before it was converted into an inn).

5. From Salthill.

6. His young Turkish valet was beginning to have to shave.

7. He was blind and mad, and his wife had died less than two months previously.

8. James Wyatt had erected two octagonal stuccoed turrets (since swept away) on the north front of the Castle, and Jeffrey Wyatt had not yet begun his work of restoration.

9. All subsequent letters until March 22nd inclusive were written in London.

10. *Harlequin Munchausen* or *the Fountain of Love*, a new pantomime by Farley at Covent Garden, featuring Grimaldi, greatest of all clowns, as Lord Humpy-Dandy, an Exquisite. It was presumably a burlesque recalling Baron Munchausen's *Travels* (1785), an early edition of which was entitled *Gulliver Revived ... containing ... an account of a Voyage into the Moon.*

11. *Harlequin Gulliver* or *the Flying Island*, the previous year's pantomime.

12. See p.237, note 48.

13. Seven Dials is the centre of St. Giles' district, then an area of terrible slums, called the Holy Land. Beggars were supposed to foregather there at night in revelry and drunkenness; Beckford may be referring to this.

14. Bindley, II 621 (more fully described in *H.P.S.* 1845): Charles I copy (with his arms) of J.C. Lobkowitz' *Philippus Prudens* <Philip II of Spain>, Plantin Press folio, Antwerp 1639. Bindley describes it as blue morocco and *H.P.S.* as red. For Bindley's sale, see below, note 34.

15. The lawyer R.S. White *Junior,* his father (Rottier) being dead; his nickname is derived from I Kings xii. 14, where the new ruler (Solomon's son) says: "My father chastised you with whips, but I will chastise you with scorpions".

16. John Boykett Jarman, jeweller, goldsmith and watchmaker in the Strand, and later curiosity dealer in St James' Street. Ruskin, who had a fine collection of illuminated MSS, bought some of them at Jarman's sale in 1864. The Missal described was at Jarman's.

17. 1815 MacCarthy catalogue, presumably Lot 396 (for this sale, see p.211, note 42).

18. MacCarthy 4264—also an illuminated manuscript on vellum, from the Gaignat sale. Dictys of Cnossos fought against Troy; his account of the Trojan War was a much later forgery.

19.   Alphonse-Louis-Philippes-Gonzaga Pignatelli (died 1808 or 1809), 19th Count of Fuentes, 19th Count of Egmont and 5th Duke of Solferino. The Pignatelli were Italian in origin (Princes of the Holy Roman Empire), but got the Spanish title of Fuentes by marriage. His mother was heiress of the Netherlandish Counts of Egmont. Like his elder brother, he died a bachelor. Beckford, who appropriately nicknamed him *The Calf,* forced him upon his daughter Susan as suitor. In giving his actual names (which are subject to endless variety in spelling and combination) I am mostly following a printed genealogy of the Egmonts in *H.P.*

20.   The Portuguese Embassy was there. The Count of Palmela (Fulibus) had probably been moved out of it because of his refusal to leave England (where he had been ambassador, and was evidently still *acting* as such) for another appointment. As a result, he was at 36 Berkeley Square (Thomas' Hotel).

21.   Louis Jacquier was proprietor of the Clarendon Hotel, New Bond Street.

22.   This was the night watchman, calling out the time on his rounds.

23.   Robert William Elliston (1774–1831), one of the greatest actors of his day, specially praised by Lamb and Leigh Hunt; a great manager of Drury Lane, 1819–26; opened the Olympic Pavilion, 1813.

24.   Elizabeth Rebecca Edwin (1771?–1854), not a great actress.

25.   *Rochester,* or *King Charles II's Merry Days,* by W.T. Moncrieff; it was a *burletta, i.e.* a comedy with music.

26.   *i.e.* lose his teeth; Scarman of George Street, Hanover Square, was Beckford's dentist.

27.   Davies, goldsmith and jeweller, York Street, Portman Square. His nickname must mean that Beckford bought from him, or at his auction, the Magnus Berg cup (see p.125, note 41).

28.   Wife of Ferdinand VII of Spain and daughter of João VI of Portugal.

29.   Maria Luisa, wife of Charles IV and mistress of Godoy, died in Rome on January 4th. According to Beckford's letter, Susan writes from Rome on January 2nd about her death (anticipated or actual); whatever the explanation of this apparent discrepancy, it is certain that Maria Luisa is meant. Beckford quotes Phipps' Sunday *News* of the 24th about her death.

30.   Presumably he means Maria Luisa.

31.   Howard Payne's *Brutus.*

32.   In the Strand, on the site of (and later called) the Adelphi. Its bill consisted of melodrama, musical farces, pantomimes, rope-dances, dwarfs, monkeys, fireworks, etc.

33. *The Judgement of Brutus on his Sons* by G.G. Lethière (1760–1832), a huge neo-Classical picture, now relegated to the Louvre cellars, was in 1816 exhibited in the Egyptian Hall, Piccadilly, where B. must have seen it.

34. James Bindley's library, sold in five portions between December 1818 and January 1821; it was rich in early English literature, especially of the period of Elizabeth and James I, and included priceless Shakespearean items.

35. Second letter.

36. George Gillow (1766–1822) of Hammersmith, second son of Richard Gillow the Elder, and grandson of Robert Gillow, founder of the famous firm of cabinet makers; he himself was a partner. His pictures were sold at Christie's in 1824 and anonymously at Stanley's on 12–13 June 1832; in 1818 he produced a folio on his collection, *Select Engravings from a Collection of Pictures ... exhibiting at the Saloon of Arts, Old Bond St,* dedicated to a famous collector, the fifth Earl of Carlisle. His warehouse was in Little Argyll Street (since submerged by Regent Street). *Father Tettone* is the nickname of a dealer or collector; *the Bard* is either George or his elder brother Robert.

37. The Oratorio at Drury Lane theatre (here ironically called a Dramatic Chapel) included selections from Mozart's *Requiem,* Haydn's Chorus *The Heavens are telling,* and an aria by Rossini, none of which Beckford mentions; and selections from Handel's *Messiah,* Beethoven's oratorio the *Mount of Olives,* arias by Paolo Bonfichi (1769–1840), a composer of religious music, and by Ferdinando Paër (1771–1839), a prolific Italian writer of operas, who was Musical Director to Napoleon. Giuseppe Ambrogetti (b. 1780) was a good *buffo* but a poor singer. Teresa Giorgi Belloc (1784–1855), married a Frenchman of that name and appeared professionally as Bellochi; she sang mostly in Milan, but was at the Italian Opera House in the Haymarket, 1817–20.

38. Pandora is R.S. White Junior. He is nicknamed Pandora because, whenever he opens his lawyer's box of tricks, some shock is in store for B., leaving only Hope remaining in his affairs. Shadwell Finch was his partner.

39. A decree by the Lords of the Committee of the Council for hearing Appeals from the Plantations. It concerned B's appeal from the decision in the case Campbell v. Beckford. This latter case had established in principle that B. must surrender certain Jamaican plantations which his family had held as mortgages for three generations; but the question still remained as to how much (if any) of the past profits and revenue B. had to disgorge. A large sum was at stake. As usual in such appeals, the decree set aside some of the pleas of each party but others were referred back to Jamaica for further investigation, so that the final judgment was again deferred.

40. House of Commons Committee to hear petitions in disputed elections which had taken place during the 1818 General Election.

41. *H.P.S.* 996 (photo), fetched £1,176.

42. The small tower Beckford inhabited.

43. G.H. Harlow (b. 1787), portrait and historical painter, pupil of Lawrence and friend of Canova, had died suddenly the previous day, and was buried under the altar of St James's, Piccadilly.

44. Martin (1789–1854) was exhibiting it at the British Institution.

45. See above, note 39.

46. Almost certainly Sir William Grant (1752–1832), who had recently retired from being Master of the Rolls, but still assisted in hearing Appeals. He heads the list of B's counsel in B's official printed Statement of his case submitted in 1801 to the same Committee hearing his appeal; Grant was probably able to conduct the appeal after he had ceased to be Solicitor-General and before he became Master of the Rolls.

47. Samuel Rogers' *Human Life* (see p.180).

48. A spencer was a a short, double-breasted, tail-less overcoat named after the second Earl Spencer (1758–1884), and was also used for a close-fitting jacket or bodice worn by women and children at this date. Beckford may be referring to some farce or interlude in the kind of winter pantomime he has already described.

49. The commonness of his name Smith makes it difficult to identify him, and without knowing the date of the letter his father received, it is difficult to guess which fort is meant; it would have been an incident in the third Mahratta War.

50. Hicks was fond of dosing with strong purgatives.

51. Psalm 180, verse 3.

52. The Censorship Office for books in Lisbon.

53. Girolamo Crescentini (1769–1846), male soprano; Anna Maria Pellegrini Celoni (d. 1835) was born and died in Rome, and wrote a singing manual, published in 1810.

54. The Duke of Blacas d'Aulps (1770–1839), staunch but moderate Royalist, was French envoy in Rome, and blacklisted Douglas because of his affair with Pauline, refusing to invite him to the Embassy. Ercole Consalvi (1757–1824) had been Secretary of State to Pius VII.

55. Giuseppe Girometti (1779–1851), Luigi Pikier or Pickler (1773–1854) and his younger brother Giuseppe, were gem-engravers and medallists.

56. Queen Charlotte died the previous November, and part of her collection was to be auctioned.

57. Sucribus would be the sugar-merchant managing Beckford's business (*i.e.* Plummer). Beckford was heavily in debt to his House, so it would not do for Hume, his buying agent at auctions, to be seen by him.

58. Pliny the Younger's *Letters*, Book II, Letter XVII, describe his villa on the Laurentine shore. A certain Bonelli was friend of Douglas and visited Fonthill in 1814, but I know nothing else about him or whether he is the man.

59. Bernard Salomon (borne *c.*1520), an engraver resident in Lyons, where he illustrated books during the last half of the 16th century. I cannot find this item in Bindley III, 1st Day (16 February), but this catalogue is badly compiled and might have omitted his name from the book he illustrated.

60. Golownin's *Recollections of Japan*, 3 vols, 1819.

61. Yeddo is Tokio; Miaco is Kyoto (north-east of Osaka), where the *Dairi* (Mikado) resided.

62. A reference to Jennings' nickname 'Dog' Jennings and to his eccentricity. For Jennings, see p.149, note 9.

63. John Cam Hobhouse, first Lord Broughton, friend of Byron. A Radical and a Bonapartist, he was contesting the by-election at Westminster against Lord Melbourne's brother (who won), after Romilly's suicide.

64. Sir Francis Burdett, political reformer, was the other Member for Westminster, and was supporting his fellow-Radical Hobhouse.

65. Archibald, ninth Duke of Hamilton, whom Beckford also calls "the snarling dog". Brother Crotchet is his younger son, Lord Archibald Hamilton (see p.103, note 55).

66. Bindley III, 1,000: *Orders of the Venetian State for the Government of Istria*, with the Governor's portrait by Tintoretto, a vellum MS dated 1543. This was Lot 378 in Edwards' sale.

67. This portrait of Rogers by Sir George Hayter ("The Phoenix") was No. 420 in the exhibition *British Portraits* at the Royal Academy, Winter 1956–7.

68. *The Champion* was a Radical Sunday newspaper which later devoted whole numbers to the enormity of the Peterloo massacre; it is interesting to find Beckford taking it in. Its severe review on February 28th (for extracts from which see p.180) of Rogers's poem *Human Life* has been completely borne out by time and, like B.'s remarks, was in strong contrast to the reviews of many better–known critics.

69. Prices had fallen catastrophically and trade was at a stand still. Nevertheless, the Government and the Bank of England were considering resuming cash payments, *i.e.* making the payment of gold coin in exchange for paper currency

obligatory if demanded. This was a severe deflationary measure, because it would further restrict credit and increase the scarcity of money, and force the Bank to discount less Bills, embarrassing the merchant banking houses named; the latter had recently undertaken very big obligations, e.g. in connection with France's discharge of her War Indemnity. These banking houses were in the centre of the controversy because Nathan Meyer Rothschild (1777–1836) and Alexander Baring, First Baron Ashburton, were during March giving evidence before the Secret Committee of the House of Commons enquiring into the expediency of the Resumption of Cash Payments; they were rightly strongly opposed to it. The fear of this measure was creating financial panic, and wild rumours were current. Messrs Hope were merchant bankers of Amsterdam who settled in England during the French invasion of Holland in 1794.

70. The banquet was at Apsley House to the Diplomatic Corps on Friday February 26th. The Duchess' reception of the ladies was a separate affair; she is called *Mater dolorosa* because she was on bad terms with her husband, from whom she largely lived apart. Lady Caroline Lamb, wife of Lord Melbourne, was nick named *Glenarvon* after her first novel, an anonymous caricature of Byron, with whom she was infatuated.

71. The Professor (Lord Roden) told Beckford of the coming sale, from June 7th, of the famous library at White Knights, Reading, formed at enormous expense by the fifth Duke of Marlborough, whose extravagance now compelled him to sell up. It was one of the finest libraries in England, he himself having acquired only four and seven years earlier respectively the Bedford Missal and the Valdarfer *Decameron*.

72. Quotation from Voltaire's *Candide*, chapter XI "The Old Woman's Story"; the reference is to her first encounter with the *castrato*.

73. From the Responsory to the seventh lesson of Matins in the Office for the Dead: *Timor mortis me conturbat, quia in Inferno nulla est redemptio.*

74. Various types of rare porcelain.

75. Beckford imagines Clarke (Boletus) successfully bidding for a lot.

76. The last novel (1736) of A.R. Le Sage, author of the more famous *Gil Blas*.

77. Perhaps on witchcraft and Satanism, or worse.

78. *i.e.* cutting down of trees.

79. Beckford hints that some books at Blenheim and White Knights had previously been sold on the quiet to dealers.

80. Morel & Co. of Brewer Street, Golden Square, oilmen and salters. An 'oilman' was a manufacturer and seller of oil, and a dealer in sweet oils and eatables preserved in them.

81.   A reference to a book in Beckford's library, *The Fortunate Youth*, or *Chippenham Croesus*, 1818. It was the true tale of Cawston, son of a Chippenham maltster, who while at Shrewsbury School invented a story that he had been left a large fortune; this enabled him to live a grand life for months on credit, before the hoax was discovered.

82.   Edward Hughes Ball (1798–1863), called "The Golden Ball" because of his fortune; one of the greatest gamblers and dandies of his day, who soon dissipated his fortune. In 1823 he married a Spanish dancer, and later disappeared to France where he died in obscurity. Educated at Eton and Trinity College, Cambridge, joined the 7th Hussars for six months, and in August 1819 assumed the additional surname Hughes. Lady Hughes, whose first husband was Captain Ball, R.N., recognised him as her grandson, but his birth is shrouded in mystery. His step-grandfather, Lady Hughes' second husband, was the distinguished Admiral, Sir Edward Hughes (1720?–1794).

83.   Philip Wyatt, nicknamed Sweetness (on whom see pp.123-4, note 28). *Philipine gem* is a reference to one of the ludicrous incidents in *Gil Blas*, when the trickster Camilla plants on the innocent and ingenuous Gil Blas her worthless ruby ring, given her, said she, by her uncle, the Governor of the Philippine Islands (Book I, Chapter 16). On p.184 B. writes of "platitudes worthy of the Philippine Islands"; although he has *Gil Blas* in mind there too, he is making a back-handed reference to the auctioneer Phillips.

84.   Or, *lawsuit*.

85.   *On the Climate of Great Britain*, 1806, by John Williams of Pitmaston, near Worcester.

86.   London.

87.   The famous firm of Bromwich, Isherwood & Bradley, which supplied Strawberry Hill.

88.   Unassailable, because Peers and M.P.s could not be arrested for debt. In contrast, Beckford was morbidly anxious to liquidate his debts, much as he hated paying out a farthing. For the first Duke of Buckingham, see p.176, note 53.

89.   Expenses at Hindon, Beckford's pocket Borough, were for the 1818 General Election.

90.   The ninth Duke of Hamilton left one of his seats (or appurtenances of it), Ashton Hall, near Lancaster, away from his heir in favour of his daughter, the Duchess of Somerset (the Hyaena), setting his whole family by the ears. She tried to hurry on a general sale there while her brother (the new Duke, *Florindo*) was still dawdling in Italy with Princess Pauline, in case the Will

was disputed. *Brother Crotchet* is Lord Archibald, and *Bouche-de-sucre* his sister, Lady Anne.

91.   Napoleon's mother.

92.   The Whigs.

93.   The Duke had a house in New Road, now Marylebone Road.

94.   *i.e.* Hicks' pills enlarge their livers. The boy referred to is one of the two sons of Beckford's friend, the second Lord Roden, by his second (Orde) wife. In the last sentence of this letter Beckford imitates Ehrhart's Alsatian pronunciation of *bourreau, bête* and *charlatan*.

95.   One of the Hamilton devices was a rose.

96.   Thomas Gwennap, dealer in pictures, antiques, etc, in New Bond Street, with a reputation for dishonesty.

97.   Possibly *Phillips*, 28th Day, Lot 1061; *Rutter*, p.11, gives the goldsmith's name as Wighels, which may well be a mis-spelling of Zacharias Weigel (pronounced Wighel), a Bavarian goldsmith working 1636–47. It had the proprietor's name engraved on it, which was perhaps Wilder or Wildercom (*com* = cup).

98.   Beckford is now back at Fonthill. The *French Horn* was an inn on the route from London.

99.   Beckford's housekeeper.

100. Poligny is in the Jura, near the Franco-Swiss frontier. For Schöll and Gibbon's library, see p.209, note 9.

101. Separate letter of same date.

102. Manuel I (1495–1521) of Portugal, during whose reign (the apex of Portuguese history) Brazil was discovered; the consequent exuberance led to the distinctive Manueline style of architecture. *Rhinoceros* is Westmacott (see p.175, note 40).

103. At Batalha.

104. Still's brother, the Rector.

105. When Beckford was due for Bath.

106. Cornelis van Poelenburgh (1586–1667) was a Dutch painter patronised by Charles I; Beckford had several of his pictures, so these two cannot be identified for certain. The Patel, father and son, were 17th-century French painters whose works cannot easily be distinguished from each other; the picture is *Bath (1845)*, Lot 309 or 310. Richard Wilson (1714–82) was one of the greatest of early English landscape painters. B. had just bought at John Knight's sale of March 23rd "a small Landscape" by Wilson (Lot 152) and it is likely to be this picture. It was either *A View on the Thames near Richmond (Phillips,* Day 26, Lot 243), now in the National Gallery, or *A*

View on the Tiber (*Bath* (*1848*), Lot 31), both of which, according to these Beckford catalogues, came from Knight's collection (in which case one of them was bought privately). Franz van Miens (1635–81) the Elder was a Dutch painter; this picture is now in the National Gallery—a lady in a crimson jacket feeding a parrot. The *new* <Velvet> *Brueghel* was bought by Beckford for £2 17s. 6d. at the Panné sale in March 1819, Day 8, Lot 1: *Christ going to Calvary*, with Jerusalem in the background and many figures, on copper 5¼" x 6½" (*Bath* (*1848*), Lot 23). For Berchem, see p.234, note 11.

107. First letter. Beckford describes the visit of William Holmes (d. 1851), Tory whip for thirty years and a great dispenser of patronage.

108. *Eight bottles* erased.

109. The small tower containing Beckford's own quarters.

110. The Duke of Hamilton.

111. Queen Charlotte's sale, Day 1, Lot 97, "a small cabinet, containing under a roof of the finest Japan lacquer, an inclosure with small folding doors, with drawers on each side and underneath; a stand for ditto on four feet, and an extra black and gold painted stand to elevate same"; bought for £20 9s. 6d. for Beckford, who was told that it belonged to or was made for Sixtus V (Pope, 1585–90).

112. Mouron and Pigault-Lebrun, the famous novelist (see p. 176, note 48), were agents at Calais. Mouron saw a great fuss going on as a skiff shot across the harbour at speed and volleyed out its passenger; realising it must be somebody important, he ran down and found Beckford. It was still Sunday.

113. From Amiens.

114. Written at his lawyer's office in Lincoln's Inn, where he stopped on his return from Paris to Fonthill.

115. From the last scene in *Vathek*, Eblis being the Prince of Hell.

116. For notes on the 1812 Roxburghe sale and the current Marlhborough sale at White Knights, see pp.122–3, note 15 and above note 71. Books referred to here are Caxton's *Mirrour of the World*, folio 1480; Valdarfer's editon of Boccaccio's *Decameron*, Venice 1471; Morlini's *Novellae ... cura Caron*, Paris 1799, bound by Roger Payne (only 55 copies printed); Froissart's *Chronicles* translated by Lord Berners, printed folio by Pynson 1525, and bound in blue morocco by R. Payne. The Missal bought by Jarman is White Knights, Lot 2822, Bruges 1531, said to have been executed for Diane de Poitiers, mistress of Henry II of France, and bound in red velvet enclosed in a silver-gilt filigree case, with an additional blue morocco case. For Jarman, see p.283,

note 16. The Persian Ambassador was Mirza Abdul Hassan Khan, who had just returned to England for his second embassy here. He was one of the lions of Society and created a sensation wherever he went, not only because he was the first Persian ambassador we had had for a very long time, and his country was a focus of political interest, but also because of his gorgeous clothing, dignity, personality and wit.

117. London Directories of the period give only Joseph Harris, senior, watchmaker and goldsmith, and Joseph Harris, junior, silversmith and jeweller, next door to each other in the Minories.

118. A parody of Portuguese pronunciation.

119. Joseph Sill, featured in the *Journal* as a Lisbon merchant, had now retired to Bath, shortly to be joined by his sister Betty, Mme Bezerra (the Cowpat), just ennobled (see p.216, note 110).

120. *Phillips*, Day 24, Lot 62, a pair by Velvet Brueghel, showing allegorically the Elements of Air and Water, on copper in ebony frames with ormolu mouldings (*H.P.S.* 55–6). For the one bought at Panné's sale, see above, note 106.

121. Chardin is grotesquely combining two of Beckford's London addresses, viz. 6 Upper Harley Street (which he had ceased to rent since May 1817), and the Hotel Jaunay, Leicester Square.

122. Two notable comets had begun to appear in June and July.

123. *Domine, labia mea aperies*, from Matins in the Breviary (not used by the laity).

124. Beckford's manuscript Reading Notes in *H.P.* show that this is the Rev. Joseph Berington's *Literary History of the Middle Ages*, 1814; *great* refers to its enormous number of pages.

125. General Orde, mourning the first anniversary of his wife's death.

126. Made at such speed in order to save inn bills.

127. Hamilton Palace—cinquefoils being one of their heraldic devices. Beckford is jealous of the idea of Franchi going there instead of to Fonthill.

128. William Robertson's *Charles V* appeared in 1769, gave him European fame and ran into many editions; its Introduction, a descriptive estimate of the Dark Ages, was one of the earliest successful British attempts at historical generalisation based on large accumulations of fact; but as a Presbyterian minister he was unsympathetic to mediaeval Christianity.

129. Probably Rook Wood, just above Splendens (*Rutter 93*). *The General* is Orde.

130. Because he had lost his teeth; he was joining Franchi in Bath on Monday.

131. Perhaps a joking reference to the treatment of asthma, rheumatism, paralysis, etc, by Galvinism, *i.e.* by electricity excited by powerful machines; at this period it was much discussed and tried. *Sampson* is Hayter, who had succeeded his brother Coxone as Clerk of the Works.

132. B. is parodying the drilling and battle-cries of the patriot volunteers, who were being armed against the discontented workers. He is also being ironical about his attitude to the soldier.

133. Farret is A. Farratt, who became B.'s house-steward in Bath. The Calf and the Soft Brother are the brothers Becket. "The two female animals" are maids.

134. Refers to the soldier in Bath mentioned in the letter of the 12th; they were going to meet him in a pub.

135. This nightmare was illustrated by Franchi in his reply (see Insert). John Cuttell was a lapidary and jeweller in New Compton Street, Soho; Samuel Coulson, jeweller and goldsmith in North Audley Street (1822 *Directory*); James Aldridge, ditto in Northumberland Street, Strand.

136. *Phillips*, Day 32, Lot 1567, describes it as a vase of Hungarian topaz executed by Benvenuto Cellini as a marriage present for Catherine Cornaro of Venice; it was mounted with a dragon-handle of enamelled gold, set with diamonds, and rested on a tripod stand of three small dragons in green and blue enamel, the feet connected by cinquecento festoons and scroll-work, set with diamonds and precious stones. The vase is sixteenth-century Florentine work, and is owned by Lord Rothschild. Illustrated in *Rutter*, p.7. Beckford had just bought it from Baldock for £285; he sold it in 1823 for 600 guineas.

137. A phallus worshipped as a symbol of the Hindu God Siva.

138. *Bath* (1845), 2nd Day, Lot 155, is a sardonyx gem portrait of her.

139. *Dell' Oreficeria e della Scultura*, Florence 1568.

140. Whitley, Brames & Milne, nurserymen, New King's Road, Fulham.

1821–1822

ALL this time, despairing attempts were being made to save Fonthill. The situation was truly desperate. Sugar was being sold below the cost of production, the price fell lower (in terms of real money) than it had ever been before, and the value of plantations was declining annually. By 1820, the annual 'free returns' from Beckford's remaining plantations had been halved since 1818 to £8,000, and the trend was inevitably downwards.

Franchi's letter of February 1821 states the position very clearly, although it needs amplification. Mortgages on Fonthill totalled £70,000; 5% interest was due on this, *i.e.* £3,500 annually, which was paid by Messrs Plummer, Beckford's West India merchants, and which helped to swell every year his enormous debt to them (on which the same rate of interest had to be paid). It can be imagined how much Beckford's indebtedness increased over a period of years merely by the addition of interest on interest already long overdue. The merchants were owed £50,000—it had been £70,000, but Harbourhead (one of Beckford's three remaining plantations) was in process of being sold for £20,000, every penny of which would go to the Merchants. The grand total of debts was brought up to £145,000 by the setting aside of at least £25,000 to meet the claim of J.G. Campbell when his lawsuit was finally settled.

The merchants could not be blamed for wanting to foreclose on these annually mounting debts. For they were secured on the wasting, shrinking assets of Jamaica, and the Parliamentary seat at Hindon; on a Wiltshire estate, much of which had originally been chalky downland and was therefore marginal farming land; and on the white elephant of the Abbey, the value of which (beyond its building material) was purely a matter of guess-work.

Fonthill had, thanks to its Abbey, immense prestige. To be master of it was a bait to the Duke of Hamilton, with his grandiose ideas of his family's importance, which he laboured unceasingly to advance. Furthermore, in those days one of the best ways of obtaining one's desires was the acquisition of safe Parliamentary seats, through which one could exert pressure on the Government. The Hindon seat was thus of some value to the Duke. In order to get the reversion of Fonthill and Hindon at Beckford's death, he was therefore asked to put up £80,000 forthwith, to liquidate the most pressing debts. He rather naturally refused. Then (as we see from Franchi's letter of October 1821) he was asked to find £30,000 to meet the merchants' pressing claims, and to pay the annual interest of £3,500 on the Fonthill mortgage. During the subsequent haggling, he wanted complete control of the estate during Beckford's life. But Franchi pointed out that planting and felling were Beckford's only hobbies now that building at the Abbey had ceased, so he must be allowed to please himself in such a small matter. However, Hamilton again declined to find the money. So another Jamaican plantation was sold, bringing the merchants' debt down to only £10,000.

But there was still the huge mortgage on Fonthill and the coming Campbell claim. Therefore Fonthill had to be sold. It was to be auctioned, with its contents, by Christie from September 17 (a date continually deferred). The View, which drew all England, began on July 1. At last the revised date of the auction was announced for Tuesday, October 8th. But on the previous Sunday local hand-bills announced its cancellation because a private sale was being negotiated. Meanwhile, the rival auctioneer Phillips was closeted with Beckford in Bath, and the sale of the Abbey with most of its contents was effected on Monday the 7th, for £300,000—a price they had never really expected to get.

1821

Franchi to Hamilton. Friday 9 February[1]

My dear Duke, ... you have left England wearied with the fatigue caused by public and private affairs, and in flying to Rome you thought to escape them. Vain hope! These enemies of your tranquillity have followed on your tracks, and it is the poor unfortunate Franchi who is charged with interrupting your happiness and detaching you for half an hour from vases, statues, marbles, pictures, Canova, Cicognara, St Peter's, the Coliseum, the Pope and all the amiable Princesses P.Q.R.S.T.U.X.Z etc, etc who make up the charm of Rome—without counting the honest Bonelli. I can hear you say "What's this all about?" Well, now for it, my dear Duke, only be indulgent over my inability at expressing myself, and rest assured that I will be as brief as possible.

... Three weeks ago the Merchants administering the Jamaican estates, being in money difficulties, wanted Bonds from M. de B— for very considerable sums. This did not please him at all because he thought it would place him in very disagreeable difficulties and too much in the power of those people, who, without directly threatening to stop his quarterly allowances, wrote a letter to Mr Fownes which produced on M. de B— the same effect, when he read it, as if they had. This brought Fownes to the Abbey. I wrote to him privately to bring with him an exact statement of M. de B—'s affairs, and this he did. The scenes which passed between us there are unbelievable, but at last, after the storm was over, we got down seriously to business and examined the accounts *au fond.* The upshot is that the interest on the debts eats up the rentals from Fonthill, Salisbury and Jamaica to such an extent, that including the above-mentioned £5,000 sterling a year which M. de B— receives and £1,200 more given to Fownes to pay pensions and legal expenses, the annual debit against M. de B— is still £1,500 sterling (at the present low price of sugar). Now if this is not stopped in time I can say at once that all M. de B—'s possessions will disappear as if they had never existed.

You can save everything by making a sacrifice which one day will pay the Duke of Hamilton a hundredfold. £80,000 sterling is the sum you are asked to find. That, with £20,000 or so more which we have in view and are almost certain of getting, will extinguish the great mass of the debts and will consequently diminish the interest on them. For this sacrifice you will have all M. de B—'s possessions at his death; after that they will be yours, although he will enjoy them during his lifetime ... But observe, Monseigneur, that this business is pressing—it must be terminated within eighteen months in the manner in which I have proposed, otherwise Fonthill must fall into the power of the first buyer. Such an idea makes my heart bleed whenever I think of it two moments on end. You may rest assured that M. de B— has only these two alternatives to follow. The one which I propose is the most advantageous according to my principles, and is what M. de B— wants. The other would give him the means of paying all his debts, which mount up to £140,000 sterling; and the residue from the sale together with the Salisbury and Jamaican rents would leave him an income of £10-£12,000 sterling net which, if only sugar rises, will increase to 18 or £20,000 ...

You know M. de Beckford, and that he has his own way of doing things and will only understand what is in conformity with it! One of his whims is never to discuss business with the person concerned, and consequently I have to broach it; after that it is for the actors at Lincoln's Inn to serve their masters. However, I am delighted to figure even behind the scenes, for, as a mere object of whom questions are asked and to whom replies are dictated, I flatter myself that I am of some use in the business, since I am very attached to M. de B— and very devoted to the Duke and to the dear Duchess of Hamilton.

You will see clearly the advantage of this transaction as regards your principle of aggrandizing your illustrious House. It is a superb prize which no usurper should snatch from you; once it is protected from caprice, it will fall to you one day. You can count on all M. de B—'s possessions, present and future, being immured in the Abbey: I will take care that you will find everything there. But if he sells, everything will be different, every thing will be changed—new houses, new caprices, new follies, new debts; everything will disappear without one being able to prevent it. Once the bird escapes from his cage he will be devoured without even a feather being saved!

... All M. de B—'s English landed property is mortgaged; the Jamaican estates are free, but their sale would not save Fonthill. The cold, the gout, the winter melancholy of this solitude and all that I have just written to you are not calculated to make me happy. But I ease my sorrow in thinking of my very dear Duke and Duchess, and I console my heart with the certainty that they love and are attached with all their —[2] to their very devoted and very attached servant the Chevalier G. Franchi.

P.S. No one has read this letter.

Saturday 10 February[3]

Knowing, my dear Friend, your abstemiousness in the present and your devotion to the future, I have authorised Franchi to make you a proposition on my behalf, which I hope will not appal you. By accepting it you will free me from a burden from which I *must* be delivered. It would be idle to pretend that such an act will not severely incommode you. On the other hand, if you find it impracticable, I would be very well off as far as income is concerned, but despoiled of Fonthill and consequently of the last atom of consideration in this country. My position would change, but the affection which I swore to you so long ago will never weaken.

<Monday> 14 May[4]

... Judging by the to-do that awaited me on your shores—the chefs, Directors of balls and illuminations etc—I did even better than I guessed by remaining in my shell. At present nothing disgusts me so much as ostentation and noise. Have I not assured you thrice over that I am more alienated than ever from the world and worldlings? But you persist in misunderstanding me. If ever I return to your country it will not be to flaunt myself in a barouche or calash. Twenty miles on horseback before breakfast fatigues me no more than it did at twenty, and it's the same with walking. The Chevalier Franchi, whom you will probably see on his return from an important mission in Italy with which his Government charged him, will tell you that I am not yet crippled. No! Thank God, I preserve the same vigour, the same terrible energy and the same *detestations*—I despise fools and fainéants of whatever nationality, titled or untitled, as I have always despised them—and perhaps even with redoubled vigour!

It would be droll to see me with these fine dispositions in the immediate neighbourhood of your brilliant Lausanne society.

That is the truth. You will find it rather brutal, but it will serve to remind you of the total difference which exists between my bearing and others'. You try in vain; neither your proposals nor your forgetfulness of my complete unsociableness will change my sentiments toward you. I am and I always will be sensible of your attachment, and I remain unchangingly, my dear Sir, your sincere friend and servant, G. de Beckford …

Franchi to Hamilton. Wednesday 17 October[5]

… You can rest assured that in the great affair he will make all the sacrifices you desire, but do not press the point about the plantations or timber-felling: you know that he cannot fell much more and that he plants more than he fells—it's the only pleasure and liberty left to him, and between ourselves, my dear Duke, it doesn't amount to much—it's not worth considering.

As for the rest, yes, he'll do it, for he cannot bear the idea of a sale of the property; the difficulty he would have in finding a place for his books and curiosities will make him endure many privations, and as for the sale of all these objects, he does not even like hearing it mentioned.

I think that everything could be saved by a sum of £30,000, which must be found immediately in order to meet the pressing needs of the Merchants; the interest on this sum would be deducted from that which you have proposed paying for the mortgages. All I beg of you, my dear Duke, is to do all you can to find the £30,000; I do not for one instant doubt that the rest will be arranged without any difficulties on his part. You must also perceive the advantage to you of getting cheaply the right of nominating the other Member of Parliament should be well considered, for it will enable you to torment those who torment you and do not spare you[6] …

1822

<Friday> *11 January*[7]

The reply, my very dear friend, that Mr Brown has just sent to my men of affairs is cruelly far from what I had expected. Taking advantage (in the widest sense of the word) of the misfortunes of the moment, he makes me feel them to the quick, treating my estates with contempt and seeking to place his foot upon my throat (in more than one way).

My dear and best friend, these are not your affectionate and loyal intentions. In the name of all that is dear, I implore you not to suffer them to be thwarted. Fownes assures me that without the sum I am asking of you, which I have limited as much as my position permits, I shall be forced to sacrifice everything to procure myself the very means of existence. Here, I live more economically than elsewhere, and even improve the properties. Hounded from here, all will become indifferent to me.

In order that the cup which I must drink may not taste too bitter, I put my trust in your generosity and your excellent and affectionate heart. In the matter of the timber, nothing will be alienated which could destroy the beauty and worth of a spot which becomes doubly dear and precious to me when I consider for whom it is destined. I know, my dear friend, that you love me too much to let me languish, suspended between heaven and earth; free me from this unbearable position, I implore you. You are the master, Brown must obey you. So order him to compromise on the only item that can render the life I am forced to live here less hard and more peaceful—my hands will be sufficiently tied without them putting even my little finger in tutelage!

But of what use are these sad details? In following the impulse of our hearts, we follow at the same time our best interests. I will owe you my salvation, my daughter will owe you the daily consolation of this spectacle, and my grandson all that I can amass and keep for him.

<*Wednesday*) *7 August*[8]

... The Holy Sepulchre has at last become one of the most animated spots in England. People go to it as to the waters; they admire it, they devour it with their eyes, they vanish into its thickets, doubtless regretting not yet being able to *retire* behind West's great dauberies.[9] Yesterday seventy waggons, each drawn by several horses, followed by innumerable gigs, deposited at the foot of the Great Portal several dozen insipid personages of that diversity of persuasions in which we glory in this blessed Isle.

According to what they tell me, a considerable number of these onlookers torture themselves in their efforts to decipher the blazons which are everywhere displayed. But they do not understand them and end up by writing in their note-books 'fancy arms'. If, then, Mr Beltz has not totally forgotten me and is not going to parade his fine tabard behind Scotland's Lord Lyon (an idea which gives the creeps to an English herald), perhaps he would go to the trouble of furnishing a short explanation, neat and well arranged, of these mysteries, entitled "Letter from a heraldic traveller" etc.[10] Now is the moment. I think the public will gladly swallow it up, for they are beginning to busy themselves with the Abbey, and they even seem disposed to panegyrize everything about it.

... What do you think of the St Albans Street procession[11] without cross or banner but with its sadly beautiful white drapery, whilst the Ecce *Sacerdos! Ecce Sacerdos!*[12] etc resounded through the neighbourhood, loud enough to topple our holy hierachy ten years sooner than we expected ...

Monday 2 September[13]

The rage is at its height. They dream only of the Abbey, they talk only of it. I doubt whether since the beginning of printing they have ever uttered such extravagances. Semiramis, Babylon, Persepolis no longer count for any thing: they proclaim that Vathek and his tower have surpassed them. The poet Bowles and God knows how many other versifiers are indulging themselves to their heart's content.[14] In short, it is a veritable Rage, and buyers present themselves from all sides.

... Before the most attractive object in the whole world (according to the frenzied impression of the day) is for ever lost to us, come and glance at it, try to glide one fine Sunday up to the demonstrator of the magic lantern, our faithful and well-beloved Franchi. He will tell you what is passing, what has passed. He will relate a thousand anecdotes which would make a fortune if one cared to print them—for the avidity with which they swallow everything which people choose to scribble about Fonthill is unexampled.

The strange things which are passing in my affairs do not cast me down. The Saint who inspired me with the Abbey will also arm me with supernatural courage to do without it, and perhaps even to erect yet another monument to his glory. It will not be for a modest sum, you may be very sure, that I will deprive myself of the fruit of so much labour and so much trouble, in fact of an object which all England beholds agape. It seems that they believe in Fonthill as blindly as in pious times they believed in the most inconceivable legends.

If by any chance the *Literary Gazette*, the *London Museum*, the *Gazette of Fashion*, the *Observer, Morning Herald, Chronicle* etc, etc come into your hands, read them and you will hear only one voice and one acclamation, and that voice the most sonorous and that acclamation the most deafening that was ever raised. And all this only costs me the trouble of reading the most ridiculous declamations and the most high-flown phrases, for neither I nor any of my satellites have paid a sou for puffing. On reading them I have cried a hundred times "The dog star rages, Bedlam is let loose". And so will you ...

Friday 13 September[15]

... 'Tis cruel how I am served by all save you. Oh my dear Gregory, how much I feel the friendly zeal and amiable ability with which you have presided over the great theatre at Fonthill. What a furore! What a concourse! It is incredible what is spontaneously written and said. Whether the King comes or not, the tickets are certainly selling—and this is the true punchinello; this morning the *Morning Chronicle* sings of the fame of the place with redoubled enthusiasm: "15,000 guineas have been received, the roads are thronged with carriages" etc. Pierrot's anecdotes are precious, and diviner still the Princess' remarks—a pity she does not return, a pity not to monopolise her completely; they say her husband is the finest gentleman in England[16] ... It looks as if Henry Hope will shew himself in a few days; receive him well, cultivate him well in order to make D. Thomas envious (he is dying with envy like a million others).[17]

The more you can find occasion to hint at and puff the MSS, the more good you will do me, the more desperate you will make Murray, and the more you will make him pay.[18]

Pien tes gomblimens à Mussy Bierod[19] ...

< ?Monday 7 October >[20]

Let us leave aside for the moment jesting, good and bad. Let me announce a great piece of news: Fonthill is sold very advantageously. I am rid of the Holy Sepulchre, which no longer interested me since its profanation; I am delivered of a burden and of a long string of insupportable expenses. At present I have only to distribute my funds prudently and await the outcome of events. For twenty years I have not found myself so rich, so independent or so tranquil.

Have the goodness to watch over the Gibbons. I do not intend to detach a single one of his books; the Purchas,[21] the Pierre de la Vallée[22] etc will remain as they are until my arrival—for nothing is more likely than my paying you a visit next summer. Now that I am more solidly than ever able to follow my whims, you only have to make the shores of the Lake of Geneva agreeable, and we will come. I have ample means and not a sou of debts. Watch your trout. MM. the Russians will have to be devilish rich to poach on my preserves; let them be content with féra[23] and a few perch. The large morsels will remain for me, be sure of that—for I am more paying and less pagan[24] than those schismatics, and a good Catholic to excess (if one is to believe the newspapers, which do not cease to debit to my account as many pranks, idle stories and extravagances as they do falsehoods). They flattered themselves that I had foundered, but they are deucedly mistaken:

Fortis superenabat Undis.

1. Franchi in French to Hamilton in Rome.

2. Franchi left a blank here.

3. Beckford in French to Hamilton, enclosing Franchi's of the 9th, above.

4. French to Dr Schöll at Lausanne.

5. Franchi from London to Hamilton in French.

6. When Hamilton inherited Fonthill, he would also obtain one of the two parliamentary seats of the rotten borough of Hindon, which would add to his nuisance value and influence with the Government (he was a Whig).

7. Beckford in French to Hamilton in Paris. Brown was the Duke's factor at Hamilton Palace.

8. From Bath in French to the Abbé Macquin, about the crowds coming to view Fonthill before its coming auction by Christie.

9. This shows that there were water-closets behind concealed doors in the wainscoting of the rooms; West's huge portraits of the Beckfords hung above, which added to the deception, and delighted Beckford's sense of the incongruous.

10. Beckford refers to George IV's coming visit to Edinburgh. The Lord Lyon King of Arms is the principal Scottish herald. The result of Beckford's request was an anonymous article with the index-title "Armorial Bearings in Fonthill Abbey" in the *Gentleman's Magazine* for September to November 1822.

11. A reference to the arrest on July 19th of the Hon. Percy Jocelyn, Bishop of Clogher, brother of Lord Roden, Beckford's friend. He was found in a compromising situation with a private of the Foot Guards, in a back room of The White Lion, St Alban's Place, St James'. They were taken through a ferocious crowd to Marlborough Street, where they were charged. The Bishop broke his bail of £1,000 and fled. After this, Bishops became a by-word in the land, and the whole affair created immense and justified popular resentment against the privileged position of the upper classes (as far as the law was concerned).

12. The full quotation from the Roman Service books is *Ecce sacerdos magnus, qui in diebus suis placuit Deo et inventus est justus*—"Behold the great High Priest, who in his days pleased God and was found righteous". This solemn phrase, taken from the Vulgate (Ecclesiasticus xliv. 16), is used in the ceremony of the Reception of a new Bishop in his Cathedral, and in the Mass of Confessor Pontiffs; perhaps it is also sung at the entry of the Pope for ceremonies in St Peter's. The crowds were of course shouting, "Look at the Bishop, look at the Bishop!"

13.   To Hamilton in French from the Claremont Hotel, New Bond Street.

14.   William Lisle Bowles has "Lines written on Fonthill Abbey" in his *Works*, ii. 321 (1855), but whether this ode was published in 1822 I do not know.

15.   From Bath to Franchi at Fonthill.

16.   *The Princess* is the Princess of Madagascar, a nickname for the third Lady Holland, the famous Whig hostess of Holland House; this nickname for her was invented by Lady Caroline Lamb in *Glenarvon*, 1816. Her husband, the third Baron Holland, nephew of Charles James Fox, was a prominent Whig and Bonapartist; he introduced a Bill for the abolition of the death penalty for stealing.

17.   Thomas 'Anastasius' Hope, author and collector, and his brother Henry Philip, also a collector.

18.   B. was angling with Murray for the publication of the *Episodes of Vathek*; and perhaps for that of *Spain and Portugal*, for Melville's *Beckford*, p.327, quotes a note to Clarke referring to this period, and Rogers' letter to Byron, 8 February 1818, suggests that Spain and Portugal may have been completed.

19.   Imitating Ehrhart's Alsatian pronunciation of "Bien de compliments à Monsieur Pierrot" (the dwarf).

20.   Original from Bath to Schöll in French.

21.   Purchas' *Hakluytus posthumus*, or *Purchase his Pilgrimes*, five volumes, folio, 1625–6. A copy of this owned by Gibbon was in the Jarvis sale in New York in 1851; but we do not know whether or not the *H.P.S.* copy was also Gibbon's.

22.   Pierre des Vallées Sernay *Histoire des Albigeois*, vellum, Paris 1569; not listed in Sir Geoffrey Keynes' *Gibbon's Library*; perhaps the *H.P.S.* copy was Gibbon's.

23.   A fish of the salmon family, plentiful in the Lake of Geneva.

24.   *Plus payant et mins payen.*

APPENDIX

Portraits of Beckford by Hoppner and Behnes

HOPPNER'S unsigned and undated picture,[1] was presented to Salford Art Gallery in 1868 as a portrait of Beckford by Sir Thomas Agnew (b. 1794), founder of the firm of Agnew's, and Mayor of Salford, a man who spent most of his life as an art dealer. He must have travelled down to London on business in Beckford's lifetime, and would have had ample opportunity to learn from printsellers, dealers and others what Beckford (who frequented their shops, art galleries and auction rooms) looked like.

If we assume that Agnew bought the picture in the Salford area, we may well ask what it was doing up there. The answer is interesting. The Marquess of Douglas, who became Beckford's son-in-law in 1810 and had been his friend all his life, had a seat, which he much frequented, forty miles away—Ashton Hall—and was M.P. for nearby Lancaster. Beckford may have given the portrait to his daughter or son-in-law, and it would then have been quite natural for it to be at Ashton. It was not a flattering or a great portrait, and in any case a portrait of Beckford could not hang in a London drawing-room or in the gallery at Hamilton Palace.

The *old* Duke of Hamilton hated his son and heir, the Marquess of Douglas, and on his death in February 1819 deliberately left Ashton Hall, or at any rate its contents, away from him (to everyone's surprise); he bequeathed them instead to his daughter, the Duchess of Somerset, who was also on bad terms with Douglas. She tried to hurry on a general sale and dismantling, whilst the new Duke was lingering in Italy, where he had been ever since 1816.[2] The pictures from Ashton Hall were sold by her at the National School Room in Lancaster on September 6th, not long after the Duke's return to Britain. He was dilatory and inattentive to business and would have been very *affairé* after so long and disastrous an absence. Is it not therefore likely that an unflattering portrait, which was in any case rather an embarrassment, may have been overlooked and gone with the rest? Lot 16, "Modern. A Portrait of a Gentleman, and a head of King Lear", bought by a Mr Cross for twenty-seven shillings, could therefore be this one.

The resemblance to the face in Romney's portrait of Beckford painted in 1782 is remarkable. The forehead, not high, sloping back; the thick eyebrows, the fine and intelligent eyes; the long nose, now becoming bridged; the short upper lip and tell-tale mouth; the angular jaw and prominent chin; the mischievous expression, although the face now has a settled melancholy; the untidy hair and cravat close up to the neck. The portrait is three-quarter length, and shows a smallish man, which Beckford was; he is holding a book of architectural prints.

A word is necessary about the other likeness of Beckford reproduced here—Behnes' drawing of 1817. When Professor Guy Chapman reproduced it in his *Bibliography of William Beckford*, he stated that the spectacles and baldness were a disguise and that it was "based on the Reynolds portrait of 1782" (p.85). There is no correspondence at all between the Behnes and Reynolds, so I do not see how one can be based on the other. But Behnes' is very similar to a head and shoulder sketch on the back of an 1803 letter[3] to Beckford, which portrays him with thinning hair and glasses. This shows that Behnes' portrait is a real one, from which we can learn what Beckford really looked like. We can also see why Beckford nicknamed the central figure, Clarke, 'The Mushroom' (*Boletus*). The figure on the right in Behnes' drawing is Caxton. This drawing illustrates *A Dialogue in the Shades*, which was printed as a separate pamphlet and also with Clarke's *Bibliographicum Repertorium* (which contains an account of Beckford's library).

1.   Described in McKay and Roberts, *John Hoppner*; 1914 Supplement, p.4.
2.   See Beckford's letters of 19 and 20 March 1819.
3.   From John Pedley, 1 April 1803; in *H.P.*

INDEX

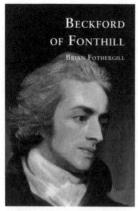

William Beckford was one of the richest men of his time and one of Britain's most eligible bachelors. However, his spectacular hedonism and disregard for convention led to an epic fall from grace. Following exile in Europe, he returned to England and set about building the grandiose Fonthill Abbey. This is Fothergill's fascinating account of a celebrated and vilified 'Fool of Fonthill".
1 85488 085 4
£18
384 pages, 16 illustrations

Ostracised by society after a scandal involving William Courtenay, in 1787 William Beckford fled England, spending much of the next decade abroad. Soon after he arrived in Lisbon and went on to spend eight months there before going to Spain. This account of his Iberian sojourn is at times scathing and often witty. It offers a tantalising glimpse into the mind of a complex and intriguing individual.
1 84588 010 2
£18
256 pages, 8 illustrations

Written by William Beckford and published in 1786, *Vathek* is the first Oriental Gothic horror novel. It relates the story of the eponymous Caliph, a man devoted to pleasure and obsessed with the acquisition of knowledge. Set in Arabia, this is a classic tale of lust for riches and power, where magic, trickery and betrayal abound.
1-84588-060-9
£6
160 pages

For further information please see www.nonsuch-publishing.com